W9-BNZ-308

Tsar Nicholas I
and the Jews

Tsar Nicholas I and the Jews

The Transformation of Jewish Society in Russia · 1825-1855

Michael Stanislawski

The Jewish Publication Society of America · Philadelphia · 5743 / 1983

Copyright © 1983 by The Jewish Publication Society of America
First edition   All rights reserved
Manufactured in the United States of America

Library of Congress Cataloging in Publication Data
Stanislawski, Michael, 1952–
  Tsar Nicholas I and the Jews.
  Bibliography: p.
  Includes index.
  1. Jews—Soviet Union—History—19th century.
2. Nicholas I, Emperor of Russia, 1796–1855—
Relations with Jews.   3. Soviet Union—Ethnic
relations. I. Title.
DS135. R9S77   1983   947'. 004924   82–16199
ISBN 0–8276–0216–2

Designed by Adrianne Onderdonk Dudden

לזכרה של

שרה פייגע בת חיים-לייב לבית ווארשא, ז"ל

נולדה בק"ק קלושין
חונכה בק"ק אסטרחן
נפטרה בק"ק מונטריאל

Contents

List of Tables

Foreword

When Nicholas I acceded to the throne of Russia in 1825, his Jewish subjects were living in blissful ignorance of Russian life and politics. They had been governed by the Russian state since the Partitions of Poland of 1772, 1793, and 1795, but the transition from Polish rule had not substantively affected their traditional way of life. Whether their putative monarch resided in Warsaw or St. Petersburg, the Jews continued to live in their own autonomous communities, governed by Jewish civil and criminal, as well as ritual, law. Whether their towns and villages bore official names in Polish or Russian, the Jews still engaged in the same limited economic pursuits, which yielded the same—if always mounting—taxes. These taxes, in turn, were still paid collectively through the Jewish communal leaders to the same local officials who had always controlled the territory, extracting the same bribes in the same patois. The Jews' existence was hardly tranquil or idyllic, but it was stable. Even the harsh expulsions from the villages periodically ordered by the government could be interpreted as only the latest manifestation of the burdens of living in Exile. The Jews were cushioned by the security of a living and vital tradition, reinforced by a legalized insularity.

However, although the Jews could not have been aware of it, the transfer to Russian administration had eroded the very basis of their society. Unlike the Polish Commonwealth, the Russian Empire was not a corporate state partaking of the feudal heritage of Roman law, which granted the right of self-rule to every component of society. In Russia there were no truly corporate estates until the late eighteenth century, when the nobility alone was granted meager rights that fell far short of the Western (or Polish) norm and did not seriously compromise the monarchy's monopoly on political power. As the empire expanded, it was forced by administrative expediency to grant the right of autonomy to several national groups, including the Jews, but in all cases these concessions were rescinded as soon as the bureaucracy was able, or felt it necessary, to impose its will on the newly conquered groups.

The inevitable recision of the autonomy—and hence the isolation—of Jewish society began in earnest only in Nicholas's reign. Until then, the Jews had been able to maintain their independence and insularity despite the efforts of Empress Catherine II to integrate them into the general legal and economic order of the empire and the attempts of Alexander I to lure them to governmental schools and agricultural colonies.[1] Almost immediately after Nicholas's coronation, however, the latent became manifest. The government embarked on an unprecedented policy of active intervention into the internal workings of Jewish life in the hope of molding the Jews in ways consistent with the emperor's overall aims and ideology.

By the end of Nicholas's reign, thirty years later, this policy had effected radical social and cultural changes in Russian-Jewish life. These changes have not been sufficiently studied in the historical literature for the simple reason that the cruelty and severity of Nicholas's methods precluded an objective evaluation of their results on the part of scholars politically and emotionally involved in the subject. As a result, the connection between developments of this reign and the new forms of political and intellectual expression that emerged among Russian Jews in the 1860s and 1870s has not been adequately explored. All studies of the later period hint that the new phenomena were rooted to some extent in the previous age but provide no clear analysis of the extent or meaning of these roots. Cause and effect are obscured in enraptured ovations to the new era.

In this study, I attempt to distinguish between the causes and their effects, to examine the connection between legal developments and social change during the reign of Nicholas I. In the process I hope to explicate the extent to which forces erupting in the third quarter of the nineteenth century were conditioned in the second. I am acutely aware that inherent in any such study of change is the danger of overlooking the forces of stasis and tradition. For this reason, I attempt at all times to chart the absence of change as well and avoid the use of any terms such as "modernization" or "secularization" which assume a model of universal development entirely inappropriate in this context. Indeed, the continuities of tradition were as complex as those of change in Russian-Jewish life.

Much of what is presented here differs substantially from the standard interpretations offered in the best works on Russian-Jewish history. These differences do not result from any revisionist fervor on my part but rather from the fact that due to the destruction of the centers of Jewish historiography in Eastern Europe in the twentieth century, the history of the Jews in Russia in the nineteenth has practically been abandoned as a subject of original scholarly endeavor since the early 1930s. A handful of studies on this period has appeared in the last half-century, but the natural process of readjusting and reweighing viewpoints and conclusions has not taken place because of the absence—in some cases, the murder—of two generations of scholars.

Consequently, it is necessary to begin this account with an investigation of the basic perceptions of Russia and its legal system shared by the major historians of Russian Jewry, and then to punctuate the essentially chronological ascent of the chapters that follow with a good deal of source criticism and historiographic analysis. My hope, in the end, is not only to study one important period of Russian-Jewish history, but also to suggest a critical methodology for that study. Unfortunately, politics continue to plague the writing of Russian-Jewish history: in our day, the interference comes in the form of barring access to archival materials. But there is, to paraphrase the Hebrew cliché, still much work to be done and sufficient reward, if the sources are approached openly, critically, and self-consciously and with the realization that "ours is not to finish the task."

Throughout this study, I use the term "Russia" as a synonym for the Russian Empire, "Russian" as its adjective, and "Russian Jews" to refer to the Jews living essentially in Lithuanian, Ukrainian, and Belorussian lands. I do so fully conscious of the imprecision involved and solely for the sake of convenience and intelligibility. Similar motives have induced me to forgo pedantic consistency in toponymy: place names are rendered according to their official nineteenth-century form, except for the several cases in which other spellings have become popular in English-language, particularly Anglo-Jewish, scholarship. All dates are in Old Style, that is, the Julian calendar in use in Russia until 1918, which in the nineteenth century was twelve days behind the Gregorian calendar. Transliteration systems follow the Library of Congress rules, except that diacritical marks are omitted in Russian and Ukrainian, and in Hebrew, the *'alef* is represented by an apostrophe, the ^c*ayin* with a raised ^c.

The appearance of this work affords me the long-awaited opportunity of thanking the embarrassingly large number of persons to whom I am indebted. First and foremost, my teachers. Yosef Yerushalmi took me under his wing when I was a college freshman and taught me not only Jewish history but also how to study history. Over the course of the years he counseled me patiently and persistently while serving as my undergraduate tutor and graduate adviser. It was he who suggested this subject as the topic of my doctoral dissertation and he who most enthusiastically urged its publication. His belief in the importance of East European Jewish history resulted in my joining him on the faculty of Columbia University. I can only hope that my work there repays in some measure my enormous debt to him. Richard Pipes inspired me to study Russian history and vigorously supported my determination to write Russian-Jewish history. His insistence that a thorough grounding in the Russian context is essential to the understanding of Russian-Jewish history informs every page of this work. In addition, his strict and elegant scholarship and teaching have served me as a model. Ben-Zion Gold knows how important his help and wisdom have been to me over the years; if I am an East European Jewish historian today, it is largely due to his love for the subject. Ruth Wisse and Robert Szulkin spurred me at an early stage to work in this field and have continued to lavish counsel and friendship on me. Dov Noy and Barbara Kirshenblatt-Gimblett provided me the rare opportunity of doing fieldwork in East European Jewish culture and thus of approaching my subject from a perspective often closed to historians; they also opened their homes to me in my frequent forays from Cambridge to Jerusalem and New York. Isadore Twersky allowed me to mine his intimate store of information about traditional Jewish life in Eastern Europe and graciously agreed to read the first draft of this study. Edward Keenan taught me both the excitement and the limits of responsible skepticism. Alexander Leyfell, Lois Dubin, and Benjamin Braude went through an early draft of this work with great care and saved me from many excesses and embarrassments. Later, Gerson D. Cohen, Michael A. Meyer, Haym Soloveitchik, Ezra Mendelsohn, Emanuel Etkes, and Shaul Stampfer contributed many valuable criticisms and insights when reviewing the manuscript. Kathleen O. Elliott taught me more than I can say, with her boundless charm and keen wit. Martin Peretz probably does not even remember enabling me to spend my first summer at the YIVO Institute. Arthur Candib long ago first directed me to Harvard, thus inadvertently determining my fate.

In a more formal vein, my thanks are due to: Dr. Charles Berlin and staff at the Judaica Division of the Harvard College Library, who for many years satisfied my every bibliographical whim; Dina Abramovitz and staff at the Library of the YIVO Institute for Jewish Research; Marek Webb and staff at the YIVO Archive; Dr. Mordekhai Navon and staff at the Manuscript Division of the National and University Library at the Hebrew University of Jerusalem; Professor Jacob Rader Marcus of the American Jewish Archives, who provided me with transcripts of unpublished letters of Max Lilienthal; and for their generous support, the Canada Council, Département de l'Enseignement, Gouvernement du Québec, the Memorial Foundation for Jewish Culture, the Institute for Jewish Policy Planning and Research, and most especially, Harvard University.

On a different, more personal and profound level, I owe more than I can possibly acknowledge to my brother Howard and sister Sheila, who have sustained me through the years, and to Marjorie Kaplan, who has made coming to New York most worthwhile.

Finally, I cannot even begin to articulate my debt to my parents, Evelyn and David Stanislawski, who raised me with all their devotion, as well as their yiddishkeit.

This work is dedicated in loving memory of my maternal grandmother, Sarah Pinkus, who personified the dignity, strength, and unbridled humanity of East European Jewry.

Michael Stanislawski
New York
Tishri 5743/October 1982

. . . the two states, the depressive and the exalted, were not inwardly distinguished from each other. They were not separate and without all connection, for the present state had been preparing in the former one and to some extent had already been contained in it—just as indeed, on the other hand, the outbreak of the healthy and creative epoch was by no means a time of enjoyment, but rather each in its own way one of affliction, of painful urgency and compulsion.

Thomas Mann, Doctor Faustus

Introduction

The Problem and Its Historiography

Before we can study the history of the Jews in the Russia of Nicholas I, we must examine the legacy of interpretation bequeathed to us by the classic historians of Russian Jewry. With the luxury of hindsight it is possible to discern that this scholarship reflected the social and political circumstances of its authors as much as history itself. This is, of course, true to some extent of all history writing, but Russian-Jewish historiography was particularly conditioned by contemporary reality: apolitical objectivity was neither its hallmark nor even its pretended goal. On the contrary, all the major historians of Russian Jewry consciously and candidly wrote history as a political and national statement, hoping to redress the tragedies by chronicling their horrors and thereby to influence in the most direct fashion the political fate of the Jews. Many of the resultant works were issued as party publications or parliamentary briefs. Most were published by openly ideological presses or periodicals. While the ideologies involved ranged across a reasonably broad spectrum of political opinion, they were all united against one common enemy, the tsarist regime and its obvious anti-Semitic bent, as exemplified by the governments of Alexander III and Nicholas II.

This exogenous stimulus to scholarship quite naturally had considerable effect on the assumptions, as well as the conclusions, of the scholars. To a large extent, their research was aimed at tracing the origins and background of contemporary attitudes and actions of the Russian authorities in regard to the Jews. This led, perhaps inevitably, to what now appears as an overidentification of the past

3

with the present, a projection backward of the context of the government's relations with the Jews. From the vantage point of today, two particularly vivid strands of anachronistic homology can be identified in this scholarship: an anachronism of centrality and an anachronism of anomaly.

By the First World War, the "Jewish question" had become one of the central issues in Russian political life. The role of the Jews in the revolutionary movement, the inclusion of their demands for civil and national rights in the general clamor for constitutional liberties, and the alleged power of international Jewry became matters of deep concern to the ruling circles of Russia. Indeed, some of the ministers of Nicholas II, if not the tsar himself, seem to have been obsessed with the Jewish problem far beyond any rational response to reality.[1]

Not surprisingly, Jewish historians and publicists, to whom the matter was of obvious crucial importance, tended to presuppose a similar centrality of the Jewish question in previous eras and circumstances. This supposition was anachronistic. Until the 1880s, the Jewish problem was an essentially marginal one in the overall context of Russian politics. In the reign of Nicholas I the policies of the government toward the Jews were mostly spontaneous, almost always unreflective, and in large part incidental to the general concerns of the emperor and his underlings.

More complex than this problem of perspective is the related problem of the uniqueness of policy toward the Jews. As in every Christian country, in Russia the Jews occupied a distinct position, determined by a theologically based enmity that infected all strata of Russian society, if at times only subconsciously. Other national or religious minorities could be persecuted as enemies of Mother Russia or the true Orthodox Church, but only the Jews were automatically and irrevocably regarded as the eternal archenemies of Christianity, the universal alien usurpers.[2]

A substratum of anti-Jewish animus in the minds of all Russian officials can thus be assumed; only its absence is surprising or particularly noteworthy. But what was critical to the history of the Jews in Russia was the reification of this animus in concrete political acts; what is critical in the reconstruction of that history is a careful differentiation between when that animus merely conditioned the application of policy, when it determined policy, and when it became policy itself.

In this analysis, it is crucial to distinguish between the unique and the anomalous. In the Russia of Nicholas I, the uniqueness of the Jews was manifest once more in a most blatant, cruel, and frightening manner. Yet at no time in this period did policy toward the Jews depart from the framework and pattern of overall governmental activity. That would come only one generation later, when the rules that had determined the governing of the empire for several centuries ceased to apply, and the caprices of prejudice—and violence—filled the vacuum. To assume that the treatment of the Jews was always anomalous within the general framework of Russian law and policy is both to misperceive reality and to obscure the vital gradations of repression.

Again, this inappropriate assumption resulted from anachronistic projection: the degree to which policy toward the Jews was anomalous seems to have been directly proportional to the centrality of the Jewish question in the general political climate of Russia. By the time of Nicholas II, treatment of the Jews was indeed both unique and anomalous.

It must be stressed that this anachronism was not a simpleminded error of naive historians but a product of the particular intellectual milieu in which the classic historians of Russian Jewry lived. Therefore, before the legal status of the Jews in Nicholas I's Russia can be described, there must be an examination of the basic perception of Russian law which Jewish historians gleaned from their milieu and set as the guiding principle of their analyses of the history of the Jews in Russia in past generations.

The Legal Context

The basic premise of all analyses of the legal history of the Jews in Russia in the nineteenth century was formulated most succinctly by the first authority on the subject, I. G. Orshanskii. In the opening pages of his *Russian Legislation on the Jews*, published in 1877, Orshanskii identified a fundamental juridical distinction between the Jews and all other citizens of the Russian state: the latter possess inherent and inalienable rights restricted by the government only in the interests of other individuals or of society at large, while the Jews enjoy only those limited rights specifically granted them by law. All other Russians enjoy the fundamental right of unrestricted residence, while the Jews are forbidden to live in all but a few regions of the country. Treated sometimes as foreigners, most of the time worse, the Jews constitute "a special class of semi-citizens, or better put, citizens of a specific part of the state—a phenomenal, one might say, unparallelled circumstance."[3]

This understanding of the legal position of the Jews seemed axiomatic to Orshanskii, who was trained as a lawyer in post-1864 Russia—as were almost all the major historians of Russian Jewry.[4] It is important to appreciate this link between the legal profession in Russia and the local school of Jewish historiography. Beyond the social pressure that encouraged Jews to study the law and the governmental pressure which inadvertently encouraged research by restricting Jews from full-fledged legal practice, there was a basic ideological confluence between the Russian bar and the Jewish historians (as well as the liberal "juridical" wing of Russian historians). All had at their core a profound belief in Western, mostly Anglo-Saxon, concepts of equality, justice, and the rule of law which would liberate all Russians, including the Jews, in an imminent Russian *Rechtsstaat*.

Unfortunately, hindsight requires a recognition that this sanguine, admirable belief resulted in a perception of the legal reality of tsarist Russia which today can serve only as material for an intellectual history of Russia, not as an acceptable analysis of its legal system. Despite their Positivist proclamations, Orshanskii and his disciples shared in the Idealist confusion between idea and reality that was the wellspring of the Russian intelligentsia. They could not see that the formal trappings of a free judicial system do not guarantee justice in the absence of liberty. As lawyers and legal theorists fighting for the entrenchment of basic rights in an essentially lawless society, they could not have accepted the fact that even in their own time there were no inalienable liberties in Russia, only inescapable obligations mitigated by the occasional privilege.

Until 1905 there were no citizens in Russia, only subjects. These subjects had no innate right to live or work in any particular manner; they possessed only those rights granted them as privileges by the emperor. Limitations on residence, economic activity, or intellectual pursuits were therefore the results not necessarily of deliberate restriction but rather of the lack of positive legislative permission.[5] To use Orshanskii's first example, but to formulate it in the objective—if objectionable—language of the tsarist legal system, the Jews were granted the privilege of living wherever they chose in a determined area of the empire; the overwhelming majority of the population was not granted the privilege of any voluntary mobility until 1861, and then just barely so. The Jews were permitted to reside in Moscow only under special conditions, with police approval; to this day, residence in this city is possible only under special conditions, with police approval.

Thus, in his protest against the travesty of justice perpetrated against the Jews, Orshanskii did not realize that he was touching upon a fundamental travesty of justice perpetrated against *all* subjects of the tsar. Guided by the noble misperception that defined his world view, he mistook the rule for the exception and set forth an analysis of the legal status of the Jews in Russia that became canonized in the historical literature but must appear seriously flawed in this wiser, if jaundiced, day.

The legal status of the Jews in Russia was in many ways the reverse of Orshanskii's formulation: they were clearly differentiated from foreigners and recognized as native subjects of the empire, liable to the general laws of the state in all cases for which there was no special legislation in their regard.[6]

To be sure, this special legislation was discriminatory, in the sense that it both distinguished Jews from other categories of subjects and exhibited a clear anti-Jewish bias. However, in a patrimonial state such as Imperial Russia, discrimination was the rule rather than the exception and hence entirely relative. Any analysis of the legal status of Russian Jews therefore must be made within the context of the entire Russian legal corpus.[7]

That corpus was astonishingly imprecise and confused throughout the imperial period, with categories and definitions assuming merely formal, not descriptive, significance. The status of the Jews was characteristically convoluted. As a result of Catherine's reforms, every Jew was simultaneously a member of an estate—that of the guild merchants, townspeople (*meshchane*),[8] artisans, or agriculturists—and of a Jewish community, and therefore subject to two different and often conflicting sets of rules and regulations. Neither contemporary bureaucrats nor later historians were able to sort out this duality and erroneously characterized the Jews as constituting an estate of their own.

This taxonomic confusion was surpassed by the chaotic muddle of Russian legislative practice. At the beginning of Nicholas's reign, it would have been well-nigh impossible for any government official to discern precisely what were the rights, privileges, and restrictions applicable to the Jews of Russia. The only codification of laws regarding the Jews was Alexander I's Statute of 1804, which was supposed to have been a comprehensive guide to the status of Jews. In fact, this statute was a confused hodgepodge of unsystematic provisions which failed even to address the basic question of where the Jews were permitted to live and conveyed the misleading impression that the communal organization of the Jews was a matter of choice, not compulsion. The statute did, however, affirm several clear principles: the Jews were considered native Russian subjects; they were permitted to own land, except for estates settled with peasants, but they would soon be forbidden from living in villages and rural settlements under any circumstances; they could send their children to the general Russian schools or maintain their own educational institutions; they were free to engage in any form of trade and commerce (except for some branches of the liquor industry) and to enroll in artisan guilds; they could participate, under certain restrictions, in the organs of municipal self-government.[9]

The 1804 statute did not even attempt to address the whole

gamut of relations between the government and the Jews—the organization of taxation, policing, judicial authority. And so, as the reign of Nicholas I began, the government did not even have a clear position on whose responsibility it was to deal with the Jews. Every Jewish community was an autonomous, self-governing entity, directed by an executive agency, the kahal, which was responsible to the local police and treasury officials who were, in turn, subordinate to the governor-general of the province. At the same time, at the start of Nicholas's reign, the Jews as a religious minority were under the jurisdiction of the Central Directorate of Ecclesiastical Affairs of Foreign Creeds, an agency recently separated from the Ministry of Religious Affairs and National Enlightenment. In 1832 the directorate became a department of the Ministry of the Interior. With the promulgation of the Statute on the Jews of 1835 an attempt was made to delegate authority over Jewish affairs to a variety of governmental institutions, but overall control of all matters Jewish was not removed from the Foreign Creeds Department. Less than a year later, this situation was recognized as juridically untenable. The typically imprecise solution was an order that the Senate refer to the Ministry of the Interior as a whole those matters concerning Jews "which by their nature require the decisions of that ministry," and restrict the province of the Foreign Creeds Department to strictly religious concerns. [10] But this did not solve the problem. Most ministries still had some authority over the Jews and at times engaged in extensive power plays to gain more.

The ministers themselves were involved with the Jews in several realms beyond the workings of their own portfolios. As with so many other problems, Nicholas was not content with the existing administrative apparatus and created special topic-oriented supraministerial committees. Soon after his accession, he reappointed the Jewish Committee set up by Alexander I, which was composed of the four most important ministers of the realm and their chiefs of staff. [11] Concurrently, he ordered the Committee for the Western Provinces to examine the situation of the Jews and to propose any reforms that it deemed appropriate. [12] Later, Nicholas convoked a second Jewish Committee, under the chairmanship of Minister of

Court Domains P. D. Kiselev, which continued to meet for a quarter of a century, well into the next reign.[13]

Almost all the members of these commissions were also members of the State Council, which in its General Assembly and Department of Laws frequently discussed and elaborated policy on the Jews and technically initiated all legislation.[14] Finally, the Committee of Ministers, in decline throughout Nicholas's reign, also deliberated from time to time on Jewish policy.

Of course, over and above all these agencies, ministers, and committees stood Nicholas the autocrat, who took a vivid interest in the status and future of Russia's Jews. This interest was by no means neutral: Nicholas's views on the Jews, cataloged by a variety of historians, were typical of the devout, chauvinistic militarist so prevalent in his service. To Nicholas, the Jews were an anarchic, cowardly, parasitic people, damned perpetually because of their deicide and heresy; they were best dealt with by repression, persecution, and, if possible, conversion.[15]

Yet Nicholas's intuitive prejudices did not always translate themselves directly and automatically into policy and law. On this issue, as on others, he was influenced to a significant degree by advisers whose outlook and ideology varied considerably. Regarding Jewish policy, it is possible to identify four distinct groups of officials in Nicholas's service: (1) the traditional militarists, including most of the governors-general of the provinces, who shared the tsar's views and supported his positions without hesitation; (2) the pragmatic traditionalists, exemplified by Minister of Finance E. F. Kankrin, who sympathized with Nicholas's opinions and objectives but viewed many of his suggested repressive measures as too costly or unfeasible;[16] (3) the objective pragmatists, led by Kiselev, who approached the subject with relatively few preconceptions and attempted to introduce some rationality into the chaos; and (4) the positive reformers, such as Count M. S. Vorontsov, governor-general of New Russia, and Minister of National Enlightenment S. S. Uvarov, who for various reasons and to differing degrees saw themselves as the active defenders or reformers of Russia's Jews.[17]

The influence of these groups varied considerably over the thirty years of Nicholas's rule. Only in the middle third of his reign did the last two groups of advisers and ministers have an important role in the formulation and execution of policy on the Jews. Until then, Nicholas determined Jewish policy by himself, moderated only by the practical limits to repression pointed out by the second group.

Nicholas's first action in regard to the Jews was his instruction that the Jewish Committee continue its work, begun in the last months of Alexander's rule, of reviewing and codifying all legislation in effect regarding the Jews. While the committee engaged in this very complicated task, most of the laws passed by the government concerning the Jews merely effected minor changes in existing provisions or dealt with specific cases that had reached the highest organs of appeal. Several of these laws were of major importance. The new Censorship Code of June 1826—dubbed the "ironclad" code by Russian historians—brought closer control over Jewish books by stipulating for the first time that one of the members of the Vilna Censorship Committee must know Yiddish and Hebrew.[18] Alexander's policy of expelling Jews from rural areas was resurrected but limited to Grodno Province on an experimental basis.[19] The requests of the merchants of Kiev that their city's privilege *de non tolerandis judaeis* be reinforced was approved, though not implemented with any haste.[20] Finally, the growth of the Jewish community of Kurland was strictly limited.[21]

All these enactments were continuations of policies previously elaborated by former governments and revealed no fresh approach to the Jews. This was not true of the most important law of this period—and one of the most significant of the century—the Statute on the Recruitment of the Jews of August 1827.

I · Conscription of the Jews

Az Nikolai Pavlovich iz keyzer gevorn,
Zaynen yidishe hertser umetik gevorn.
(When Nicholas Pavlovich became emperor,
Jewish hearts became sad.)

Yiddish folk song[1]

The Decision

In Western Europe the conscription of the Jews was either a by-product of their emancipation or an important milestone on their road to legal equality. Thus, the first recruitment of the Jews into a European army was ordered by Joseph II of Austria in 1788, six years after the promulgation of his *Toleranzpatent,* which extended civic rights to the Jews of Bohemia and Moravia. Similarly, French Jews began to be drafted after their emancipation in 1790 and 1791, and the Napoleonic invasions of Holland, Italy, and the German principalities subjected the Jews to compulsory military service as a consequence of their political liberation.[2]

Only in Russia was the conscription of the Jews neither ordered nor received as a herald or harbinger of their civic betterment. Military service in Russia, unlike the West, was not a duty borne equally by all citizens in exchange for the protection of the state and its laws but a burden selectively imposed by the government for social and economic, as well as strategic, reasons. Thus, even though Russia was the first country in Europe to introduce compulsory service, it was one of the last to implement universal conscription. Until 1874 each category of Russian subjects was liable to a different set of military regulations. The nobility, after 1762, and the clergy were exempt from any compulsory service; the guild merchants were permitted to pay a special tax in lieu of personal service; the peasants were drafted not personally but by commune, at the discretion of their landlord.[3]

Throughout the centuries of Jewish life in Poland, the question of the military duties of the Jews was never raised, since there was no compulsory draft in the Polish Commonwealth. When the Polish Jews were transferred to the Russian Empire, however, they had to pay for the luxury of not serving. In September 1794 the government set the exemption tax for merchants at 500 rubles per recruit and extended this tax to the Jews. All Jews, regardless of economic classification, were, for the purposes of recruitment, regarded as merchants and accorded a privilege generally reserved for a small part of the population.[4] This departure from general practice was explicitly affirmed by another law passed four months later.[5]

This extension of privilege did not result from a benevolent concern for the welfare of the Jews or even from fiscal considerations. Rather, the Jews were exempted from service since they were assumed to be incapable of being soldiers because of their physical weakness, cowardice, religious fanaticism, and suspect loyalty. The notion that some military use could be extracted from the Jews despite these drawbacks was voiced by several bureaucrats during the reign of Alexander I but was not accepted by the emperor, due primarily to the consistent refusal of the Ministry of War to consider any participation of Jews in Russia's armed forces.[6]

These objections were overruled by Nicholas almost immediately after he became tsar for reasons only secondarily concerned with the Jews themselves. Nicholas predicated his life on a fervent and unswerving belief in the superiority of the military life and the conviction that no problem was insoluble if approached through the army, that even the most recalcitrant criminal or coward could be trained to be a useful soldier. Faithful to this guiding principle, he imposed a military model on most aspects of Russian life, even on those for which it was eminently unsuitable.[7] "The government of Russia," wrote the French critic Astolphe de Custine, "is camp discipline substituted for the order of the city, a state of siege transformed into the normal state of society."[8] Nicholas extended obligatory service to several problematic groups previously exempted—including the inhabitants of the Kingdom of Poland, the Ukrainian Cossacks, the declassé gentry of the Western Provinces, the military colonists, and even some clergy[9]—and widely expanded the use of recruitment as a punitive measure in a variety of criminal offenses.

To Nicholas, the traditional objections to drafting the Jews, whether cultural, religious, or military, seemed self-contradictory. How better to deal with an anarchic, feeble, and heretical group than through the army, where, as he wrote in another context,

there is order, there is a strict unconditional legality, no impertinent claims to know all the answers, no contradiction, all things flow logically one from the other; no one commands before he has himself learned to obey; no one steps in front of anybody else without lawful reason. . . . [10]

Tactically, therefore, Nicholas's decision to draft the Jews was a natural corollary of his general policy of standardization through the military.

Of course, standardizing the Jews had an added psychic and religious dimension for Nicholas, not present in regard to other groups. From the outset it was clear that the recruitment of the Jews was also the most efficient way to convert them to Christianity. Indeed, one member of the Third Section of the Imperial Chancellery—the secret police—wrote an anonymous memorandum that detailed the unparalleled missionary possibilities provided by army life and discipline and recommended that only young Jews, less entrenched in their faith than their elders, be conscripted, at double the usual quota.[11]

Other members of Nicholas's staff were not quite so enthusiastic about the prospect of recruiting the Jews. When Nicholas ordered the Jewish Committee to draft legislation conscripting the Jews, the committee stalled and failed to produce such a law. Thereupon, Nicholas turned to his brother Constantine, who as commander in chief of the Western Provinces was in charge of the areas inhabited by the Jews. Constantine delegated the matter to his deputy Novosil'tsev. Two months passed, and Novosil'tsev, too, failed to prepare any legislation.[12]

It is quite likely that the delay in both these cases was caused by the intensive lobbying activities of Jewish intercessors in St. Petersburg. Nicholas's intention to draft the Jews was hardly a secret. One bureaucrat reported that

everybody knew about it and discussed the impending conscription of the Jews. The latter had known for a long time what was being prepared for them and had their agents in St. Petersburg in order to avert the blow or at least to postpone it *ad calendas Graecas*.[13]

This same bureaucrat claimed that Novosil'tsev had received 20,000 rubles from the Jews for his cooperation; another report held that Admiral N. N. Mordvinov, a member of the State Council, had received 200,000 rubles for his silence during the debate on this question.[14]

Nicholas's will could not be thwarted by such obstacles. He simply bypassed the usual legislative channels and exercised his autocratic prerogative by ordering his chief of staff to draft the necessary legislation. The Recruitment Statute of the Jews was published on August 26, 1827, along with the first general draft levy of Nicholas's reign.[15]

The Legislation

The preamble to the recruitment statute announced its unprecedented departure from previous policy on the Jews:

. . . considering it just that for the relief of all Our loyal subjects, the recruitment duty be equalized for all categories of subjects liable to it, We order that Jews be required to fulfill the recruitment duty in person.[16]

In other words, the privilege previously enjoyed by the Jews of being treated as a unified group not subject to the same social and economic differentiation as the rest of society was now rescinded in the name of the equalization of civic duty.

Nicholas undoubtedly was not conscious of the far-ranging implications of this new approach to the Jews. While significantly different in intent and scope from the Western model of conscription as a by-product of emancipation, the recruitment of the Jews in Russia did substantially broaden the extent of their legal and social inclusion into the general polity of the empire. In the West, a similar process of differentiation and integration was—or at least seemed at the time to be—a progressive development, replacing corporate distinctions with individual rights. In Russia, where there were neither corporate nor individual rights to enjoy, this same process of integration took on a repressive character, leveling the Jews to the lowest common denominator of rightlessness. In both cases, however, the critical factor was the revolutionary dismemberment of the legal integrity of Jewish society; the social repercussions of this process were remarkably similar, irrespective of political context.

In Russia's extraordinary legal system, equalization of duty did not result in the uniformity of obligation. Only the requirement to serve in person was common. Each category of subjects liable to personal service was still governed by a separate series of military regulations. Special military ordinances were issued for each of these groups—the residents of the Baltic provinces, the inhabitants of Poland, the declassé gentry of the Western Provinces, the Finns, and the Jews.[17] The "general military regulations" in fact only applied to the Great Russian peasants and townspeople.[18]

The multiplicity of these rules, their complexity and intricacy, render comparative analysis extremely complicated. The 1827 statute on the Jews itself consisted of 157 articles, and it was amended or superseded by an additional 116 laws passed during Nicholas's rule. Yet even with all these exceptions and clarifications, the Jews were regarded by the military authorities as being subject to the general regulations and not in a different category of military law, as were the Poles and the Finns.[19]

For the sake of clarity, the most important aspects of the military regulations applicable to the Jews are summarized here under ten headings and compared, when possible, to the rules regarding other groups:

1. Quotas. It has been a standard claim of historians on the subject that the Jews were recruited at a higher, or double, quota than the non-Jews.[20] In fact, this was not the case. The 1827 statute did not stipulate any quota at all for the Jews, leaving them liable to the general norm. This norm, established by yearly laws for the entire empire, was calculated in different ways over the thirty years of Nicholas's rule but generally required that four to eight recruits be presented for every thousand tax souls in a community.[21] In the last four years of Nicholas's reign, the Jews were subjected to the higher draft rate that had been in effect for a decade for other elements of the population of the former Polish provinces.[22]

2. Age of recruits. The statute set the draftable age for Jews at between twelve and twenty-five. Recruits over the age of eighteen were to be enrolled in the regular forces for the standard term of twenty-five years; those under eighteen would serve in special units known as Cantonist battalions until they reached majority, at which point they would commence their full term of service.[23]

   This was the most important departure from the other sets of regulations, which set the standard draft age of recruits between twenty and thirty-five.[24] There were several circumstances in which Russians below the age of twenty could be recruited. Unmarried boys of seventeen could be offered as replacements for married members of their families; any peasant could be drafted by his lord at eighteen; younger boys could be recruited into the navy at any age.[25] More importantly, several categories of children were conscripted into the Cantonist battalions.

   These battalions were introduced into Russia from Prussia by Peter the Great to serve as the training schools for the sons of soldiers and some nobles. Under Nicholas, these battalions were transformed and expanded: in addition to their original constituency, they now included all criminals and vagabonds under the age of eighteen, the minor sons of the Polish and Ukrainian gentry who had participated in the Polish Uprising of 1830, the sons of prisoners sent to Siberia and of gypsies imprisoned in Finland, any abandoned boys from the age of eight up, and various categories of illegitimate children.[26] In sum, the Cantonist battalions were used by Nicholas as a broadly applied means of social and police control. It was not surprising that Nicholas decided to send Jewish children to these battalions. Only with regard to the Jews, however, was this device used systematically against an entire population. This exception was clearly motivated by the missionary aspect of the conscription, detailed in the anonymous Third Section memorandum.

3. Exemptions. The statute exempted from personal service Jewish guild merchants and rabbis in accord with the general practice. In addition, several categories of Jews were released from the recruitment duty for reasons not paralleled in any other regulations: those who completed courses in state-sponsored academic institutions of any level were permanently exempted from the service duty; Jewish children studying in these schools or serving as apprentices to Christian masters were released from duty for the duration of their training; Jewish colonists and their children were exempted from active service for twenty-five or fifty years, depending on the size and locale of their colonies; later, pupils in the government-run Jewish schools and rabbinical seminaries were also exempted.[27] These exceptions reinforced the unconscious integrative aspect of the conscription: any Jews who participated in one scheme of the government aimed at reforming the Jews were automatically exempted from liability to another.

4. Replacements. In accord with the general rules, a Jew could volunteer to serve as a replacement for another Jew if the arrangement was voluntary and if the proposed substitute belonged to the same community and to a family which had already fulfilled its military duty or had another male eligible for service.[28]

5. Duties of the Jewish community. As was the case for all groups liable to the draft, the Jews were required to present recruits by communities, each acting individually from the other and from the non-Jews in its environs. The recruitment was to be supervised by specially elected members of the Jewish community.

The statute contained an important provision which permitted the Jewish community to draft any of its members at any time for vagrancy, irregularity in the payment of taxes, and for any other offense not tolerated by the community.[29] This was entirely in keeping with the procedures established for all other categories of Russian draftees. Unique to the Jews, however, was the additional stipulation that no one may be drafted merely for actions in conflict with the religious "superstitions" of the Jews.[30]

6. Order of the draft. All Jewish families eligible for conscription were to be listed in special queue books that would rank the families in descending order of the number of males they contained. A copy of this book was to be kept in the Treasury Department at all times; it had to be written in Russian, but a Yiddish copy was to be made available as well. If two families had the same number of males, their order would be set by lot.[31]

This procedure was in keeping with the rules established for all other groups, at least until May 1828, when an amendment to the statute was passed which permitted the Jewish communities to divide large families into smaller ones and to combine several small families into a large one in the queue books, even when these permutations had no basis in real life. At the same time, the kahal leaders were allowed to draft village Jews before city Jews.[32] No explanation was given for these extraordinary provisions, which legalized social discrimination.

7. Oath of service. Every Jewish recruit, like his non-Jewish comrade, was required to swear an oath of allegiance and obedience to the emperor; this oath would be taken either at induction or upon attaining majority. The text of the special oath prepared for Jews was fascinating:

In the name of Adonai, the living, omnipotent God of the Israelites, I swear that I desire to serve and shall serve the Russian Emperor and State wherever and however I shall be instructed during my service, in full obedience to the military authorities, as faithfully as would be required for the defense of the laws of the Land of Israel. . . . If, by my own weakness or the influence of another, I shall transgress this oath of faithful service, may my soul and that of my entire family be damned perpetually. Amen.[33]

This text was to be read in Hebrew, but a Yiddish translation was to be recited beforehand, and the Russian officials were to be presented with a Cyrillic transliteration of both versions. The oath was to be administered by a rabbinical court, with witnesses present from the Jewish community and the local government. The recruit was to stand before the Holy Ark, clad in prayer shawl and phylacteries, and to swear on an open Torah scroll. After the ceremony, the full range of *shofar* blasts was to be sounded.[34]

8. Travel instructions. Regulations unique to the Jews were appended to the statute, stipulating that all Jewish recruits were to be billeted only in Christian homes during their travels and prohibited from having any contact with local Jews.[35]

9. Religious freedom. According to the standard military rules, Jews were to enjoy absolute religious freedom while serving in the army. They were to be permitted to conduct their own services or to pray at established synagogues; rabbis were to be appointed as chaplains, paid by the government. Officers were instructed to ensure that their Jewish charges were not hindered or criticized in their observances.[36]

10. Privileges after service. The statute ordered that Jews who complete their full term of service satisfactorily would be eligible to serve in the civil service, a privilege withheld from other Jews.[37]

The Implementation

Even in Western Europe, the Jews viewed the introduction of compulsory military service with deep ambivalence. On the one hand, they applauded it as a positive mark of their political progress; on the other, they recognized the difficulty, if not the impossibility, of reconciling the demands of army life with the requirements of traditional Jewish observance.[38] Indeed, even in an independent Jewish state, universal conscription has been the subject of extensive religious controversy.

In Russia the imposition of any conscription duty would have been an extremely harsh blow to the Jewish community. Under the best of circumstances, the implementation of the recruitment statute would have evoked much sorrow and pain. In fact, that legislation was so systematically breached by both the Russian authorities and their Jewish deputies that the recruitment of the Jews into Nicholas's army resulted not only in great suffering but also in unprecedented social turmoil and dislocation.

The most flagrant violation of the conscription regulations concerned the religious freedom of the Jewish soldiers. From the very first year of the new conscription system, the missionary motives of the government manifested themselves in both overt and covert ways. In July 1829, Nicholas instructed all commanding officers to separate Jewish recruits who would convert to Russian Orthodoxy from those remaining in their faith.[39] At the same time, he issued a secret circular which permitted army priests to depart from a standard procedure and baptize Jews without prior authorization from their bishops.[40]

In the first fifteen years after 1827, such baptisms occurred at a steady rate. For example, of the 1,304 Jews serving in the Saratov Cantonist battalions during these years, 687 were converted; 101 of the 301 Jewish children in the Verkhne-Vralik battalions from 1836 through 1842 were baptized; in the years 1842 and 1843 alone, 2,264 Jewish soldiers and Cantonists were converted to Russian Orthodoxy.[41]

Nicholas was disappointed with these figures and let it be known through the ranks that more Jews ought to be baptized. Beginning in January 1843, he requested a monthly report on the rate of conversions of Jews in the army and personally evaluated the results. In April of that year he noted "very few" on the report; in June, "very little success"; in July, reading that only twenty-five

Jews had been baptized, he informed the Procurator of the Holy Synod that he was "disappointed at the lack of successful baptisms of Jewish Cantonists and soldiers, and this fact should be brought to the attention of the responsible clergy."[42]

At the same time, the minister of war wrote an unpublished memorandum to the procurator relaying the emperor's wishes that the number of priests assigned to Cantonist battalions be increased and that detailed instructions on converting Jews be provided to all chaplains.[43] The latter task was assigned to the chief priest of the army and navy, Vasilii Kutnevich, who produced such instructions in October 1843. These instructions, covering twenty-five pages, advised the priests that a more sophisticated psychological approach would yield better results. Each Jewish soldier had a unique personality and a different degree of grounding in the Jewish tradition; each Jew must therefore be dealt with individually in order to discern the most effective manner of leading him to the baptismal font. At all times, Kutnevich concluded, conversions must be handled with respect and gentility, without the use of force.[44]

This last suggestion was dictated by the formal requirements of dogma but had little practical resonance as the emperor's personal interest in the success of the mission to the Jews became more and more apparent. From the memoir literature and from the careful archival research undertaken by Shaul Ginzburg immediately after the Russian Revolution, it is possible to summarize the main incentives used to convince Jews of the superiority of Christianity. From the moment that Jewish soldiers, and particularly Cantonists, were brought to their camps, they were subjected to constant pressure to convert. In clear violation of the original regulation, all signs of their former life—phylacteries, ritual fringes, prayer books, prayer shawls—were taken from them, and they were forbidden to speak Yiddish. Every official they met alluded to conversion at the slightest opportunity; every punishment they received was preceded by a promise of repeal upon baptism. They were forbidden visits with relatives or with other Jews in the area of their camps; they were ordered to write home in Russian and often were denied letters written to them in Yiddish. Several former soldiers testified that the only meat they received was pork and that most food was cooked in lard. Jewish prayer meetings were permitted only to adult soldiers; Cantonists were prohibited from initiating their own services or from praying with the older Jewish soldiers.[45]

Following Kutnevich's directives, the chaplains held private meetings with each Jewish recruit during which they read special missionary literature provided by the Synod in St. Petersburg. The army priests often complained that the Jews were better versed than they in Holy Scripture and requested additional help from their superiors.[46]

Apart from these psychic incentives, physical torture was used as well. The memoirs of former soldiers abound with descriptions of whippings in the name of religion. One former Cantonist related that while bathing in the river, his corporal forced Jewish children to remain under water for long periods of time unless they agreed to convert; another Jewish soldier was stuffed into a sack, thrown down a flight of stairs, and then dragged back up by a rope when he refused to convert. Several former Cantonists recalled being tortured by being fed salty fish and then being forced into sweat baths for extended periods.[47]

Affidavits submitted to the authorities by converted soldiers wishing to return to Judaism testified to additional types of torture. Evsei Groykop claimed that he agreed to be baptized after he was beaten and then forced to walk barefoot on hot coals; Dmitrii Kaufman had needles forced under his fingernails and was denied food for days on end; Lazar Golin was beaten by officers and denied medical attention until he converted.[48]

These methods had their desired effect. From 1845 to 1855 baptisms of Jewish soldiers and Cantonists became so common that fonts and godparents could not be provided to meet the demand. The Saratov Cantonist battalion was singled out for praise by the government for its efficiency in converting Jews en masse: in July 1845, Nicholas noted "Thank God!" on a report that 130 Jews were converted in that battalion alone. In 1853 the local bishop reported that "God willed 134 Jewish Cantonists to accept Russian Orthodoxy on Whitsunday, and on that day, the Christian Church baptized them all in the waters of the Volga with extraordinary zeal."[49] Similarly, 223 Jewish children were baptized in the Volga on October 21, 1854.[50]

The exact number of Jews who were converted in Nicholas's army cannot be determined with any precision. From the archival resources available, the impression emerges that at least half of the Jewish Cantonists and a substantial number of adult Jewish soldiers were baptized during their service.[51]

Since the success of conversionary techniques was so closely linked with the age of the recruits, it was inevitable that the Russian authorities would encourage the induction of children rather than adults. Indeed, the few extant official statistics coincide with the impression of the memoir literature in estimating that approximately two-thirds of the Jews drafted into Nicholas's army were under the age of eighteen and thus were sent to the Cantonist battalions. On the basis of the published recruitment levies for the empire as a whole, it appears that some 70,000 Jews were conscripted in Russia from 1827 through 1854; of these, approximately 50,000 were minors.[52]

Although the Russian officials preferred recruits under the age of eighteen, the actual choice of conscripts was the responsibility of the Jewish communities. There is no evidence that the government applied any specific pressure on the Jewish officials to comply with its preference for child-recruits; that the leaders of the Jewish communities did comply was one of the most significant occurrences in Russian-Jewish history.

Their reasons for doing so were complex. At times, there simply were not enough grown men to fill the recruit quotas. But even when there were, the kahal officials seem to have presented more children than adults to the induction centers. The basic reason was demographic: the marrying age of Russian Jews was extraordinarily low, and most Jewish males over the age of eighteen were married and heads of families. The brutal decision facing the Jewish leaders was whether to conscript fathers or their children. In order to minimize the social and economic strain that would result from any loss of manpower to an already impoverished society, the decision was reached to draft the children.

In this connection there occurred the second most important type of violation of the recruitment laws, the widespread conscription of Jewish children under the age of twelve. Birth certificates were an extremely rare commodity among Russian Jews at this time, and there was no legal way to establish one's age. When a recruit was presented for induction, his age was set in one of two ways if he had no documents: the presiding officer would estimate the age of the recruit based on his appearance, or witnesses would be called to testify to his age. Both of these methods were open to irregularities. It is difficult to imagine any army official disagreeing with Jewish representatives presenting a child for induction; in any case, the proclivity of Russian bureaucrats for bribes was legendary. And although the bearing of false witness was considered a severe offense in Jewish law, the poverty-stricken Pale of Settlement never lacked persons willing to perjure themselves—especially in a gentile court—for a price.

Consequently, a substantial number of Jewish children below the age of twelve were drafted into the Cantonist battalions. Memoirs and contemporary accounts abound with examples: I. Itskovich entered the Irkutsk Cantonist battalion at the age of seven; the Cantonist Nizherovskii was converted in the Pskov battalion at the age of eight; the Cantonists Reshtik, Bentshik, and Nefedov were already baptized in the army at the ages of nine, ten, and twelve, respectively.[53] One memoirist even recalled the drafting of a boy of five.[54]

In all such cases, the appropriate number of years was simply added to the child's age on his induction papers. In 1829 the minister of war asked the chief doctor of the Kiev Military Hospital why the sickness and mortality rates of Jewish Cantonists were so high. The doctor replied:

Of the 1,600 new Cantonists who arrived in 1828, half were brought from distant regions. Their registration lists stated that they were ten years old, but due to the fact that their baby teeth were still falling out, it was clear that they could not have been older than eight. There were no resources to send them back to their far-off parents, and so the battalion was forced to retain them, registering them with the ages given on the lists.[55]

The most vivid description of the ages and condition of Jewish children in Nicholas's army can be found in the memoirs of Alexander Herzen. In 1835, Herzen was exiled to Viatka for three years. Near this town, one thousand versts from Moscow, Herzen encountered a group of children being taken to Kazan. He asked the convoy officer who these children were and where they were going, and the following conversation ensued:

"Oh, don't ask; it'd even break your heart. Well, I suppose my superiors know all about it; it is our duty to carry out orders and we are not responsible, but looking at it as a man, it is an ugly business."

"Why, what is it?"

"You see, they have collected a crowd of cursed little Jew boys of eight or nine years old. Whether they are taking them for the navy or what, I can't say. At first the orders were to drive them to Perm; then there was a change, and we are driving them to Kazan. I took them over a hundred versts farther back. The officer who handed them over said, 'It's dreadful, and that's all about it; a third were left on the way' (and the officer pointed to the earth). 'Not half will reach their destinations,' " he said.

"Have there been epidemics, or what?" I asked, deeply moved.

"No, not epidemics, but they just die off like flies. A Jew boy, you know, is such a frail, weakly creature, like a skinned cat; he is not used to tramping in the mud for ten hours a day and eating biscuits—then again, being among strangers, no father nor mother nor petting; well, they cough and cough until they cough themselves into their graves. And I ask you, what use is it to them? What can they do with little boys?"

I made no answer.[56]

Herzen continued with a description of the children:

They brought the children and formed them into regular ranks: it was one of the most awful sights I have ever seen, those poor, poor children! Boys of twelve or thirteen might somehow have survived it, but little fellows of eight and ten. . . . Not even a brush full of black paint could put such horror on canvas.

Pale, exhausted, with frightened faces, they stood in thick, clumsy, soldiers' overcoats, with stand-up collars, fixing helpless, pitiful eyes on the garrison soldiers who were roughly getting them into ranks. The white lips, the blue rings under their eyes bore witness to fever or chill. And these sick children, without care or kindness, exposed to the raw wind that blows unobstructed from the Arctic Ocean, were going to their graves.[57]

Children were also presented as recruits in cases for which adult recruits were required by the law, such as voluntary replacements for other recruits. One shoemaker's apprentice, for example, was persuaded by his master to "volunteer" in place of a rich man's son. The child's guardians objected at first but soon bowed to the will of their ward, perhaps after having been promised a share of the spoils.[58]

This last case points to another important aspect of the conscription of the Jews. Wherever possible, the recruits were taken from the ranks of the poor and unemployed, who had no influence on the communal leadership. This was accomplished primarily by ordering the queue books in such a way that the poor families would always remain at the top of the list, and the turn would rarely reach the richer families. Although such practices elicited the vengeful condemnation of contemporary intellectuals and later populist historians, they were sanctioned and even recommended by the government. Conscription was viewed by the tsarist authorities as an effective means of social and economic control, and the kahal, like the communes of townspeople and peasants, had the right to recruit anyone for failure to pay taxes, for rebelliousness, or for any kind of unsociable conduct. In addition, the 1828 amendment to the Jewish Recruitment Statute specifically permitted the kahal leaders to combine small families and divide large ones at random.

The few communal recruitment records that have survived testify to the prevalence of such discrimination. For example, the Grodno kahal filled its 1828 quota entirely with "undesirables."[59] The archives of the Minsk community, preserved in the YIVO Institute, provide more graphic detail of such procedures. In 1827 the Minsk kahal, combined with several smaller neighboring communities, presented a list of seventy potential conscripts to the authorities. Of these seventy, forty-one were over eighteen, but forty-four were either unmarried or living alone; thirty had no occupation, thirteen were listed as servants, three as beggars, three as unskilled laborers, and fourteen as tailors, tradesmen, or cobblers; forty-nine of the seventy were registered as living in the city, twelve were vagabonds, and eight were living in nearby villages.[60] When the actual draft call was issued, however, most of these men and boys could not be located or had some valid exemption, and so the communities compiled another list of fifty-two possible recruits. Of these, almost half were under eighteen, but only twenty-three lived alone; their occupational distribution was roughly the same as their predecessors, but now only twenty-four were listed as city dwellers, while the remaining twenty-eight were living in villages or were vagabonds.[61] Since the total male population of these communities was approximately six thousand at this time,[62] and the quota for the year was four per thousand,[63] the kahal had no problem disposing of its obligations without seriously compromising the economic stability of its population. This was, of course, merely the first year of the conscription of the Jews.

At times, the kahal leaders did overstep the wide discretion allowed them by the law and extended the designation "undesirable" to those who displayed religious laxity—a usage specifically forbidden by law. The Hebrew writer Avraham Ber Gottlober related in his memoirs a story of the Hasidic kahal leader of Old Constantine who tricked the non-Hasidic children of the community into the draft by spreading rumors of the repeal of the conscription decree.[64] In the town of Ryzhan, Grodno Province, the communal leaders were planning to draft a poor tailor known as "Leybechke der treyfnyak" since he did not observe the laws of Sabbath and kashrut, but they were forbidden to do so by the local rabbi.[65] In Vilna, the traditionalist kahal authorities later attempted to forestall the opening of the government-sponsored rabbinical seminaries by drafting the sons of several of its proposed teachers, but this was discovered by the local administration and forbidden.[66]

Since the proportion of underage recruits in the ranks of the conscripts was so high, and parents fought the recruitment of their children so strenuously, the kahal leaders had to hire special deputies to find and abduct suitable candidates for the draft. These posses, called *khappers* by the Jews (from the Yiddish verb *khapn*, to catch), soon became permanent fixtures in the Pale and earned the hatred and the scorn of the masses of Jews. In the early years of Nicholas's regime, the main duties of these *khappers* were to search out fugitives and to kidnap young children from their mothers' arms. The work was lucrative; apart from the rewards paid by the government and the salary from the kahal, the *khappers* frequently released kidnapped children for ransom money and replaced them with others.

Specific examples of the treachery of the *khappers* abound in the memoir literature of the period. The following two accounts are paradigmatic. In Kamenets, despite the efforts of his friends and schoolmates, the *khappers* caught Yosl, the eight-year-old son of a rich coachman who had died. Yosl's mother followed him to Brest-Litovsk, but she was sent back to Kamenets, where she died a few days later. A year passed, and Yosl returned to Kamenets with a battalion of soldiers, but he was now an unresponsive idiot, doomed to die within a short time.[67] The Hebrew writer Y. L. Levin was walking along the streets of Minsk when he saw six men emerge from a coach and enter a Jewish house. A few moments later the men came out, dragging a child whom they had gagged. The child's mother soon followed, screaming and sobbing, but the *khappers* threw her to the ground and rode off with the child.[68]

The institution of the *khappers* flourished, however, after the introduction of a law in July 1853 which allowed the Jewish community to present any Jew found traveling without a passport as a substitute for a recruit required from the community.[69] Groups of *khappers* would roam through the streets abducting anyone who passed by. Often, an ordinary Jew would capture a child or adult and hand him over to the *khappers* as a substitute for a son or a brother.

Specific incidents provide shocking tales of horror. One poor woman with two small children in her arms entered a store in Zhitomir one Friday afternoon to beg for bread for the Sabbath. When the storekeeper heard that the woman was from Kiev Province, he winked to his son who grabbed the older child and carried him off to the *khappers*.[70] In Volhynia one *khapper* captured and sold ten young boys in three months; later, he himself was caught without a passport in Zhitomir and drafted.[71]

Such stories could be multiplied indefinitely, but one last example will suffice to characterize the tragic chaos which prevailed among Russian Jews as a result of Nicholas's new policy. A poor peasant woman asked a Jewish butcher's wife for some kosher meat to feed two Jewish boys who were hiding in her village. The butcher's wife, assured by her husband that their own two sons were hiding in town with a Christian friend, seized on the opportunity of finding replacements for her sons and asked the naive peasant where the two boys were hiding. She then hurried to inform the local *khappers* of her discovery. When the *khappers* returned with the boys, the butcher's wife was astonished to see that these were her own two sons.[72]

The Reaction

Before such acts of desperation became common, the Russian Jews reacted to the conscription policy within their traditional world view. Their initial response to the 1827 decree, therefore, was a mixture of gloom, fear, and mystical speculation. "All artisans' shops were abandoned," reported the Yiddish writer A. M. Dik in Vilna,

no matches were made, and many were broken off. Many Jews prepared to go to Palestine, others rushed to join the merchant guilds. A cripple was considered a saved man, an only son a joy, a hunchback an aristocrat.[73]

The natural tendency of the pious Jews to view such an edict as a punishment from God was reinforced by the coincidence of the publication of the recruitment statute with the beginning of the penitential Seliḥot period of the Jewish year. Preachers found ancient texts which proved that the decree would be revoked if the Jews would repent. Synagogues were filled day and night, fasts proclaimed and prolonged, contributions to charity increased, all in the belief, as the liturgy has it, that "penitence, prayer, and charity annul a severe verdict." While the communal leaders called meetings to discuss the crisis, the masses flocked to the cemeteries to plead for the intercession of their deceased parents. One town solemnly watched a folk preacher place a letter to God in the hands of a corpse in the hope that this would convince Him to change Nicholas's mind. [74]

When it became apparent that penitence alone would not suffice, the Jews did not resign themselves to serving the tsar obediently. The methods they used to evade the draft were similar to those employed by the Russian peasants. They hid in forests, amputated their fingers or toes, or escaped across the frontiers. The governor of Volhynia reported that such evasions were so widespread among the Jews of his jurisdiction that it was quite common not to find even one eligible recruit in many Jewish communities during the conscription season. [75]

When the Jews could not escape the draft by such means, they found refuge in their traditional channels of resistance to external threat, an adamant consolidation and intensification of their religious armor. Consequently, the number of students in the traditional Jewish schools, the *hadarim* and yeshivot, rose significantly during Nicholas's rule. Many parents who previously could not afford to send their children to school for long periods of time now realized that they could not afford not to keep them in school, fearing that they would be conscripted without a sufficient knowledge of Judaism to resist conversion and calculating that the kahal leaders were reluctant to draft good Talmud students. [76]

This inward-directed response to the actions of Nicholas's government was symptomatic of the deep-seated, intuitive distrust of gentile authority common to Jews throughout the Diaspora. To the Russian Jews, the new conscription decrees were horrifying but not surprising: evil edicts aimed at converting Jews were the natural and expected products of Exile. Entirely unexpected and astonishing, however, was the role that the Jewish leaders played in the new recruitment system: the fact that Jew was pitted against Jew in ways previously unimagined and that the suffering was not shared equally by all Jews. The strength of traditional Jewish society had always been its solidarity. Although there were definite social and economic divisions among the Jews, these had never resulted in a true polarization of the community along class lines (despite allegations to the contrary of Marxist historians). To be sure, the various sectarian movements and political crises of the eighteenth century had effected some weakening of Jewish solidarity and cohesiveness—though its scope and nature are far from certain and the subject of much historiographic debate.[77] It is clear, however, that at the beginning of the nineteenth century the essential fabric of Jewish unity had survived intact. The opposing groups always came together in the end to unite against a common, external enemy. The antagonisms that resulted from the conscription system, on the other hand, were never truly assuaged for they were of an entirely novel order. Now it was Jew oppressing Jew.

Perhaps the most poignant evocation of the shock that resulted from this new predicament was provided by the Hebrew writer Buki ben Yagli (Y. L. Katsenelson) in his description of his grandmother's response to the *khappers*. At first, the old woman believed that the *khappers* in her town must be Philistines or Amalekites; soon she discovered, as she told her grandson,

No, my child, to our great horror, all *khappers* were in fact Jews, Jews with beards and sidelocks. And that is indeed our greatest problem. We Jews are accustomed to attacks, libels, and evil decrees from the non-Jews—such have happened from time immemorial, and such is our lot in Exile. In the past, there were Gentiles who held a cross in one hand and a knife in the other, and said: "Jew, kiss the cross or die," and the Jews preferred death to apostasy. But now there come Jews, religious Jews, who capture children and send them off to apostasy. Such a punishment was not even listed in the Bible's list of the most horrible curses. Jews spill the blood of their brothers, and God is silent, the rabbis are silent. . . . [78]

This shock was soon translated into anger and bitterness, which could not be vented through the time-honored modes of internalized protest. As a result, an entirely unprecedented breaking of the ranks occurred in Jewish society; numerous riots and attacks against the *khappers* and their kahal employers erupted throughout the Pale, cases of informing to the government mounted both in frequency and in scope, and several groups of Jews even took the radical step of applying for legal separation from the rest of the Jewish community. These actions seriously debilitated the autonomous communal structure, whose powers were steadily being diminished by the government.[79]

As the old organization of Jewish society in Russia lost its coherence, a new institutional order had to be found. As the traditional world view was complicated by the exigencies of the new political and legal context, new ideas and ideologies had to be invented. In these parallel processes, the experience of the recruitment policy played a critical role. But in the court and St. Petersburg, conscription was only the first round in the government's emerging new policy on the Jews.

2 · Political Offensive

. . . le despotisme n'est jamais si redoutable que lorsqu'il prétend faire du bien, car alors il croit excuser ses actes les plus revoltants par ses intentions, et le mal qui se donne pour remède n'a plus de bornes.

Custine

The Statute of 1835

The two main poles of Nicholas's Jewish policy were conscription and conversion through the military. After assuring the implementation of these two goals, he gave very little thought to the Jews and withdrew from any active determination of policy in their regard. When any new problem arose, he had a simple solution: conscript the offenders, raise the quotas, convert.

When these simple measures were not applicable, Nicholas favored a passive, patient reliance on the precedents of his predecessors. These precedents, however, were often not accessible or very clear owing to the absence of a systematic code of Russian law. Therefore, in line with his general policy of codifying and editing the law books, Nicholas ordered the Jewish Committee to bring into order all the laws affecting the Jews.

The purpose of this codification was not to innovate, merely to clarify, but in the course of sorting out the laws, a divergence of opinion did emerge in the highest bureaucratic circles. The Department of Laws of the State Council put forward several alleviative amendments to a draft statute on the Jews prepared by the Jewish Committee. These amendments called for the cessation of all expulsions from the villages, the extension of the residence rights of

Jewish merchants of the first guild to include all of Russia, the recision of the expulsion of the Jews from Kiev, and various reductions of the rigors of the conscription system, particularly the recruitment of underage recruits.[1]

Unfortunately, exactly who proposed these changes and why are not known, but it seems safe to assume that they were motivated by economic considerations: the fear of loss of revenue to the treasury combined with the expectation of personal remuneration from grateful Jewish lobbyists.[2]

Of course, Nicholas was in no way bound to accept these recommendations. However, he did accept the first, which advised him to cease the expulsion of the Jews from rural settlements. The second amendment was rejected by two-thirds of the members of the council and by the emperor, although the amount of time permitted guild merchants outside the Pale was extended. The third recommendation was rejected in the council by a surprisingly tight majority of one; the emperor declined this counsel, along with the last amendment.[3]

The final result of these deliberations, therefore, was not so static as might have been predicted. The resulting Statute on the Jews, published on April 13, 1835, did contain some important innovations, along with a restatement of most of the provisions of Alexander's 1804 statute collated with the laws passed in the interim.[4]

First, the Pale of Settlement was finally clearly delineated,[5] its borders remaining in effect until World War I. It consisted of the provinces of Grodno, Vilna, Volhynia, Podolia, Minsk, and Ekaterinoslav in their entirety; the Bessarabian and Belostok oblasts; the Kiev Province, except for the city of Kiev; the Kherson Province, except for Nikolaev; the Taurida Province, except for Sebastopol'; the provinces of Mogilev and Vitebsk, except for the rural settlements; the Chernigov and Poltava provinces, excluding the Crown and Cossack settlements; and the existing Jewish communities of Kurland, Riga, and Shlok, and all villages and rural settlements within fifty versts of the western frontiers of the empire (nos. 3–5). Within these areas, the Jews were permitted to move from place to place as they desired and to acquire land and property of any sort, save estates settled with serfs (no. 12). There was to be no more forced resettlement, that is, expulsions from the villages; this most important provision was enacted in a separate law preceding the full statute.[6] Temporary sojourns outside the Pale were permitted for the acquisition of inheritance, the securing of rights at judicial venues, study at academic institutions, and some commercial affairs. First-guild merchants were permitted to travel to both capitals and to seaports and to reside in Moscow for periods of up to six months at a time—a substantial extension from the one-month period previously allowed (no. 51). For the first time, Jewish merchants were officially permitted to travel to the important commercial fairs outside the Pale, at Nizhnii-Novgorod, Irtbits, Koren', Kharkov, and Sumsk (no. 51).

In a reversal of policy, Jewish merchants and townspeople were permitted to participate in the organs of municipal self-government "on the same basis as persons of other creeds" (no. 77)—a direct contravention of a large number of local traditions which restricted the access of Jews to a number of posts in most municipalities and disenfranchised them completely in others. For the first time, a limitation was introduced on the marrying age of Jews: no Jewish male under the age of eighteen or female under sixteen could marry (no. 17).[7] New, too, were the requirement that every rabbi take an oath of allegiance to the Russian state and its laws and the corollary provision that if a rabbi could not fulfill all the functions of his office, the community could elect several learned Jews to assist him in his clerical and ritual duties (no. 90).

In addition to these innovations, the statute reaffirmed the 1804 provisions on other matters. Jews were still forbidden to retain Christian servants, except in agriculture, factory industry, and various commercial posts (no. 15). Colonizing was encouraged as before, with increased access to land and greater tax concessions (nos. 121–47). Tax farming in all its guises, including the crucial liquor trade, was open to Jews on the same basis as before (no. 64). The power, authority, and obligations of the kahal and synagogue were also unchanged (nos. 67, 98–103), as were the laws on taxation, except that a new tax ordinance was promised (no. 75). The provisions of the 1804 statute that permitted Jewish children to attend any educational institutions were retained, as was the supremely important right to maintain a separate Jewish educational system of *ḥadarim* and yeshivot (nos. 104–17). Finally, foreign Jews visiting or residing in Russia were to be governed by the previous laws and restrictions (nos. 118–21).

The Revisions and Amendments

The Statute of 1835 had been intended as a brief Code of Laws for the Jews, a comprehensive guide to their status in the empire. However, it soon became clear that the drafters of the statute had dealt ineffectively or incompletely with several important areas of contact between the Jews and the government. Almost immediately after the statute's publication on April 13, a series of clarifying regulations began to be issued, which, in effect, restored the ad hoc, haphazard manner of dealing with the Jews supposedly superseded by the statute.

Thus, on April 22, 1835, the State Council again took up the question of the Jewish guild merchants and proposed a 20 percent reduction in the dues to the first—that is, the most privileged— guild, in compensation for the limited field of activity open to Jewish merchants in comparison with their gentile competitors. This reduction for Jewish merchants alone was approved by Nicholas on May 31.[8]

A more revealing revision was necessary in connection with the election of Jews to the organs of municipal self-government. It is most unlikely that the authors of the statute knew exactly what they were doing when they drafted its article 77. They could not possibly have breached traditions dating back to the latter years of Catherine II's reign without having the authorization of the State Council and the tsar, and neither would have approved such a move. The framing of this article seems to have been one of those not uncommon blunders of an essentially incompetent bureaucracy neither overly familiar nor particularly concerned with Jewish life. Immediately after the publication of the statute, local officials began to protest the equality provision. Since new regulations for self-rule in general in the Western Provinces were then being formulated, an amendment was appended to these regulations reinstating the previous stipulation that only one-third of the members of any city magistracy or town council could be Jewish, and none in Vilna or Kiev.[9]

This correction was not at all satisfactory to the protesting local authorities: there were many more offices previously closed to Jews and important local traditions not dealt with. Most important, the Jews in the Lithuanian provinces had never been permitted to hold municipal office at all, as was pointed out most vigorously by Governor-General Dolgorukov, who simply refused to enforce the new law pending further clarification and correction from St. Petersburg. This finally came in July 1839 in the form of a new definitive law. In elections to be held separately from those of the Christians, Jews could be elected members of the city council or magistracy, except in Vilna and Kiev; they might be elected as members of the Billeting Commissions and Taxation Committees and as representatives of their estates to various forums; in all cases they could not constitute more than one-third of the members of any body and nowhere could they hold the office of *burgomister*, city head, or delegate to the regional and police councils. These last two restrictions had been suggested by Dolgorukov, who had but a Pyrrhic victory in the end; the rules were now to be applied equally in all of the Western Provinces, including his own.[10]

Concurrently, a different kind of revision took place regarding articles 27 and 32 of the statute, which permitted Jews to become agriculturists on lands assigned to them from state property by the minister of finance. Since the Pale was composed of territories with an acute shortage of virgin arable land, the minister of finance, Kankrin, decided to implement these provisions without delay by colonizing Jews on the empty plains of Siberia. This plan was approved by the Committee for the Western Provinces late in 1835 and then by the Committee of Ministers, and 15,154 *desiatiny* (approximately 40,915 acres) were set aside for Jewish colonization in the Tobol'sk Province and Omsk Oblast of Siberia.[11] As was the case every time a new tract of land was offered to Russian Jews, a surprisingly large number of them applied to move to the new lands; so many did that Kankrin had to allocate 13,363 more *desiatiny* to provide the requisite quota of land per settler.[12]

When this second grant of land was submitted for approval to Nicholas, he astonished all his advisers by ordering a halt to all settlement of Jews in Siberia. Apparently, Minister of Internal Affairs D. N. Bludov and Chief of the Third Section A. Kh. Benkendorf had convinced Nicholas that it was inappropriate to send Jews to Siberia to improve their moral status; a more likely result would be the transplantation to Siberia of the commercial practices of the Jews in the Pale to the detriment of the native population. Moreover, it was a bad precedent to introduce Jews into areas not permitted them by the statute.[13] As a result, Nicholas soon ordered not only the cessation of all settlement of Jews in Siberia but also the transfer of the Jews already there to lands in New Russia.[14]

As promised in article 75 of the statute, a new regulation of the *korobka* tax was issued in October 1839.[15] The *korobka* was the basic internal tax of the Jewish community, used to pay taxes to the government, dispose of debts, and provide for the communal and philanthropic needs of the community. The intricacies of the administration and collection of this tax had become so complex over the years that the Russian government was loath—or unable—to attempt to regulate it completely from above and had issued only partial decrees in regard to particular aspects of the tax. Only in the latter part of the 1830s did the Ministry of Finance undertake a comprehensive investigation of the *korobka,* culminating in a law that stipulated that the *korobka* belonged to the Jewish community but was to be administered under the control of the local authorities. There were to be two types of *korobka:* the general tax, obligatory in all Jewish communities and obtained from a surcharge on the slaughtering and sale of kosher meat, and the auxiliary tax, optionally imposed at the discretion of each kahal and collected as a percentage on all commercial and property transactions and on the manufacture of the special Jewish garb. Both types of *korobka* were to be farmed out to tax farmers, supervised by the kahals. In addition, estate taxes and revenues from communal bathhouses, as well as fines paid to the community treasury, were to be added to the *korobka*, but these were to be paid directly to the authorities.

The statute had completely overlooked one critical area of Jewish life, last the subject of legislation in 1826—the censorship of Jewish books. Although control over publishing and importation of Jewish books had increased since the accession of Nicholas, censorship of these books was far from effective, because of the large number of Hebrew presses in small towns in the Pale and the close ties of Russian Jews with their coreligionists across the Austrian and Prussian frontiers. In the early 1830s, a number of reports had reached various ministries in St. Petersburg regarding the large number of uncensored books in Jewish libraries. These reports—actually denunciations—were made by maskilim, proponents of the Jewish Enlightenment movement, the Haskalah, in the hope of enlisting the aid of the authorities in counteracting the influence of the Hasidim, who produced a prodigious number of devotional and hagiographic tracts that eluded the censors' control.[16]

At this stage, the government had not yet developed any relations with the maskilim. Various ministers periodically extended help to an ambitious maskil who petitioned the authorities for subsidies—as was the case with the Hebrew writer Isaac Ber Levinsohn in 1828[17]—but this was done without any conscious taking of sides in internal Jewish debates; anyone who informed on the subversive Jews was rewarded. The sectarian squabbles between "enlightened" and "obscurantist" Jews were regarded by the government as oversubtle: the minister of internal affairs, Count Bludov, for example, reacted to these denunciations of uncensored books by stating that he could see no difference between the Hasidim and their opponents—they were all fanatic, ignorant Jews.[18]

The large stores of uncensored books, however, did engage Bludov's interest and whet his bureaucratic appetite, regardless of their provenance. As a result, he introduced a new censorship law in October 1836, which went far beyond any previous legislation. All books held by Jews that had been published without censorship or imported without permission were to be presented within a year to the local police; a special commission of rabbis would examine these works and report any unsuitable ones to the Ministry of Internal Affairs. Thereafter, any uncensored work found in the possession of a Jew would constitute grounds for serious punishment. In addition, in order to facilitate supervision over Jewish books, all Hebrew printing shops were to be closed, with the exception of one in Vilna and another in Kiev (later changed to Zhitomir), where special censors would be appointed.[19]

The maskilim were disappointed; relegating censorship to rabbis was self-defeating from their point of view. But the proposed rabbinical supervision did not occur, since the number of books presented to the police was so large that Bludov was moved to order his officials to dispose of the problem by burning all the accumulated books.[20]

Such an order was typical of Nicholas's censorship policies of the 1830s and 1840s, when the infamous Third Section of the Imperial Chancellery gained more and more control over the enormous censorship apparatus of the Russian state.[21] Yet despite their number, imperial Russian censors were notoriously inefficient; as Isaiah Berlin has noted, censorship in nineteenth-century Russia

was an obstacle, at times a maddening one. . . . But because it was, like so much in Old Russia, inefficient, corrupt, indolent, often stupid or deliberately lenient—and because so many loopholes could always be found by the ingenious and desperate, not much that was subversive was stymied effectively.[22]

Indeed, an enormous number of Jewish books were published in Russia in Nicholas's reign despite the intervention of the police and their informers: literally hundreds of rulings in Jewish law, Hasidic Hagiographa, Yiddish chapbooks, et cetera.[23]

The importance of this episode, therefore, was not so much its practical effect as its adumbration of a dramatic new alignment of forces: the government working in consort with the enlightened Jews against traditional Jewish society. At this point, the development was merely in embryo; the government was not yet conscious of the potent possibilities offered by the growing split within the Jewish community. Within a very short time, however, this consciousness did appear and led to radical changes in the lives of Russia's Jews.

The Kiselev Reforms

It was not only the maskilim who submitted proposals to the government regarding the Jews. Because of the increasingly dismal economic situation in the Western Provinces, the scapegoat theory of Jewish responsibility for Ukrainian and Belorussian penury became more popular than ever among local officials, who recommended a variety of old and new repressive measures against the Jews in their reports to superiors. By the middle of 1840, a considerable number of such reports had accumulated at court, and Nicholas ordered the State Council to consider whether any new policy ought to be developed in regard to the Jews. The council stood by its former work and rejected the recommendations of the officials, finding that the existing legislation was sufficient.[24]

Thereupon, Nicholas turned to his most creative adviser, Count P. D. Kiselev, then in the midst of a radical reform of the status of the state peasants, to review all these reports. Within a short time, Kiselev submitted to the emperor the memorandum "On the Ordering of the Jewish Nation in Russia," which changed the course of the government's Jewish policy.[25]

The memorandum was based on a pastiche of misinformation that had been submitted as evidence to the former Jewish committees and incorporated the standard misrepresentations of Jewish religious traditions and economic behavior found in all such analyses since the Polish Partitions. Thus, according to the memorandum, the causes of the "estrangement of the Jews from the general civil order" were (1) the religious teachings of the Talmud, which taught the Jews not only that they were the Chosen People but also that as a result of their election they were to dominate all other nations politically and economically and therefore were released from any moral obligation to gentiles or responsibility to non-Jewish courts; (2) the existence of the kahal, which camouflaged the subversive Jewish court and exercised unlimited control over the Jews, exceeding that of the rabbis; (3) the *korobka* tax, which was secretly controlled by the kahal and which reinforced the servility of the Jewish masses to their leaders; and (4) the unique dress of the Jews, which had no religious significance and served only to separate the Jews from the rest of the population.[26]

Although Kiselev's diagnosis was traditional, his prescription was revolutionary. For the first time, a high Russian official enjoying the confidence of the tsar came to the conclusion that repressive measures could not solve the Jewish problem in Russia. Kiselev argued that the Jews had withstood the severest persecutions and repression throughout the ages and had maintained their national unity and character; the former policies of the Russian government had been unable to change that by means of renewed oppression and would continue to fail if they remained within the same framework. The solution was to abandon police restrictions and "on the example of other states to begin the fundamental transformation of this nation, i.e., the removal of those harmful factors that obstruct its path to the general civil order."[27]

According to Kiselev, the actions of the government must be devoted to two goals: the moral and religious reeducation of the Jews and the abolition of those legal impediments to the "rapprochement" of the Jews with the rest of the population. In order to achieve the first goal, the government should establish a network of schools for Jewish children in which special attention would be given to the teaching of Russian language and history, and Judaic subjects would be taught from a new Jewish catechism that would stress duty to the monarch, loyalty to the state, and the superiority of "useful" occupations. In addition, the government should extend its control over the private education of Jewish children, invite enlightened Jews from Prussia and Austria to teach in the new schools, and require that all rabbis be certified by the new schools. Moreover, provincial rabbis should be appointed throughout the Pale, and the separate Jewish dress outlawed.[28] The second goal would be even easier to legislate: the kahal and the *korobka* should be abolished immediately by the government.[29]

These proposals, Kiselev confessed, would take some time to

effect the desired transformation of Jewish society. The government would have to wait for the maturation of a new generation of Jews, enlightened and economically restratified. In the interim, several measures would be required to spur the productivity of the rest of the Jews, dividing the useful Jews from the nonuseful. Jewish townspeople would therefore be given five years to establish their usefulness; this could be accomplished either by proving stable residence through ownership of property or by becoming artisans, agriculturists, or guild merchants. At the end of the five-year transition period, any Jew who failed to establish his usefulness would be conscripted for longer terms than usual and then forcibly retrained in one of the useful occupations.[30]

This last recommendation clearly contradicted Kiselev's rejection of repressive police measures, but this was the least of the self-contradictions inherent in the memorandum. Kiselev—most probably under the tutelage of Uvarov—had studied the experiences of Western European countries with their Jews and was consciously emulating the policies of Prussia, Austria, Bavaria, Baden, and, to a lesser degree, France. Basically, the intent of the new policy was to reproduce in Russia the social metamorphosis which had taken place in Western European Jewry: to transform the Jews into—idealized—German Jews, educated in the language and culture of their country, integrated into its economy in productive professions, moderate in religion, perhaps even more receptive to Christianity.[31] In some parts of Germany, Kiselev observed with admiration, there had emerged a new sect of enlightened Jews who had developed a sort of Jewish Protestantism, and in North America the Jews had progressed so far that they had even switched their sabbath to Sunday.[32] "Believe me," Uvarov told Max Lilienthal, "if we had such Jews as I met in the different capitals of Germany, we would treat them with the utmost distinction, but our Jews are entirely different."[33]

Neither Kiselev nor Uvarov recognized, however, that there were also crucial differences between the governments they were emulating and their own, which cast the Jewish policies they were mimicking in an entirely different light. In Western Europe, the transformation of Jewish society had been effected as a quid pro quo: Jewish communal autonomy was exchanged for individual civic rights; educational and religious unity was weakened as the perception of the possibilities for at least partial integration into a new "semi-neutral society" became apparent.[34]

In Kiselev's rather naive reformulation of the policies of the Western powers, this essential reciprocal character of the transformation of Jewish life was entirely ignored. Significantly, in his overview of the Western policies, Kiselev discussed the French case only under Napoleon, omitting any mention of the precondition of his actions, the emancipation of French Jewry.[35] There is no evidence that either Kiselev or Uvarov thought out with any clarity what the actual results of adopting these policies in Russia would be. They spoke only in the vaguest way of an eventual rapprochement between the Jews and Russian society, never detailing the legal or social consequences of that process. Those historians who assumed that the goal of the new policy was simply the conversion of the Jews presupposed a clarity of purpose in the minds of Kiselev and his colleagues that was entirely absent. When Russian officials intended their policies to lead to conversion, they were not at all shy about saying so in their internal correspondence and drafted legislation which pursued this goal rather efficiently—as can be seen with regard to conscription.

Kiselev's memorandum, therefore, began with a kernel of rational analysis that was all but entirely overwhelmed by an overarching superficiality of vision and understanding. Nonetheless, its recommendations were approved by the emperor, who then appointed Kiselev as the head of a new committee whose title reflected the acceptance of the argument of the memorandum: the Committee for the Determination of Measures toward the Fundamental Transformation of the Jews in Russia.[36] Besides the chairman, the committee consisted of the head of the Second Section of the Imperial Chancellery, Bludov; the acting minister of internal affairs, A. S. Stroganov; the assistant minister of finance, F. P. Vronchenko; General L. V. Dubal't; and—as an afterthought—the minister of national enlightenment, Uvarov.[37] The fact that Nicholas did not immediately think of appointing Uvarov to this committee testifies to the novelty of the notion of using education as a tool of policy toward the Jews in the minds of Russia's leaders. Soon, this would become one of the dominant motifs of Jewish policy.

By the end of 1841, the committee had met several times to discuss Kiselev's recommendations and sent the following priority listing of legislation to Nicholas: (1) reordering the *korobka* and abolishing the kahal, (2) establishing state-sponsored Jewish schools, (3) appointing provincial chief rabbis, (4) colonizing the Jews on state lands, (5) dividing the Jews into useful and nonuseful categories, and (6) outlawing the traditional garb of the Jews. Nicholas accepted these recommendations and ordered each member of the committee to work on legislation in his own area of competence. He changed the rank order of the legislation slightly but significantly by raising the reclassification scheme from fifth to third place but also stipulated that the nonuseful Jews be conscripted at five times the normal quota, rather than at merely double, as the committee had suggested.[38]

Within a short time, these recommendations began to bear legislative fruits. The rapidity with which this policy produced results was not solely due to Kiselev's persuasiveness. Rather, these measures were implemented immediately since they fit into a general, though unconscious, pattern of Russian policy after the Polish Uprising of 1830, when the frightened Russian government introduced a series of measures in the Western Provinces that were intended to quell further subversive activities in these formerly Polish territories. Until 1830 the local administration of this area was governed by provisions of the Magdeburg Law, the Lithuanian Statute, and Ukrainian common law. Beginning in 1831, this judicial autonomy was steadily diminished, and it was rescinded altogether in 1840.[39] At the same time, a major reclassification of the local gentry was begun, and some sixty-four thousand petty polonized nobles were stripped of their status and downgraded to the category of taxable landholders (*odnodvortsy*) in the countryside and urban dwellers (*grazhdane*) in the cities. These newly declassed nobles were then subjected to a series of stringent regulations: conscription at double the usual quota, forced resettlement, imposed russification of their schools, and renewed interference into their religious affairs.[40]

With a time lag of about ten years, all these measures were introduced in parallel though distinctive ways for the Jews, as the legislative results of Kiselev's recommendations. Except for the increased draft quotas, issued together for the Jews and the *grazhdane* and *odnodvortsy* of the Western Provinces, the two problems and policies were never linked in the published laws or internal writings of the bureaucrats. It may well be that there was never even any covert but conscious link between the two; the uniqueness of the Jews in the minds of even the most liberal Russian bureaucrats precluded such rational comparison. In retrospect, however, there can be no doubt that the parallels between the measures taken to solve both problems were anything but coincidental. Rather, the true nature of Russian policymaking was revealed through this unconscious parallelism: a deep structure which effectively precluded innovation.

Thus, although Kiselev's original—if shallow—ideas broke entirely new ground in the history of Russian governmental attitudes toward the Jews, when his recommendations were translated into law, their radical novelty was diffused by the form given by the bureaucracy. Kiselev had dared to suggest that the reform of Russia's Jews follow the example of the civic betterment of Western European Jewry. As each of his recommendations was implemented, any vestigial resemblances to their Western model were all but obscured by the techniques borrowed by the tsarist officials from their tactics of neutralization of the Ukrainian gentry.

3 · Beginnings of the Russian Haskalah

Quelques zélés israélites que nous soyions dans l'intérieur de nos temples, soyons de bons citoyens dans les relations de la vie extérieure.

Joachim Tarnopol, Odessa, 1854

The first plank in the program of Kiselev's Committee for the Transformation of the Jews to be legislated was the reeducation of the Jews through a network of government-sponsored schools and rabbinical seminaries. In order to understand the impact and results of this policy, it is necessary first to survey the extent of the enlightenment of the Jews in Russia before the 1840s and then to analyze in greater detail the purpose and evolution of the school system.[1]

From the early eighteenth century, there appeared within German Jewry individuals who cultivated the German language, secular studies, and European manners while expressing novel criticisms of Jewish life and thought in the spirit of the nascent Enlightenment. By mid-century this trend had coalesced into a fully articulated movement, known as Haskalah—Hebrew for Enlightenment—and perhaps best personified by Moses Mendelssohn. The radical innovation of this movement was not its recourse to German, natural science, or rationalist philosophy per se but a new intellectual and social ideology: an acceptance of the authority of non-Jewish thought and mores as at least equal to traditional Jewish teachings and behavior and a concomitant commitment to a fundamental reform of Jewish life according to "European" dictates and standards.

49

As the Haskalah spread through the German principalities and the Austrian Empire, it gained adherents in the neighboring Jewish communities of Russia and Poland. Yet until the 1820s, there were so few identifiable maskilim within the Russian Empire that there seemed to be no place in that Jewish society for them. Some, like Solomon Maimon, Solomon Dubno, and Zalkind Horowitz, were forced to spend their adult lives in Western Europe; others, like Leib Nevakhovich and Gregory Peretz, chose to convert to Christianity and remain in Russia.[2]

These were lonely, exceptional figures, who left no legacy or even means of communication to Russian Jewry. Beyond them, however, there was a large number of Jews perched on the borders of traditional society, influenced to some degree by the Haskalah but not willing or able publicly to declare allegiance to its controversial principles.

This border area was especially populous since—contrary to popular image—Eastern European Jewry had never been completely cut off from foreign intellectual developments and scientific learning. Through the ages, a small but important strain of Jewish scholars in the Polish-Lithuanian lands had displayed an awareness of philosophy, mathematics, natural sciences, and foreign languages and had composed tracts on these subjects in Hebrew.[3] This elite stratum of scholars, represented in the late eighteenth and early nineteenth centuries by the Gaon of Vilna and his disciples at the yeshivot of Lithuania, permitted access to such study only to those with the most thorough grounding in traditional Jewish sources and an unquestionable purity of intent. These investigations were to be undertaken as an ancillary tool in exegesis, not as a competing system of authority; lessons gleaned could only elucidate Jewish sources, not supersede them.

Yet, as the struggle between rabbinical Judaism and Hasidism intensified, this intellectual orientation developed into an important ideological force. In addition to its profound philosophical and religious disputes with the Hasidim, the Lithuanian school often focused its public criticism on the pedagogic deficiencies of Hasidic society. These criticisms were very similar to the specific educational proposals of the Haskalah: a stricter emphasis on the study of Hebrew grammar and the Bible, in addition to the Talmud; a moderation in the use of the hermeneutical technique of *pilpul;* the admission, on some level, of the study of secular subjects and languages.

As a result of this similarity of means, if not ends, it is often quite impossible to differentiate in the early years of the nineteenth century between a traditionalist of the Lithuanian school and a maskil. For example, scholars have long pondered the thought of one such ambiguous figure, Menashe of Ilya, who seems to have held maskilic views while functioning on the whole within the traditional community.[4]

In such cases, the historian's obsession with neat definitions and classifications may prove counterproductive, obscuring the most important aspects of the issue. Until the second quarter of the nineteenth century, it was possible for some thinkers to accept some of the ideas of the Haskalah but not its radical conclusions; more important, even full-fledged maskilim deliberately couched their arguments in the language of tradition in order to propagate their views more effectively and to protect themselves from the wrath of their opponents.

More vital than the search for precursors of the Haskalah or proto-maskilim, then, is an analysis of precisely when and why this fluidity between traditionalism and enlightenment was blocked, how the Haskalah in Russia changed from an amorphous body of ideas into an ideology and a movement. This transition occurred in two stages during the reign of Nicholas I, in large part as a direct result of the policies and actions of the government.

Intellectual developments in Judaism have rarely been so intimately linked with external forces, but the nexus between the Haskalah and the Russian government was recognized as critical by both supporters and enemies of enlightenment. In this connection, it is important to examine a paradox of Russian-Jewish culture. Russian Jews developed a mythology of the political importance of the maskilim which was independent of, and often contrary to, reality. Owing most probably to the role played by the German and Austrian governments in the propagation of Haskalah in the West, in Russia a maskil was viewed by his opponents by definition as a man of political muscle, if not an agent of the government. Even in 1810, for example, when the Hasidic master Naḥman of Bratslav met three early maskilim in the town of Uman', his followers reported that "these heretics were important men close to the government."[5] In fact, these maskilim were utterly devoid of any influence with the authorities. Even twelve years later, when they attempted to open a school based on the principles of the Haskalah, the local government officials heeded the objections of the traditional community and forcibly closed the school.[6]

The presupposition of the power of the maskilim was pervasive, however, and when the government actually did intervene on the side of the Haskalah, the effect on Russian-Jewish society was electric. This first occurred in 1828, when the Hebrew writer Isaac Ber Levinsohn was awarded a grant of 1,000 rubles by the government.

Levinsohn was born in Kremenets, Volhynia, in 1788, to a prosperous family tinged with a bit of enlightenment. His father spoke Polish and insisted that Isaac study the Bible and learn Russian. In 1807, Levinsohn moved to the border town of Radziwiłłów to join his new bride and there studied German, Latin, and Greek. During the Napoleonic invasion, he served as an official translator to the Russian forces. His intellectual position was formulated after the war and beyond the frontiers of the empire. From 1813 to 1820 he lived in several cities in Galicia, where he associated with the most important maskilim of his time, including J. L. Mieses and Isaac Erter in Brody, Joseph Perl and M. M. Lefin in Tarnopol, Nakhman Krochmal and Meier Letteris in Zółkiew.[7] The lessons he learned from these teachers began to bear fruit upon his return to Kremenets in 1820, when he composed the first Russian grammar in Hebrew and several satires aimed at the Hasidim.[8] At the same time, he began his major work, *Teʿudah be-yisra'el* (Testimony in Israel), which argued for the permissibility of secular study and the necessity of a "productivization" of the economic activities of the Jews.

Levinsohn completed this book three years later. Since he lacked the funds to publish it himself, he appealed to two different constituencies for material aid. First, he issued a call to the Hebrew-reading public for prepublication orders; next, he wrote a series of letters to the highest officials of the empire, summarizing the reforms proposed in the work. Neither Grand Duke Constantine nor the Warsaw branch of the Jewish Committee answered his letters with any tangible support, but Admiral A. S. Shishkov, the minister of national enlightenment and head of the Central Directorate of Ecclesiastical Affairs of Foreign Creeds, passed Levinsohn's letter and manuscript to the St. Petersburg headquarters of the Jewish Committee. The members of this committee judged that the work was useful and recommended that it be published upon the completion of the proposed legal reorganization of the Jews. In addition, the committee voted to award Levinsohn 1,000 rubles as compensation for his efforts. Upon imperial assent, this grant was made in 1828.[9] Meanwhile, Levinsohn had managed to publish his work with the help of friends.

To Levinsohn, the cooperation of the government came as no surprise. Moved by an image of the gentile world and its leaders gleaned from Lessing, Goethe, and Schiller, Levinsohn assumed that the rulers of Russia shared the same European world view and thus were naturally predisposed to a beneficent reform of the Jews. To the traditional Jews, on the other hand, the subsidy was also viewed without surprise. Since maskilim were ipso facto agents of the government, what could be more natural than the government joining forces with the heretic to destroy the Jewish religion? In the words of the family tradition of the powerful Liubavich dynasty, the grant was a reward to Levinsohn "for slandering [his brethren] as being devoid of morals."[10]

In retrospect, it appears that the actual intent of the government in supporting Levinsohn was somewhere between these two readings and a bit closer to the second. Levinsohn labored under a misconception that was fundamental to the relations between the maskilim and the authorities throughout the nineteenth century. With only isolated exceptions, the Russian bureaucrats who dealt with the maskilim were completely alien to the political and literary culture of the Enlightenment. More importantly, these bureaucrats were entirely ignorant of Jewish life and not interested in learning about it. Therefore, much of Levinsohn's letter to Shishkov, written in poor Russian but in the jargon of the Haskalah, misperceived its audience and in turn was misunderstood. Criticism aimed by Levinsohn at part of the Jewish people was taken to apply to all Jews. Thus, when he wrote that "the folly and fanaticism of our rabbis and commentators have diverted our religion into a direction injurious to themselves and to the common good," his readers did not understand that he meant only some of the rabbis; when he stated that "some parts of the Talmud seem to reinforce views harmful to our Fatherland," his audience did not mark his qualification that this was a misreading of the Talmud; when he commented that he had "always lived among that numerous body of Jews who provide the safest refuge to superstition and prejudice" and thus understood what "means are appropriate in order to destroy them," the members of the Jewish Committee were simply not knowledgeable enough about Jewish life to decode this reference to the Hasidim.[11]

Clearly, at this stage the government had no comprehensive policy on the Jews, no commitment to their enlightenment, and no interest in their sectarian squabbles. The very same minister who approved the grant to Levinsohn was to state emphatically eight years later that he could detect no substantive difference between the Hasidim and their opponents, since they were all benighted Jews.

As the traditional Jews intuitively understood, the award to Levinsohn was in fact a reward for denouncing the moral ills of his people. But what neither the traditionalists nor Levinsohn could understand was that the government was not consciously supporting the Haskalah as part of a deliberate policy of dividing and conquering the Jews. The grant to Levinsohn was merely an undirected shot in the dark, a payment, or rather payoff, to an informant before a strategy of prosecution was decided upon.

Nevertheless, the fact that Levinsohn had been singled out by the government was sufficient to establish the reputation of *Te'udah be-yisra'el* as the gospel to the enlightened. Several writers testified to the critical influence of this one book on their intellectual development. The most flamboyant description was written in a letter to Levinsohn in 1834 by the scholar Mattias Strashun:

From the day that your book appeared, I read it from beginning to end, and could not put it down. I read it twice and thrice and could not have my fill: I wished that I were a dove, that I could fly to you, to be with you and embrace you, to be your dutiful servant forever. . . . Your book alone made me into a man.[12]

Though important, such direct conversions to Haskalah were not the most critical results of the publication of this book, which did not contain many ideas or arguments not previously elaborated by other maskilim. The appearance of *Te'udah be-yisra'el* and the spread of the news of its governmental imprimatur initiated a process that would entirely transform the cultural history of Russian Jewry: the gradual, but persistent, obliteration of the fluidity between traditionalism and enlightenment.

On the one side, the traditional community began to increase its guard against signs of heresy, which it clearly equated with ideas such as Levinsohn's; in the coming years, unorthodox figures of any sort would be called "Teudahkes" after his title. Bit by bit, public collaboration with enlightenment became more and more problematic—and rare—for even the most moderate representatives of traditional authority. While *Te'udah be-yisra'el* had received the customary rabbinical approbation from the moderate Rabbi Avraham Abele of Vilna, no subsequent overtly maskilic tract could be approved by a rabbi. Levinsohn's next book, *Bet Yehudah* (The house of Judah), was completed in 1828 but could not attain a rabbinical endorsement and so remained unpublished for a decade, until it was printed privately by a wealthy supporter of its author.[13]

On the other side, those who had harbored similar views now felt empowered to proclaim them in public. In the major Jewish cities and towns, young Jews began to meet together and to develop ties as members of a new intellectual force. In Vilna, a group of Hebrew writers who had previously expressed themselves only through traditional genres or innocuous translations now published plans for an annual Haskalah review that would spread its message through poetry, biblical exegesis, and historical and scientific articles; in Berdichev, a Jewish doctor named Rottenberg announced that he was forming a Society of Seekers after Enlightenment which would unite all maskilim in Russia.[14]

Clearly, Levinsohn's collaboration with the government had opened wide the gates of Haskalah in Russia, permitting the emergence into the open of ideas previously held in silence. Most of these ideas came into Russia from Galicia or East Prussia, whose Jewish communities had always had very strong cultural and economic ties with Russian Jewry. Like Levinsohn, several of the maskilim who began to appear in the 1820s and early 1830s came from families that had business dealings with Galician Jews and thus easily gained access to the new currents in germanized Jewry.

Regrettably, this link between Haskalah and commerce has largely been explored by historians who espoused a rather vulgar brand of economic determinism. Whether adherents of Soviet Communism or Marxist-Labor Zionism, these authors attempted to force their data to comply with rigidly predetermined schemes of historical development. They posited that the Haskalah was simply the ideological expression of the class interests of an emerging Russian-Jewish bourgeoisie and even attempted to prove that the spread of Haskalah was conditioned by the distribution of factory industry in Russia.[15]

These naive and often crude analyses have misrepresented both the economic and the cultural history of Russian Jewry. To begin with, those Russian Jews who traded with Galicia and Prussia were not the originators of new economic forces within the Pale. They were engaging in the same forms of petty trade that had always been relegated to Jews in Eastern Europe. At times this trade was lucrative, at times not, but it never could break through into large-scale international commerce owing to the severe legal limitations imposed on Jewish businessmen. Only later in Nicholas's reign did there develop a small Jewish bourgeoisie occupied in new types of economic activity. Many of the members of this new bourgeoisie supported the already established Haskalah, others did not.[16]

The economic link with Galicia and Prussia served only as a medium for the spread of new ideas, which appealed to Jews well beyond the circle of merchant families. Wealthier Jews could, of course, better afford the luxury of heresy than those who were dependent on the community for sustenance, but most wealthy Jews did not accept the new notions or bear their consequences. From the beginning, the Haskalah gained adherents from all segments of Jewish society, and for most maskilim there was no economic aspect to their ideology. On the contrary, their break with the mainstream often led to their impoverishment. Levinsohn, again, was symptomatic; though his family's economic position may have facilitated his original enlightenment, his acceptance of the goals and values of the Haskalah condemned him to a life of poverty.[17]

For only one group was there a direct link between economics and Haskalah: the Galician Jews who immigrated to Russia seeking business opportunities. From the beginning of the nineteenth century, Jewish doctors trained in Lwów, Breslau, or even Padua moved to Russia to seek their fortunes in a medical desert; while some of these physicians remained traditional Jews, most were of a more modern temperament and contributed significantly to the spread of Haskalah in Russia. More numerous were the wheat dealers from Brody who settled in Southern Russia, particularly in Odessa, during the 1820s. Brody had long been a center of Haskalah of an unusually radical bent, and the Brodyites who came to Odessa immediately established cultural institutions on the model of those they left behind. Under their influence, Odessa soon became, after Vilna, the second most important center of Haskalah in Russia. Yet even in Odessa, economics played only a partial role in the spread of enlightenment. More important was the fact that Odessa and New Russia as a whole were frontier territories with no traditional Jewish communities of any note. As a result, the Galician Jews who came there were able to fashion an entire communal structure based on their variety of Judaism; Haskalah flourished there by default. Soon, the news spread throughout the Pale that "Hell burned fifty versts around Odessa," and Jews from other parts of the empire flocked to Odessa to partake of its free spirit.[18]

The number of maskilim in Russia mushroomed in the late 1820s and throughout the 1830s, but they were still a tiny minority in Russian Jewry, with little coherence as an intellectual or social group, no independent means of support, virtually no power base, and very little ability to propagate their views. Although they continued to believe that the government was on their side, the regime for its part gave them no substantive evidence of such support. A second request for a grant to Levinsohn was denied in 1836 by the same minister who had supported the first, and contrary to the wishes of the maskilim, this minister appointed rabbis as the agents of his new censorship policy.[19] Most Hebrew presses were still closed to the maskilim because of their lack of rabbinical endorsement. By 1840, only eleven original works, five translations, and a handful of poems by Russian maskilim had been published anywhere.[20] The Vilna group's grandiose plans for a Haskalah periodical floundered: the first issue appeared in 1841, the second and last in 1844.[21] Neither the Society of Seekers after Enlightenment nor a similar society proposed by Levinsohn had any success.

The most significant, if meager, results of the Haskalah were in the critical realm of educational reform. In the first decade and a half of their open activity in Russia, the maskilim were able to open four modernized schools. The most successful was in Odessa. Founded in 1826, the school flourished after the immigration from Galicia three years later of its influential director, Bezalel Stern. By 1835 an official report listed 289 students at the school. With the addition of Russian, the curriculum consisted of the standard fare of Haskalah schools in Galicia: Hebrew grammar and composition; the Bible with Mendelssohn's translation and commentary in German; selected tractates of the Talmud; Jewish moralistic literature; German, French, and Russian language and literature; mathematics; physics; rhetoric; Russian and world history; geography; calligraphy; and mercantile law.[22] Three of the teachers of this school opened a branch for girls in 1835, which attracted 60 pupils.[23]

In 1838, Stern supervised the establishment of a school in Kishinev with the same curriculum as its model in Odessa.[24] In Uman', the maskilim again attempted to open a school in the 1830s but once more were rebuffed by the local authorities upon the protest of the traditional community.[25] Finally, in 1838 the officers of the Jewish community of Riga received permission from the Ministry of National Enlightenment to bring to their city a German-Jewish rabbi trained in the spirit of "pure Enlightenment" to head a German-style school for this small, germanized community. Upon the recommendation of Ludwig Philippson, the editor of the *Allgemeine Zeitung des Judentums* of Leipzig, a twenty-three-year-old graduate of the University of Munich, Max Lilienthal, was hired for the position. Lilienthal set out for Russia in October 1839 and arrived in Riga at the beginning of January 1840, after spending some weeks in St. Petersburg, where he established good relations with the minister of national enlightenment, S. S. Uvarov. He set about his task as teacher and preacher to the Jewish community, but his position was very modest. A year after his arrival, the school counted only 37 students in three grades.[26] Lilienthal did not remain in Riga very long; in 1841 he was called to the capital by Uvarov to head the proposed reform of the educational system of the Jews throughout the empire.

Uvarov's summons to Lilienthal marked the end of the first stage of the history of Haskalah in Russia. In fifteen years the movement had grown from a handful of individuals hesitantly revealing their views to a small community spread thinly over an enormous territory, making marked progress mostly in areas without an established Jewish presence. That situation was now to change most drastically: for the first time, the government, in the person of Uvarov, was consciously and seriously embarking on a policy of spreading enlightenment to Russian Jews.

The Problem of Uvarov

This strategy was arrived at only in the course of the governmental debate on the redirection of policy toward the Jews. The idea that the regime should intervene actively in the education of the Jews was formulated by Uvarov and then accepted by Kiselev and the rest of the Committee for the Transformation of the Jews.

In the historiography of Russian Jewry this reorientation of policy has for the most part been explained as part of a simple, straightforward morality tale: an evil, devious Russian minister, bent on converting the Jews to Christianity, attempts to lure them to barely disguised missionary institutions that ultimately collapse in failure because of the perspicacity of the Jews.[27] This analysis found support in the picture of Uvarov painted by nineteenth-century liberal Russian historians and their latter-day advocates. To their mind, Uvarov was the consummate reactionary bureaucrat, the coiner of the slogan Orthodoxy, Autocracy, Nationality, who tried to suppress the advance of Russian education and culture.[28]

Recently, historians have called into question this image of Uvarov. Two American scholars independently studied his work closely and concluded that far from being a stereotypical reactionary of the Nicholaevan ilk, he was a moderate, prudent, and enlightened patriot who rejected obscurantism and xenophobia and actually promoted the advance of the Russian educational system.[29] Two Soviet scholars came to similar—if surprisingly more sophisticated—conclusions. Analyzing his correspondence with Joseph de Maistre, they convincingly refuted the view that Uvarov had evolved from a liberal of the Alexandrine era to a typical reactionary of Nicholas's court and depicted him as a consistent, moderate, and cosmopolitan conservative who differed substantially from his colleagues and his master.[30]

This attempted rehabilitation of Uvarov has been only partially successful. But the questions raised do necessitate a closer look at him to understand his role in the promotion of enlightenment among the Jews.

Uvarov was born in Moscow in 1786 to a highly placed aristocratic family: his father was an aide-de-camp of Empress Catherine II, who held the infant at the baptismal font. He entered governmental service at the age of fifteen and spent his formative years at the embassies in Vienna and Paris. In 1811 he was appointed curator of the university district of St. Petersburg, a post he held even after he became president of the Imperial Academy of Sciences in 1818. After retiring briefly from service in order to write, he was recalled as deputy minister of national enlightenment in 1832 and was promoted to minister a year later.[31]

Like so many other Russians of his background, Uvarov's intellectual and cultural home was Germany, and he considered himself part of the vanguard of European culture. He spoke French, German, Italian, and English as fluently and more willingly than

Russian and wrote almost exclusively in the first two tongues. Fashioning himself an orientalist and a classicist, he wrote many essays, which he collected in two volumes published in Paris in the 1840s.[32] This work, as well as the presidency of the Academy of Sciences, gained him the status of "associé étranger" in the Institut de France and membership in the academies of Göttingen, Copenhagen, Rome, Madrid, Naples, Munich, Brussels, Tuscany, and Washington, D.C.

Despite these affiliations, it is clear from his writings that Uvarov was not an original thinker or scholar. His essays were pallid imitations of contemporary scholarship, marked by a superficiality of content and an utter lack of wit. At best, Uvarov was a littérateur, at worst, a dilettante. Herzen put it more scathingly: "a veritable shopkeeper behind the counter of enlightenment."[33] Uvarov's intellectual wares were as eclectic as they were self-important, but they were consistent. The heroes of his youth were the great figures of post-Napoleonic conservatism: Jean-Victor Moreau, Karl Freiherr von Stein, Pozzo di Borgo. Throughout his life he tried to emulate their combination of cosmopolitanism and patriotism, philosophy and statesmanship. In 1814 he wrote that Bonaparte had failed because he had misunderstood the march of history. Political systems had to conform to the three fundamental characteristics of any nation, its religion, its patriotism, and its national honor.[34] In the 1830s he translated this triad for Russia as Orthodoxy, Autocracy, and Nationality.

By each of these terms, Uvarov meant something very different than that understood by Nicholas and the other standard-bearers of "Official Nationality." S. Soloviev pointed out the incongruity of this slogan in the mouth of Uvarov: "Orthodoxy—while he was an atheist, not believing in Christ even in the Protestant manner, autocracy—while he was a liberal, nationality—although he had not read a single Russian book in his life. . . ."[35]

This was not quite exact. Uvarov did believe in God and Providence in a strictly rationalist, antimystic fashion. But he was not a deist. When Maistre accused him of being a Protestant, Uvarov replied that as a member of the Orthodox Church he was equally well disposed to Catholicism and Protestantism but was closest in beliefs to Jansenism, with one qualification: "If the men of Port-Royal, and the Jansenists in general, would have, like the Jesuits, submitted to a civil or ecclesiastical authority, their role would have been nobler, purer, and more Christian.[36]

This was the key to his faith: Christianity consisted not in a specific theology but in a perfect moral creed, which, submitted to the proper authority, would lead toward an ideal state of grace in which man and citizen were united in a Christian polity.[37]

This statist, nonpartisan Christianity was a universal goal, but each nation could only reach it along a separate path, determined by its own traditions. Espousing a simplistic Herderianism, Uvarov maintained that every people had its unique spirit, manifested in a set of institutions which define its appropriate government. Nations could not change these institutions by force, and when they attempt to do so, God intervenes to redirect them—witness the collapse of republicanism throughout Europe. Political dislocation is not only wrong for ideological reasons but also counterproductive:

History tells us that great political changes are the slow fruit of time, the free activity of the national soul, the interchange of mutual benefits of all the state's classes; it tells us that emancipation of the soul through enlightenment ought to precede the emancipation of the body through legislation . . . that civic and political freedom . . . come only in the years of ripe and real maturity.[38]

Russia has not yet reached such maturity, Uvarov held, but this was a blessing, given the instability of Europe in the aftermath of the revolutions of 1789 and 1830. If Russia would adhere to a policy in consonance with its national spirit, it could attain true enlightenment.

This confused popularization of Romanticism led Uvarov to a distinctly idiosyncratic educational philosophy. The task of the Ministry of National Enlightenment, he wrote to Nicholas in 1837, must be to blend European civilization and the Russian spirit, "to efface forever any antagonism between European enlightenment and the needs of our own situation."[39] This he proceeded to do as minister by introducing classical studies into the curriculum of the gymnasiums and the universities, by raising the admission standards of these institutions, and by spreading enlightenment to the Jews.

For Uvarov alone among the ministers of Nicholas I, policy toward the Jews was an integral part of an overall approach to government. Precisely why this was so is impossible to ascertain; there is simply not enough material on Uvarov's life to establish any positive reason for his deep interest in the Jews. It may well be that this interest was a by-product of his research into ancient civilization and "oriental" cultures: many scholars of the ancient Israelites, including Uvarov's model, Herder, moved from a fascination with the ancient Jews to a keen interest in their modern descendants.[40] Indeed, in his first published essay Uvarov stressed the centrality of the study of the Hebrew language and its literature as "the key to all the divine and human sciences."[41]

Whatever the cause, Uvarov repeatedly expressed his concern with the history and future of the Jewish people. In his ministry's official journal of 1835, Uvarov revealed his general views on the Jews in a review of a recently published history of medieval Jewry:

The existence of a nation dispersed over the face of the earth for centuries, persecuted and despised by all, but energetic and industrious, to whom we are all indebted for many important discoveries, must occupy an important place in the history of European enlightenment. [The author] has masterfully portrayed the tyranny, oppression, and torture suffered by the Jews, as well as the spirit of their society, mores, life, and beliefs—their crafty, cunning, and greedy politics, as well as their moral bitterness. . . . This survey of the literary activities of the Jews proves that despite the mystical gibberish of their rabbis, this nation has displayed a splendid imaginativeness, which only lacked judicious guidance.[42]

This guidance Uvarov set out to provide to the Jews of Russia. In 1838 he met with the leaders of the Vilna maskilim, Nisan Rosenthal, Hirsh Zvi Katzenellenbogen, and Israel Gordon, and discussed with them the possibilities of collaborating on a new educational program for Russia's Jews. The minister promised his full cooperation: "Give us a finger, and we shall stretch out our whole hand."[43] At the same time, Uvarov met with influential German maskilim and solicited their opinions on the reform of the schools of Russian Jews.[44]

Even before launching his own program, Uvarov took active measures in support of the education of the Jews. In 1839, for example, the maskil Leon Mandelshtam came to Vilna to study at the university there but soon found that it had been closed in response to the Polish Uprising. He then requested permission to take the examinations for the University of Moscow in the Vilna gymnasium. The local curator questioned this unusual procedure and appealed to Uvarov, who approved the setting of the admission tests. A year later, Uvarov followed up on this case, writing to the curator to see if Mandelshtam had made any progress.[45]

Even those historians who viewed Uvarov as an evil missionary felt compelled to remark on the sympathy and seriousness of his commitment to the education of the Jews. One such scholar wrote:

When one recalls the harsh restrictions on Jewish education which came into effect later, in the time of Alexander III, it is difficult to believe that once, and especially during the reign of such a tsar as Nicholas I, the situation could be so different.[46]

This difficulty in suspending perfectly understandable preconceptions about the evil designs of Russian bureaucrats has led to a widespread and serious misreading of Uvarov's goals in undertaking the reform of the education of the Jews. More specifically, the texts cited to prove that his goal was to convert the Jews through the schools have been misunderstood.

The first such text is the report which Uvarov made to Nicholas on March 17, 1841, "On the Transformation of the Jews, and on Opinion on This Subject Abroad."[47] Uvarov began the report with a description of his contacts both in person and in writing with "educated Jews in Germany." From these men he had learned that the major obstacle to the reeducation of their coreligionists in Russia is the self-interest of the rabbis and their erroneous prejudice that the Talmud is essential to the education of every Jew. This is not so, advised his informants. The Talmud is necessary only to future rabbis; other Jews should instead study the Bible and the ethical and moral teachings of Judaism. Such a curriculum has been instituted with great success in three Jewish schools in the empire, in Odessa, Kishinev, and Riga, and these could serve as the models for another 146 schools throughout the country. Two hundred Russian Jews are already qualified to teach in these schools; the rest could be imported from abroad, from the "New Jewish School" (*novoiudeiskaia shkola*), that is, the maskilim or early Reformers, whose leaders have already expressed keen interest in such an endeavor.[48]

Uvarov then reproduced his memorandum "On the Education of the Jews," which he submitted to Kiselev's committee. From this text, we can see precisely what his influence was on the final report of that body. Here he stated that for many centuries, governments have attempted to solve the problem of the Jews by force, but "nations cannot be destroyed, especially not that nation whose current history began at the foot of Golgotha."[49] But nations can be reduced to moral degradation, and this has happened to the Jews as the result of previous governmental actions.

Does it follow from this that it is possible to hope that the Jewish tribe can improve itself by itself, and must the government undertake the complex and enormous task of lessening, if not obliterating, the obstacles separating them from us?[50]

A positive response to these two questions, he asserts, must lead to the belief that the only appropriate solution is the reeducation of the young generation of Jews in schools based on the principles of those already established in Odessa, Kishinev, and Riga. According to the "best Jews," these schools counteract the negative influence of the Talmud and lead to the complete transformation of the Jews. He then goes on in a paragraph most often cited by Jewish historians:

Thus directing the activities of the schools against the effects of the Talmud, [the question arises:] should this purpose be openly announced. It seems to me that it need not and ought not to be, for that would result in pitting the majority of the Jews against the schools from the beginning, as well as losing the support of those who sense the damage caused by the Talmud and grasp its absurdity but would not separate themselves so sharply from their brethren from the outset. This position is supported by the testimonies and opinions of all those whom I have consulted with on this matter. They all agree that the very operation of the new schools will weaken and soon destroy the power of the talmudic traditions. I must explain at this point that I have found several well-intentioned, enlightened Jews who are ready to oppose the Talmudists under the leadership of the government, but I have not met one who would prematurely proclaim such opposition. Consequently, in the Odessa, Kishinev, and Riga schools, the teaching of some parts of the Talmud has been retained for the sake of appearances, while the real teaching is very far from the spirit of the Talmudists, to the extent that the Jewish elders say: "These schools are fine, their spirit is pure Jewish, but learning leads to Christianity." In the language of these inveterate adherents of Jewish prejudices and superstitions, these words mean: "The teaching in the newly established schools may slowly destroy in the Jews the fanaticism of separation and introduce them to the general principle of civility [*grazhdanstvennost'*]." In this they are not mistaken, for is not the religion of the Cross the purest symbol of universal civility?[51]

This passage must be closely parsed. Uvarov is not speaking of the goals of the projected government-sponsored schools but rather is referring to the accomplishments of the schools already established by the Jews themselves in Odessa, Kishinev, and Riga. He interprets the fears of traditional Jews that these schools will lead to Christianity to mean that they fear the disavowal of Jewish separatism and the acceptance of the Jews into general culture. He accepts this judgment in this revised form: the enlightenment of the Jews will indeed lead to the gradual improvement of their civic and cultural status and thus to their acceptance of the general principles of "civility." He does *not* say that the Jews will or should be converted to Christianity in these schools or that such is their purpose; rather, in accord with his general views on the inexorable link between civic society, true culture, and Christianity, he affirms that Christianity is the purest manifestation of civility.

This statement is imprecise, obscure, and fallacious. The traditionalist Jews were not afraid of civility, but of gentile learning at an unbearable cost to their beliefs and way of life. But on the basis of this statement it is not possible to impute any missionary motive in the establishment of the new schools, as all the major historians of Russian Jewry have done.[52]

These historians also cite another passage in support of their interpretation; it is out of chronological order, but pertinent to the discussion. This is the first sentence of Uvarov's memorandum of

November 13, 1844, generally referred to as his "secret report," in which he confessed his true motives—although in fact this memorandum was no more or less secret than any other official document in Russia, where even the state budget was (and remains) a tightly guarded secret. The sentence in question reads: "The goal of the education of the Jews consists in their gradual rapprochement (*sblizhenie*) with the Christian population and the eradication of the superstitions and harmful prejudices instilled by the study of the Talmud."[53] The term *sblizhenie* is both etymologically and semantically identical with the French-English *rapprochement* and is therefore just as ambiguous. Russian writers used this word to denote a wide variety of possible relations between groups, ranging from assimilation (an equally imprecise and hence useless term) to integration to emancipation.[54] It is not clear what specific political arrangement Uvarov meant by this term because he never detailed the future relations between the Jews and the Russians. This was not his concern. He believed in principle that political changes cannot be anticipated before they are grounded in cultural changes. What is absolutely clear from the context of this citation, however, is that *sblizhenie* did not mean for Uvarov the conversion of the Jews through the schools, but their europeanization through education.

Moreover, according to Uvarov, this education had to conform to the *Volksgeist* of the Jews, and he had learned from the maskilim that this had been perverted by the emphasis on Talmud study. Only by teaching the Jews their own true culture through enlightened eyes could they achieve enlightenment. His purpose, as he told the Warsaw Jewish community in 1843, was "die Israeliten durchaus israelitisch zu bilden" (to educate the Hebrews in a thoroughly Hebrew fashion).[55]

This does not mean that Uvarov did not hold out the hope that the education of the Jews would lead to their conversion to Christianity—only that there was no indication of this hope in the texts already cited. One other source, previously undiscovered, does shed light on this matter.

Uvarov's *Journal of the Ministry of National Enlightenment* contained a section devoted to news of educational and cultural developments around the world. In this section of the 1836 issue an anonymous report was published announcing the founding of a new journal, *La Regeneration*, by the Jewish community of Strasbourg. The author of this report—most probably Uvarov, who wrote most of the articles in the journal and censored all the others to conform to his views—remarked:

This undertaking will have important consequences. It will provide the means for the moral and intellectual rapprochement [again, *sblizhenie*] of the Jews and Christian society and thus reinforce the civil and political ties already uniting the two in many countries in Europe and will render more assistance to leading the Jews to the truth of Christianity than the system of separation and estrangement that has been followed until now in their regard.[56]

In order to interpret this statement correctly, we must differentiate in general between two conversionary goals: one that advocates an immediate, direct, exogenous conversion of the Jews—that is, a missionary policy—and one that holds that the political and intellectual amelioration of Jewish life will gradually but inevitably convince the Jews of History's verdict, the superiority of Christianity.

From the 1836 report it can be seen that Uvarov held the second hope. The rapprochement between the Jews and their neighbors will reinforce the political ties which they have with the Christians, dissolve their separatism, and inevitably bring them to the truth of Christianity—which Uvarov believed was simply the perfect civil order. For him, active missionizing among the Jews would be useless. In the 1841 report he wrote, "The Jews have always been suspicious of any intervention of Christians into their faith; we can await changes in their religious beliefs only when they themselves grasp their errors."[57]

This position was strikingly similar to that of the most famous proponent of the reform of the Jews of the West: the Abbé Grégoire, who believed that converting the Jews—his long-term goal—had to be preceded by practical changes that could only be harmed by an open insistence on missionizing.[58] Uvarov would have subscribed to Grégoire's statement that "truth is only persuasive when it is subtle," although he would undoubtedly have disagreed with

Grégoire about the exact content of that "truth"—the Jansenist credentials of both were rather flimsy.

Uvarov's purpose in establishing the new schools was not to convert the Jews. Rather it was to transform them into educated Europeans, to bring them in line with their West European counterparts who had already been "united" with their Christian compatriots on a moral, intellectual, and ultimately political level. Like Grégoire and so many other proponents of the reform of the Jews, Uvarov hoped that the transformation of the Jews would one day lead to their recognition of the truth of Christianity. But in this hope he was no more malevolent—or accurate—than the other sanguine soothsayers of the ultimate dissolution of the Jewish community.[59]

Max Lilienthal in Russia

From the first, Uvarov's new policy actively encouraged the participation of Jews in the determination of the programs of his ministry. In 1840 he requested that the minister of the interior instruct the governors-general of each of the areas inhabited by Jews to convoke a committee composed of local bureaucrats and Jews to discuss future educational and rabbinical policy. Six such committees were established, in Odessa, Kiev, Poltava, Vitebsk, Vilna, and Mitau, and they were supposed to submit their recommendations by the beginning of January 1841.[60] It is impossible to determine how many of these committees actually were convened in the proposed form; only one—not surprisingly, in Odessa—is known to have filed a report in the name of both its governmental and its Jewish members.[61] In Vilna a group of forty-five maskilim sent a letter to Nicholas supporting the educational and religious reform proposals of the local committee, but it is not clear if this circular had any official status.[62]

Other Jewish communities, by far in the majority, boycotted the committees altogether in protest against the unprecedented intrusion into the internal workings of Jewish society and out of fear of the inevitable conclusions. Rabbi Yizhak ben Haim of Volozhin, possibly the most important rabbinical figure of the time and the leader of the moderate wing of the Lithuanian school, came to Vilna to organize a campaign against the committees—or, as one maskilic source put it, to gather funds for the subornation of its members.[63]

Faced with these disappointing results, Uvarov decided that the educational and intellectual regeneration of Russia's Jews must be spearheaded by the Jews of the West. To this end, in the beginning of January 1841, he summoned Max Lilienthal back to St. Petersburg and spent five weeks with him formulating a new strategy for the enlightenment of the Jews: invitations would be extended to German Jews to accept positions in Russia, and specific plans and curricula would be elaborated for the new schools.[64]

Lilienthal immediately set about both these tasks. He wrote to some of the most influential intellectual leaders of Western European Jewry—Leopold Zunz, Abraham Geiger, Ludwig Philippson, Samuele Davide Luzzatto, among others—requesting their help in locating teachers for the schools. In these letters he revealed his unbridled enthusiasm with the new project and a rather naive misunderstanding of its possibilities. To Luzzatto, for example, Lilienthal wrote a rather pompous letter asking for a detailed plan of the Collegio Rabbinico in Padua and the names of any of its graduates who would be willing to move to Russia:

If it were ever possible for Russia to have the benefit of seeing some men from your seminary who have as yet no positions, appointed as directors of the eight hundred schools which are to be founded, I would consider myself happy both to have rendered the state such a service and to have found for these men a sphere of activity in which they could exercise their proper functions, with good fortune and success. Moreover, these men would have a better prospect here than could be equalled elsewhere. They would be installed and salaried by the state: Russia would reward them for the diffusion of knowledge and culture and exceeding that reward would be the gratitude of the state. They would in time find here the fulfillment of their most ardent hopes. Will such men as feel themselves disposed to take part in this great mission of *kiddush ha-shem* please send me post-paid, immediately upon the receipt of this letter their certificates and recommendations, also their addresses, in order that they may be informed of the government's decision without delay? But haste is necessary—*et la°asot la-shem* [the time for God's work is nigh].[65]

The drama was overstated, the haste unnecessary. But the twenty-five-year-old Lilienthal was flushed with excitement, intoxicated with his almost messianic mission. To Luzzatto and the others he spoke of the impending emancipation of the Jews of Russia: "Once they have attained culture, they are offered emancipation; in the wake of knowledge—the rights of man."[66] The graduates of the schools

are to receive all the rights of citizenship without trammel. This is a great and glorious thing, the like of which our history has not yet produced; not a too sudden deliverance from the bonds of the Middle Ages without being able to make use of the freedom, as happened in France; not a restless exertion and struggle without obtaining the least advantages, as in Germany.[67]

Lilienthal had hardly obtained such promises. In his memoirs he recalled that when he boldly proposed to Uvarov that the hesitations of the Jews would disappear if they were granted emancipation or at least some amelioration of their civic status, Uvarov merely assured him that the tsar's intentions were honorable.[68] However, Lilienthal was often given to extreme exaggeration and overstatement.

His letters caused a major stir in the Western European Jewish intelligentsia. Luzzatto, normally the most sober and cautious of the maskilim, replied in a generous letter bemoaning the lack of graduates from his seminary, suggesting that Lilienthal send Russian students to study there, and proposing that the tsarist government fund a Hebrew periodical dedicated to the spread of enlightenment that he could edit.[69] Although bidden by Lilienthal to keep the news of the proposed reforms secret, Luzzatto leaked the contents of his letter to Zunz and Isaac Jost, suggesting that this would ease the plight of the unemployed maskilim of Germany.[70] Philippson and others quickly compiled lists of available candidates for the teaching posts;[71] Jost in Frankfort even began to study Russian in preparation for the trip.[72] Within a short time,

Lilienthal had a list of over two hundred German Jews willing to move to Russia to join his school system.[73]

At the same time, Lilienthal was busily composing detailed plans for the schools, which he sent off to the ministry after he returned to Riga. Here too Lilienthal stressed the need for German Jews to guide the schools. He proposed that the language of instruction should at first be German, with Russian gradually introduced; he recommended that the schools be free and include instruction in horticulture, agriculture, and technical drawing; and he advised that the graduates of the schools be permitted to join the civil service, to study at any university, and to live outside the Pale upon their graduation. Uvarov agreed to all these points, except the last, which he admitted was impossible.[74]

At the end of 1841, another dimension was added to Lilienthal's mission. Nisan Rosenthal, a powerful early maskil of Vilna who had recently been appointed an Honorary Citizen for his services to the empire during the Polish Uprising,[75] was then engaged in a power struggle over the communal educational institutions of Vilna. In December 1841 he petitioned Uvarov for permission to found a new modernized school in Vilna; the minister approved and instructed Lilienthal, then in Riga, to accompany Rosenthal to Vilna to assist in the establishment of the school and to report on the receptivity to enlightened education on the part of the community as a whole.[76]

Although Lilienthal had been in Russia for over two years, he had never come in contact with traditional Russian-Jewish society. The small Jewish community of Riga was entirely westernized in culture and outlook; St. Petersburg had no Jewish community at all at this point, except for Jewish soldiers posted there. When he arrived in Vilna, Lilienthal was spellbound by the sight of a city largely inhabited by Russian Jews. Echoing Napoleon's remark upon entering Vilna on a Friday afternoon in 1812—"Gentlemen, I think we are in Jerusalem!"—Lilienthal wrote,

I never before had witnessed such a large number of Jews to almost the entire exclusion of Christians. Wherever I looked, out of every corner, out of every house there came Jews, some with their *talit* and *tefilin*, returning from the *bet ha-midrash*, others hurrying to their business, most of them earnest, gloomy faces, absorbed in their various thoughts and occupations. . . . Coming from Germany, where in all the cities Jews are in the minority, entirely disappearing amongst the larger majority of their Christian fellow citizens, I did not know what to make out of this swarming beehive of Jews. I too believed myself to be in Palestine instead of in Russia, so entirely and thoroughly Jewish appeared to me the city of Vilna.[77]

This lack of familiarity with Russian Jews did not restrain Lilienthal from instructing them on how to reform their lives. Two days after his arrival in Vilna, he met with the leaders of its kahal to discuss the government's new educational policies. This was the first time that the Jews were publicly informed of Uvarov's plans; their response was the first indication of the major realignment of the politics and ideology of Russian Jewry.

Unfortunately, there is no reliable account of the deliberations of this meeting. Many historians have described it relying exclusively on Lilienthal's own recollections of its discussions, without subjecting these to any critical scrutiny.[78] Lilienthal's memoirs as a whole were replete with self-justifying embellishments and highly questionable transcriptions of conversations, and so can only be used with caution.[79]

It is possible to reconstruct only the broad outlines of the encounter. The elders of the community were sent into a panic by Lilienthal's arrival but recognized that it was imprudent to ignore him and boycott the meeting. They appeared and attempted to convince him that as an outsider he did not understand the special circumstances of Russian Jewry and the true—that is, missionary—motives of the regime. The maskilim, of course, supported Lilienthal enthusiastically and were able to elicit a compromise from the assembly: the community would attempt to raise 5,100 rubles from its charity funds to found a new school, pending the approval of a general meeting of all Vilna Jews.[80] This session ended without a definite resolution.

Meanwhile, the leaders of the kahal of Minsk had invited Lilienthal to explain his position to them. The Vilna maskilim warned Lilienthal about accepting the invitation, since Minsk had an insignificant number of maskilim and was entirely under the control of the traditionalists, including a substantial Hasidic community. Doubtless, the invitation was part of a plot to subvert the reforms of the government.[81]

Lilienthal did not heed their warning and arrived in Minsk at the end of January to confront the greatest shock of his life. Meetings had been held to coordinate strategy against him; the entire community seemed to be united against him and willing to express their feelings openly. At a public meeting, Lilienthal became the target of fierce opposition:

The greatest indignation against the proposed reforms of the schools was unanimously manifested. The leading members of the *Beth Hamidrash* threatened with banishment and excommunication anyone who dared support such a frivolous scheme. The *Melamdin*, unfaltering and united as a phalanx, described in gloomy colors the future punishment awaiting those who would lead the children to apostasy. The *Shiur* rabbis could not quote enough Talmudic sentences proving the wickedness of those who would indulge in the reading of *Terefa Posul*, and the determination to defeat any motion made in my favor was general.[82]

Lilienthal escaped from the meeting before it concluded and returned to Vilna three days later. The last sounds he heard in Minsk were the "scorn and derision of wanton children" shouting a mixture of Russian and Yiddish that he could not but understand, though he knew neither language: "*Shkoles nie zhelaem*" (we don't want any [secular] schools).[83]

Reporting this encounter to Uvarov, Lilienthal stressed that it stemmed from the fanaticism of the masses, whipped up by the traditional teachers who feared for their own jobs. To his mentor, Ludwig Philippson, Lilienthal confessed that the Minsk kahal leaders had expressed a more profound and sober argument: so long as the Jews were not granted civil rights, secular education would bring them only misfortune since it would raise expectations that could not be fulfilled, given their inferior legal status.[84] This rather sophisticated rebuttal to Uvarov's naive ideology was not relayed to the minister.

The news of the outburst in Minsk quickly reached Vilna and encouraged the traditionalists there to oppose Lilienthal more vocally. At the general meeting called to discuss the tentative resolutions of the first session with Lilienthal, the traditionalists arrived en masse. One maskil who was present recorded the proceedings with ironic detail:

A large crowd filled the meeting hall and overflowed into the yard: old and young, artisans, teachers, even the blind and the lame. . . . Soon, they began to speak their minds about the infidel who came to take their sons to impure schools and to mislead them from the truth. . . . The tailor said: gouge out his eyes with a needle; the cobbler: pierce his ears with an awl; the butcher: bind him like a goat to the slaughter; the locksmith: lock his mouth so that he cannot open it . . . and the teachers in the forefront said: Be strong, brothers! Be strong for the sake of our nation and youth! Strengthen the customs of our fathers. We want no part of Lilienthal and his followers and their ways. The crowd chanted: We don't want, we don't want![85]

Soon, the meeting degenerated into chaos, and the police were called in. The sexton of the community was arrested, and the fire department dispersed the crowd by dousing it with water. Lilienthal again fled for his life and left for St. Petersburg soon thereafter.

This massive failure in public relations did not sway Lilienthal from his mission. On the contrary, he realized that it provided him with the opportunity that he had been seeking to extricate himself from the unsatisfactory post in Riga and to become an official of the ministry. In a letter to Uvarov, which has hitherto not been published, he explained that the fierce opposition of the masses of the Jews to the school reform would condemn the government's plans to utter failure unless he were to receive official authorization to head a campaign to force the Jews to attend the new schools.[86]

In the capital, Lilienthal elaborated on these principles. He recommended that the government subject all Jewish educational institutions to the control of the Ministry of National Enlightenment and then convoke a rabbinical synod, based on Napoleon's Sanhedrin, to approve the ministry's plans for the reform of the Jewish schools.[87]

Uvarov accepted these recommendations, not only because they conformed with his plans for the reeducation of the Jews but also because they substantially increased the power of his ministry, divesting its rival, the Ministry of the Interior, of a part of its jurisdiction. On June 22, 1842, Nicholas approved a law which extended the supervision of the Ministry of National Enlightenment to all Jewish schools, including the *hadarim* and yeshivot, and "any others of whatever appellation in which Jews either study the interpretations of their Law and Scripture, or teach children" and called for the convocation of a rabbinical commission to be held in St. Petersburg for the "swift implementation of the goals of the government." This commission would be composed of four rabbis, one from each of the four regions inhabited by the Jews, and would be named the Imperial Commission for the Education of the Jews of Russia.[88]

At the same time, Uvarov surprised Lilienthal with a new task: he was to tour the entire Pale of Settlement as an official of the Ministry of National Enlightenment in order to canvas the Jewish communities for appropriate candidates for the commission and to report on the extent of enlightenment among the Jews and the availability of teachers for the new schools. As a full-fledged representative of the government, Lilienthal was to enjoy the protection of the police authorities and all the privileges of the imperial service. His task was to convince the Jews that the intention of the government was "to prepare them for a truly civil and moral life, which consists merely in the approach to a universally acknowledged civilization, without infringing on their religion."[89]

Lilienthal was understandably hesitant about returning to the sites of his humiliation and tried to ease his way by announcing his message in a polemic tract published in Vilna. Since his Hebrew was weak, Lilienthal wrote this pamphlet in German and had it translated into Hebrew by the maskil Sh. Y. Fin under the title *Maggid yeshuʿah* (Herald of salvation).[90]

On one level, this work was merely a reiteration of Lilienthal's previous arguments to the Jews: Nicholas, in his infinite wisdom, had decided to uplift the Jews by granting them the right to a decent education, which will allow them to improve their desperate economic situation. The Jews had nothing to fear from such an education, which would not infringe on any of the commandments of the Torah or even any custom developed by the rabbis. The new schools would bring only happiness to the Jews, prosperity, and security.

At the same time, *Maggid yeshuᶜah* was an unambiguous warning that the government would not brook any interference with its plans or any insults to Lilienthal during his imminent trip. This visit was not designed to survey the Jews' opinions on the reforms or to request their compliance but merely to inform them of the government's beneficent purposes. Any improprieties such as those that occurred in Vilna and Minsk would have the most dire consequences. The tsar and his ministers were prepared to overlook the previous intransigence of the Jews, but any further opposition would only prove the accusations of the Jews' cupidity, degeneracy, and lawlessness which are continually heard at court. Only if they would obey the commands of the government and follow the recommendations of Lilienthal and the proposed rabbinical commission would they be safe.[91]

Maggid yeshuᶜah was printed in thousands of copies and distributed to all the communities Lilienthal would visit. Although reportedly burned by one Hasidic group,[92] it seems to have had its desired effect of muting any public opposition to Lilienthal's trip—reinforced, no doubt, by his constant police escort. From July to December 1842, Lilienthal crisscrossed the Pale: Riga, Mitau, Kovno, Vilna, Minsk, Grodno, Belostok, Zhitomir, Berdichev, Kamenets-Podol'sk, Kishinev, Odessa, Kherson, Uman', Kiev, Chernigov, Mogilev, and Vitebsk. Everywhere, even in Vilna and Minsk, the communities welcomed Lilienthal, heard him out, and nominated candidates for the commission. In most cities his reception was cordial but not warm; in the southern strongholds of the Haskalah he was greeted triumphantly.[93]

An important cause of the positive reception given to Lilienthal by the traditional Jews was the early support he received from the leader of Lithuanian Jewry, Rabbi Yizḥak ben Ḥaim of Volozhin. In a private encounter between the two on the eve of Yom Kippur 1842, Rabbi Yizḥak did not quite express approval of the government's plans but consented to participate in the rabbinical commission to be convened in St. Petersburg.[94]

His reasons for doing so were complex. To begin with, he was the most influential representative of his time of the moderate wing of rabbinic Judaism. His yeshivah was renowned as the most enlightened in Russia, and some reports even held that he approved the use of Mendelssohn's biblical commentary and translation in the academy.[95] Although he was far from an adherent of the basic tenets of the Haskalah, he was much more positively inclined to some of their suggestions on educational reform. This receptiveness to moderate change apparently led him to consider cooperating with the government in this venture in order to attempt to control the reforms from within. This ideological moderation was not the only factor in his decision, as many scholars have assumed. He previously had refused to participate in the committees convoked by the regime barely two years earlier. It appears that in their meeting, Lilienthal had elaborated on the dangers of opposition detailed in *Maggid yeshuʿah*. He told Rabbi Yiẓḥak that Nicholas had wanted to subject all of the Jews of the empire to forced penal service but was dissuaded from doing so only by two ministers, Uvarov and Kiselev, who proposed instead the reform of the Jews through education. If Lilienthal were resisted, he told the rabbi, the emperor's will would prevail.[96] Faced with so grave a threat, Rabbi Yiẓḥak decided that collaboration with the government was the only solution and hoped that some benefit might even accrue to the Jews if they maneuvered carefully.

The other rabbinical nominee to the commission, Menaḥem Mendel Schneersohn, also agreed to participate but for entirely different reasons. Stopping in Vilna on the way to St. Petersburg, the Liubavicher rebbe announced that he was starting on a holy mission to counter the designs of the government, to preserve intact the Jews' traditional way of living and learning.[97]

The commission met in St. Petersburg from May 6 to August 27, 1843. Besides the two rabbis, its official members were the traditionalist financier Israel Halperin of Berdichev and the director of the modern Odessa school, Beẓalel Stern; representing the government were Uvarov, his assistants, and Lilienthal, with the Jewish university student Leon Mandelshtam serving as interpreter and scribe.[98] Lilienthal had invited the two most powerful leaders of Western European Jewry, Adolphe Crémieux and Sir Moses Montefiore, to attend the sessions as observers, but both declined the invitation.[99]

The commission met in secret, and there is no official record of its deliberations or specific recommendations. The published descriptions of the archives of the Ministry of National Enlightenment—opened to scholars for a brief period after 1917—merely list six "projects" drawn up by the commission, without detailing their contents. These projects dealt with the basic guidelines for the education of the Jews, additions to the laws on education in the code, proposals for the division of teaching hours and the funding of the schools, the organization of the rabbinical seminaries, reforms of private Jewish education, and regulations for the *hadarim* and yeshivot.[100] When these projects were discussed by the Jewish Committee, several points were objected to by various ministers and defended by Uvarov: that Jewish subjects be taught twenty-eight and one-half hours a week, and secular studies fifteen; that the rabbinical schools be called seminaries; that the inspectors of the seminaries be Jews; that there be secondary schools for the Jews on the level of the gymnasiums; that foreign Jews be permitted to become Russian citizens.[101]

Uvarov successfully defended all these recommendations, except the last.[102] This was not surprising, as it is most likely that they were drafted by him and his staff and merely rubber-stamped by the members of the commission with minor amendments. At the end of the sessions, one of Uvarov's assistants lauded the Jewish participants:

Having almost daily contact with them, I became convinced of their boundless loyalty to the Crown and their absolute obedience to the Imperial will, not only out of fear, but motivated by their conscience. All four are loyal men, honest, with character and without servility. Their work promoted the goals of the government and merit reward.[103]

The only direct testimony of the participants themselves are two letters written by the rabbis on the commission. On November 3, 1843, Yizhak of Volozhin wrote to Uvarov that he had heard from Lilienthal of a rumor spreading through the capital that at the commission the rabbis did not dare to express their opinions openly. He hoped that the ministry would not pay any attention to this "unsubstantiated twaddle," since he had repeatedly told some of the most authoritative persons that it was crucial to hasten the introduction of the new school system and had promised various communities help in doing so and in founding agricultural settlements.[104] The second letter is of an entirely different character. In 1847 or 1848 (the Hebrew year 5608), Rabbi Schneersohn wrote to Leon Mandelshtam, Lilienthal's successor as "learned Jew" at the ministry:

In the Commission which the government convened in 1843, and in which we participated, the curriculum of the schools for our children was set and approved by the government, and according to the will of our Emperor it is not to be depleted or amended, and in truth, the curriculum that we set was the one that we found to be essential for the instruction of children in accordance with the Torah and the Talmud, from which nothing, God forbid, may be deleted.[105]

This letter seems to refer not to the curriculum established for the new, modernized schools but to the rules elaborated for the ḥadarim and yeshivot, which were permitted to continue as before under the supervision of the ministry, with the stipulation that the study of Russian be gradually introduced.[106]

The members of the commission apparently had less success in fashioning the direction of the new governmental schools. According to one historian who referred to manuscript sources but gave no citations, the members of the commission informed the ministry's officials that Jewish tradition requires every father to teach his sons Jewish law, which must be done in Hebrew and Aramaic with glosses permitted only into Yiddish. Once that religious obligation is fulfilled, there is no legal objection to secular studies, so long as they are taught only to older students and in special quarters removed from the venue of religious instruction. The ministry accepted only part of these recommendations, increasing the number of hours devoted to Jewish studies, promising to replace a proposed catechism based on that used in the German Reform schools with the study of the Talmud, and deciding to accept pupils at the age of eight instead of six, as originally planned.[107]

The disciples of the two rabbis who served on the commission compiled various accounts of their masters' participation. Though infused with hagiographic inaccuracies, these stories reveal a great deal about traditional Jewry's reaction to the commission. The most detailed such account, written by the great-grandson of Rabbi Menahem Mendel Schneersohn, claims that the rabbi was put under house arrest twenty-two times during the course of the commission's meetings, as punishment for his courageous and outspoken defense of the tradition: "refusing to countenence changing the most minute custom."[108] While Rabbi Yizhak of Volozhin, the chief contemporary opponent of Hasidism, abstained on a crucial vote advocating the abridgement of the liturgy, Menahem Mendel, the story continues, challenged the very legitimacy of the question:

Do not rush to record this decision! I have already been punished several times for insisting that the Ministry of Culture invited these selected Jewish citizens to hear them out on Jewish law and custom. The Ministry desired to hear their opinions and did not summon them to inform them of the Ministry's opinion on these matters. These matters are not known to the Ministry from their authentic sources, but through the corrupted well-springs of atheists and Torah illiterates. The information on the Jewish religion given the Ministry by these atheists is erroneous and confused, and ridiculous to any Jew learned in Torah. I must repeat my earlier statement: the Ministry of Culture has no authority over Jewish law and custom. If the Ministry usurps the prerogative to cast the deciding vote, I hereby—as I have warned you before—resign from this Commission, and request permission to leave.[109]

Such permission was not granted; instead, the rabbi was summoned to Uvarov to face charges of insubordination. He denied any wrongdoing and was arrested once more. The sessions of the commission were indefinitely postponed. Only through the intercession of an old friend of the Liubavich dynasty, Count A. N. Golitsyn, were the charges dropped and the meetings reconvened.[110] The account ends without mentioning what the rabbi's role was in the final decisions of the commission.

The followers of Rabbi Yihzak of Volozhin were far less triumphant in their recollections, mentioning nothing of his actual voting record, preferring instead to record his wise retorts to Uvarov's barbs. Thus, when the minister tried to insult the Jews by asking God why He ever created such a despised and weak nation, Rabbi Yiẓḥak broke out in joyous laughter. Asked to explain his bizarre response, he explained to Uvarov that he had long been waiting to hear such a question, for it fulfilled Balaam's prophecy: "In due time it shall be said to Jacob and to Israel, What hath God wrought?" (Num. 23:23).[111] The only substantive report found in the recollections of Rabbi Yiẓḥak's disciples records his mood after the conclusion of the commission's hearings. Stopping in Vilkomir on the way home from St. Petersburg, he confided to a small group of intimates who were pressing him for details of his experiences:

Believe me, I have nothing at all to tell you—one does not discuss failures. Salvation has not yet come, let us only hope that no further evil decrees befall us. A wind of destruction is prevailing over our nation, and only prayer and mercy can help us now. And I have no more to say to you, my brothers.[112]

It is not clear if Rabbi Yiẓḥak himself concluded that his collaborationist, moderate policy had been erroneous.[113] It is certain, however, that this was the overwhelming consensus of traditional Russian Jewry, Hasidic or mitnagdic. The battle lines were now drawn more starkly than before: the government and the maskilim on one side, God and His people on the other.

The maskilim accepted this assessment—although they too believed that the Lord was on their side. They celebrated the commission as the final blow of their victory over the obscurantists, the harbinger of imminent salvation.[114] The commission of 1843 thus served as the second and decisive turning point in the relations between the traditionalists and the maskilim: Haskalah was now the official policy of the Russian government.

This was confirmed by the law of November 13, 1844, "On Establishing Special Schools for the Education of Jewish Youth."[115] Without affecting the access of Jews to Christian academic institutions, there would now be established special Jewish primary schools which would correspond to the Christian parish schools and secondary schools corresponding to the district schools, as well as rabbinical seminaries for the training of teachers of Jewish subjects and rabbis, which would be run according to the general rules of the ministry, "taking into account, when necessary, the laws and customs of the Jews." Jewish subjects would be taught by Jewish teachers; other courses by either Jews or Christians. The Christian teachers would receive the same privileges as if they were employed in a Christian school; the Jewish staff would be exempted from military service. The students would be granted the same privileges as those accruing to Jewish students at Christian schools: a ten-year exemption from the draft for those at the secondary level, fifteen years for those who graduate from a gymnasium, and permanent release from conscription duty for those graduating the last levels with exemplary performance in Russian language and philology. These schools were to be funded by special monies collected by the ministry. Private Jewish schools and home tutoring would also be subjected to the control of the ministry. In order to supervise the smooth functioning of the new order, special temporary commissions staffed by Christians and Jews were to be convened on the provincial and district levels. The law concluded: "We hope that this new demonstration of Our concern for the moral improvement of the Jews will convince them to cooperate with these plans aimed at their true benefit."

Along with the publication of this law, the ministry issued detailed instructions on each aspect of the legislation.[116] These instructions ran 286 paragraphs. The following were the twelve most important points:

1. The controversial phrase—"the goal of the education of the Jews consists in their gradual rapprochement with the Christian population and in the eradication of the superstitions and harmful prejudices instilled by the study of the Talmud";[117]

2. The primary schools will be established in every Jewish community where it shall prove possible to do so and the secondary schools only in those provinces in which the large population of Jews renders their attendance at Christian institutions unlikely;[118]

3. Two rabbinical seminaries will be founded, one in Vilna and another in another site;[119]

4. (Contrary to the alleged promises made to the Rabbinical Commission of 1843), the customary method of teaching Jewish law shall be replaced wherever possible by the use of a catechism such as that drawn up by the Jews of Germany;[120]

5. The inspector of the primary and secondary schools and the director of the rabbinical seminaries must be Christian;[121]

6. The teachers of Jewish law may be brought to Russia from abroad, especially from Bavaria, Prussia, and Austria;[122]

7. A "learned Jew" will be appointed at the ministry and in every university district to interpret Jewish matters; these might be either Russian or foreign Jews;[123]

8. The curriculum of the primary schools will be Jewish law, Russian literacy and grammar, Hebrew literacy and grammar, arithmetic, and calligraphy; in the secondary schools, Russian and general geography and history and mechanical drawing will be added, and bookkeeping, geometry, mechanics, natural history, physics, chemistry, and commercial and technological studies might be offered as supplementary courses;[124]

9. The rabbinical seminaries will begin with a four-year preparatory class which, in addition to Jewish courses, will study Russian philology, logic, Latin, German, French, mathematics, geography, statistics, world and Russian history, physics, calligraphy, and technical drawing; this will be followed either by a one-year pedagogical course or by a two-year rabbinical course;[125]

10. The Talmud Torahs, or communal schools for orphans and the poor, will be supervised by the ministry but left to run according to their present system;[126]

11. The *hadarim* will be officially broken down into two categories: primary—for children up to the age of eight—and secondary—for those older than eight; within six months after the publication of these instructions, every *melamed* or director of a *heder* must report to the ministry in writing the number and names of his students and receive a certificate of good behavior from the local civil authorities; those who fail to do

so, as well as those wishing to become *melamdim* or to open a ḥeder, must pass an examination to be administered by the local temporary commissions;[127]

12. The heads of every yeshivah must provide yearly lists of students and curricula to the authorities and prepare their students for a public examination which may be held at the end of every academic year.[128]

Barely eight months after the promulgation of this ukase, Max Lilienthal left Russia, spent a short time in Germany, and went on to the United States, where he became an important leader of the Reform movement. Since 1845, historians and commentators have pondered Lilienthal's actions and have advanced ten different hypotheses to explain them:

1. Lilienthal became disillusioned with the aims of the government and realized that he had been duped by a hypocritical regime dedicated to the weakening of the Jewish religion, not the betterment of the Jews (the most popular thesis);[129]

2. He had become convinced that the aim of the schools was the conversion of the Jews (a stronger version of this same argument);[130]

3. He was angered by the government's attempt to convert him personally to Russian Orthodoxy (the second most often proposed explanation);[131]

4. He was bitter that the proposed plans for the schools did not conform to his own vision;[132]

5. He was humiliated by the government's failure to invite German teachers to teach in the schools;[133]

6. He was horrified by the edict that banished the Jews from regions within fifty versts of the western frontiers of the empire;[134]

7. He was afraid of the anger of the Jewish masses;[135]

8. He had no position in Russia;[136]

9. He had learned of the so-called secret memorandum in which Uvarov revealed his true missionary motives;[137]

10. He was convinced to leave by the exclusion of the Talmud from the curriculum of the schools.[138]

None of these hypotheses survives a close examination of the sources. Most are based on no hard evidence and can easily be refuted by the evidence available; three are based on problematic sources that must be analyzed carefully.

The first group can be disposed of quickly. The notion that the curriculum of the schools was inconsistent with Lilienthal's proposals is disproven by a reading of the countless memorandums he sent to Uvarov, which reveal an uncompromised confluence of purpose and method with the plans as published in the November 1844 law.[139] Similarly, he could not have been disillusioned by the exclusion of Talmud from the schools, since it was included in precisely the amount and form that he himself had recommended.[140] The opinion that he left because of the lack of invitations to German teachers is untenable. Just before he left Russia, he stated that he still expected these invitations to be forthcoming, and in fact, the decision not to hire teachers from abroad was made a considerable time after Lilienthal left Russia.[141] That he learned of the "secret" memorandum is equally baseless. Apart from the fact that he never once referred to this document and that it was no more secret than any other intraministerial report, there was nothing in the memorandum that would have surprised him in the least. On the contrary, Lilienthal shared much of Uvarov's ideological and intellectual bent.[142] Finally, the idea that Lilienthal was afraid of the anger of the masses was an anachronistic projection of populist historians with no basis in fact or logic.

Three hypotheses merit serious consideration. The first is the view that he was outraged by an attempt to convert him to Christianity, which is based on two sources. The *Allgemeine Zeitung des Judentums* reprinted a report from Königsberg, first published in the *Deutsche Allgemeine Zeitung*, which detailed in an inaccurate and nearly hysterical manner the policies of the Russian government in regard to Catholics, Protestants, and Jews. At the end of the article, the anonymous correspondent revealed that the Russian authorities had attempted to convert Dr. Lilienthal.[143] Such an unsubstantiated rumor from a questionable source is hardly sufficient proof, as is conceded by the proponents of this thesis; they hold, however, that the rumor was confirmed by Lilienthal himself, in a letter that he wrote to Ludwig Philippson shortly after his arrival in America, in which he said,

The Lord, to whom I sacrificed my position in Russia, for whose holy name I surrendered livelihood, honors, a life position, He, the father of all, to whom I entrusted my fate, and who forsakes none who trust in Him, has helped me in His mercy and has given me a second sphere of activity.[144]

This statement is highly dramatic—and highly ambiguous. Surrendering a job or sacrificing a position to the Lord can mean a variety of things, especially in the mouth of a German Reform rabbi given to heavy-handed hyperbole. To view this statement as an uncontrovertible allusion to resisting conversion is to fall prey to circular reasoning: one assumes that Lilienthal was pressured to convert and then reads this into an ambiguous text.

This ambiguity would leave the question open were it not based on a logical incongruity. This reading would only be plausible if one could explain who attempted to convert him and why. None of the advocates of this theory has attempted to do so, and for good reason. If the traditional view of the missionary motives of the school policy is accepted, this belief hinges on the essential covertness of these motives; if that reading is doubted, the problem is, of course, even sharper. In either case, it is known that the government was well aware of the opposition to Lilienthal and the schools on the part of the overwhelming majority of Russian Jews. As a result, it went out of its way to mute this opposition, to convince the Jews that its policies were absolutely not conversionary in motive or execution. To convert Lilienthal would have been to assure the complete alienation of all the Jews, including even the maskilim, from the schools, and to doom the entire policy to certain failure. Without reliable evidence to the contrary, this hypothesis must be rejected as both unproven and illogical.

The most popular theory—that Lilienthal was disillusioned with the government—is also attended by a combination of textual and logical complications. Up until the time Lilienthal left Russia, he never expressed anything other than complete and absolute confidence in the aims and policies of the government. Only several years after he came to America did he first express negative feelings about Nicholas and his regime. Not only negative, but vituperative. In a series of articles, he reviewed the entire history of the Jews in Russia as a chronology of unrelieved persecution and suffering and concluded that there was no hope at all for the Jews of Russia, save the grace of the Lord.[145]

However, Lilienthal never linked this later realization directly to his abandonment of the Russian mission, and there was absolutely no reason to be reticent on this subject on the pages of the *Allgemeine Zeitung* or *The Occident*. In fact, a close reading of these articles—which, interestingly, are never cited by the proponents of this explanation but merely alluded to in passing—further complicates any such link. In the last installment of this series, first published as "Russisch-jüdische Skizzen," Lilienthal wrote:

So long as the Emperor did not either reject the requests of his ministers or sanction their plans with his signature, there was still hope; when these hopes were dashed, nothing remained but the absolute certainty—if God does not intervene—that Judaism will be ruined in Russia.[146]

However, on the preceding page, Lilienthal provided a firm dating for this supposed change in imperial policy, Nicholas's assent to these hopeless policies—November 13, 1845, a full five months *after* his departure from Russia.[147] That is, according to Lilienthal's own testimony, the decisive change in Russian policy which caused his disillusionment occurred after he had already left the country.

Historians predated this disillusion by falling prey to a simple, if specious, syllogism. In his memoirs Lilienthal recalled that during his first reception in Vilna he promised his audience that he would resign immediately if he learned that the government had in mind anything harmful to the Jewish religion.[148] Although there is absolutely no independent corroboration of this promise, it has been accepted as fact by every scholar describing the encounter. The reasoning was then inexorable: (1) Lilienthal promised that he would abandon his work if he discovered any dangers to the Jewish religion; (2) he left Russia and later expressed disillusionment with the government on these grounds; therefore, (3) he left Russia because he discovered such dangers.

Further confutation of this logic is provided by Lilienthal's own unambiguous statement about his abandonment of the mission. In an article in the *Jewish Times* of 1870, Lilienthal described the edict issued by Nicholas in April 1843 expelling the Jews from the territory within fifty versts of the Prussian and Austrian frontiers of the empire and described his shocked reaction. In this account, the heroes and devils of the previous account are reversed; the ministers were equally horrified by the tsar's decision and attempted to dissuade him by appealing through the Senate and the Committee of Ministers. At the end, however, Lilienthal recalled that he

received a note from Councillor Vronchenko to call on him at once, and when I entered his room with a downcast air he told me that the Emperor had rejected the petition of the council and that all hope for a repeal was gone. I then made up my mind to leave the Imperial service, and in July 1845 I left St. Petersburg for the shores of the land of human rights and liberty.[149]

This statement, which has nothing to do with the educational policies of the government, is the evidence for the sixth hypothesis cited above. However, when this account is examined in the light of the actual chronology of the promulgation of the expulsion law, it cannot withstand critical scrutiny. The edict was published on April 20, 1843, as Lilienthal noted, and was followed by an appeal that extended for several months. While Lilienthal did not provide the date of the resolution of this appeal, according to official sources, it was January 10, 1844.[150] If Lilienthal indeed had reached the decision to abandon the Russian service immediately after hearing of the outcome of the appeal, he would have had to do so in early 1844.

Yet a full six months later, on July 6, 1844, he wrote a letter to his fiancée's father in Munich, mentioning his disappointment with the fifty-verst edict but nevertheless predicting a glorious future for himself in Russia:

It seems certain that the new Jewish legislation [that is, on the schools] will be finished by the end of the year. . . . I can therefore repeat to you here what I communicated heretofore, viz., that a position commanding 1,000 rubles salary is assured me.[151]

And some five months afterward, in December 1844, he wrote to his fiancée, Pepi Nettre:

From my letter to your father you will see that I have an appointment, and in May, God willing, I hope to bring you home with me. . . . My stay [in Munich] will be at the most three weeks, my work will not permit me to remain longer unless I should receive orders from the government that would require a longer stay in Germany. . . . Make all the necessary preparations: get your trousseau ready. . . . A fur coat cannot be finished in Russia in time. . . . Furs are very expensive here; at home they cost only half as much. I believe the ladies wear foxes.[152]

Three months later, on February 19, 1845, he again wrote to Miss Nettre:

Thank your father heartily in my name for attending to the fur coat for you. As regards your dresses, the best materials will be wool and silk. You know I am bitterly opposed to the latter, but St. Petersburg with its fashions cannot be ignored.[153]

Clearly, a full thirteen months after the resolution of the appeal of the fifty-versts expulsion, Lilienthal still intended to remain in Russia in the service of Nicholas I. Why did he not, and why did he never reveal why?

First, the question posed by all the previous analyses must be rephrased: the problem is not why he left Russia. From the time he arrived in Riga, Lilienthal planned to return to Munich to marry Miss Nettre and bring her to Russia. Until 1844, it seemed, he could not receive permission from the government to leave Russia. Therefore, he repeatedly postponed the trip and the wedding date, for which he apologized profusely and repeatedly in his many letters. When he finally did leave on the trip, his departure was not secret or stealthy, as it is always described.[154] On December 8, 1844, he received permission from the Russian government to take a vacation in Germany and therefore wrote the second letter cited above. After another short delay—by now Miss Nettre was very impatient—he left Russia for a holiday in July 1845 and married Pepi Nettre in Munich on August 27.[155] Thirteen days before the wedding, however, Lilienthal's father wrote Uvarov requesting an extension of his son's holiday leave, because of sickness.[156] Two months later, on October 25, 1845, Lilienthal sent his resignation to Uvarov.[157] Soon thereafter, he left for America and arrived in New York in November.[158]

The question, properly posed, therefore, is not why did he leave Russia, but why did he decide not to return?

In order to propose an answer to this question, it is necessary substantially to redraw the portrait of Lilienthal that is common in the historical literature. The passions evoked by the Lilienthal venture—the questions of the role of the Russian government in the reform of the Jews, the character of the Haskalah itself, the relations between German and Russian Jews—turned all the participants in the episode into national and moral symbols and precluded their consideration as ordinary human beings displaying the mundane emotions of mortal existence. Since these particular passions have long been exhausted, it is possible to restore these people to their human proportions.

This can be done from the letters Lilienthal wrote to his family and fiancée from Riga and St. Petersburg, only parts of which were published in his biography, its author explaining that they "contain passages which are of too intimate a character for the public eye. Hence only portions of the letters have been selected as were felt to be of public interest."[159] Fortunately, Lilienthal's daughter-in-law Sophie felt no such scruples when she restored this correspondence in her privately printed *Lilienthal Family Record*.[160]

Max Lilienthal was twenty-three years old when he left Munich for Russia. His appointment in Riga was his first steady job—he had applied to several rabbinical posts but was refused because of his known sympathies with the growing Reform trend, then out of favor with the Bavarian authorities. Soon after he arrived in Riga, however, he realized that his future there was not very promising. The small local Jewish community was embroiled in a complicated lawsuit that threatened its very existence, and prospects for a positive outcome were not good. In a letter written to his brother Samuel, Lilienthal revealed his solution to this lack of prospects:

. . . convinced that it would be very difficult for the community to carry out its project, and that thereby the position of the schools would be very precarious, . . . I tried to open for myself a future of great promise by presenting to the above-named Minister [Uvarov] a plan for the erection of consistories, which was accepted with great approval. . . . I made myself known in this way to the Minister—one must never let the opportune moment pass without making use of it.[161]

In Munich, however, the families were not impressed. His father and, equally important, his prospective father-in-law were highly dubious of the entire Russian venture. Would he make a living sufficient to support him and his future bride? His father wrote him several "awful, unpleasant letters . . . hurting [him] by bitter reproaches," urging him to demand greater pay and apparently instructing him to return to Germany should his position not improve. Max was adamant: "You will say, 'Return,' " he wrote, still from Riga.

All right, but do you think that that can be so easily done? Where are the many vacant situations, where the places where one can immediately find employment? And further, shall I give up so quickly my chosen career? Shall I believe that God in mere capricious mood has taken me a blind puppet of fate, thrown me into Russia in order, in another mood, to throw me out again? I believe otherwise when I review what I have accomplished in seven months.[162]

And in the same letter:

When I think of my relations to the authorities, of how I am favored by the Minister and treated by him with real fatherly kindness; when I recall with what kindly consideration I, the Jew, am judged, how the effort is made to encourage me; when I consider what the future may have in store for me, I would not then exchange my situation with that of any of my compatriots in Germany, and feel myself richer in honors and reputation than they.[163]

However, the spectacular and lucrative career never materialized. Lilienthal did have a position in St. Petersburg, but it was not that of a freewheeling reformer of the Jews, as he anticipated. Instead, he became the first "learned Jew" at the Ministry of National Enlightenment. This was hardly the grandiose position that he kept awaiting and of whose imminence he kept assuring his family. Although his salary was respectable enough—rather equivalent to that of a skilled laborer at a St. Petersburg plant at the time—it never was raised from the time he joined the service until he left and was hardly commensurate with his ambitions and expectations or with the society life in the capital to which he aspired.[164]

Moreover, although there is no evidence that his relations with the government were anything but impeccable throughout his stay in Russia, there is overwhelming proof of a growing rift between him and both camps of Russian-Jewish society. His problems with the traditionalists were predictable and unavoidable, but his massive lack of support among his natural constituency, the maskilim, was the opposite of what both he and they expected.

Some of the problems stemmed from personal jealousy and economic competition. The founder of the first Haskalah-based school in Vilna, Hirsh Kliaczko, joined in a denunciation of Lilienthal and Nisan Rosenthal submitted to the government in April 1842, charging them with illegal activities.[165] The director of the Odessa Jewish school, Bezalel Stern, was openly disdainful of Lilienthal and deliberately avoided him when he came to Odessa, choosing instead to embark on a study of Karaite antiquities in the Crimea.[166] At the rabbinical commission, the two clashed openly and repeatedly. Allegedly, during one discussion, Stern said to Lilienthal, "You know nothing," to which the latter replied, "I know one thing better than you, Herr Direktor—how to shut up."[167] Although this animosity was probably also rooted in professional jealousy—until Lilienthal's appearance, Stern was the most respected maskil and influential modern educator in the Pale—there was a profound ideological disagreement involved as well. Based on his own experience in Galicia and Odessa, Stern believed that reformed education could only be successful when it reflected the wishes of an already enlightened community; reforms from above and outside would be rejected by the Jews and collapse in failure. Accordingly, Stern was much less sympathetic to the government's proposals at the St. Petersburg commission and—according to the Liubavich tradition, which was hardly well-disposed to Stern's brand of Judaism—often sided with the traditionalists against Lilienthal.[168]

Even the Russian maskilim who completely supported the government's policy of enlightenment from above came to oppose Lilienthal. One of the leaders of the moderate group of Vilna maskilim, Mordekhai Aaron Ginzburg, penned an attack on Lilienthal so vehement that it had to be published outside Russia. This attack, titled *Maggid ᶜemet* (Herald of truth) in deliberate rebuttal of Lilienthal's *Maggid yeshuᶜah*, focused on two related issues: Lilienthal's incompetence as an uninformed outsider and his disregard of local maskilim. Who is this German come to tell the Russian Jews that we cannot save ourselves, Ginzburg asked in disgust:

This is not the man whom we need: he knows less Torah than young students, and even his philosophical knowledge is not great. . . . One can't deny that these doctors speak German fluently, for it is their mother-tongue, as well as French and often English as well, and they know Latin and logic, history and geography, etc.—but these are matters which gymnasium students know as well; what has this knowledge to do with the name "Doctor of Philosophy"?[169]

This was a fundamental cultural antagonism between the autodidactic Russian maskilim and the university-trained German Reformers. "May God in His mercy forgive our German brethren," Ginzburg continued, "for with their rabbis they have transgressed the laws of the Torah as much as the inhabitants of Poland have transgressed against the laws of wisdom with their old rabbis."[170] And Lilienthal compounded this ignorance with his pomposity and dishonesty. In his *Maggid yeshuᶜah* he neglected to mention the crucial support given him by Nisan Rosenthal and claimed that the educational reform was proposed by the emperor himself, not his ministers, which was clearly not true. Finally, in his tour of Russia he completely ignored all the Russian maskilim, hobnobbed only with the rich, and fraternized to the point of absurdity with the Hasidim. He was well suited to his position in Riga but utterly inappropriate and ineffectual in the role which he took on in his conceit.[171]

Even the most radical and westernized of the Russian maskilim soon turned against him after pinning their hopes on him and disregarding his egotism. To them his decision to call the rabbinical commission, however, was intolerable:

What have we got to do with rabbis? How will these "righteous" men save us? Does Israel lack Torah—are we missing any commandment in the Code of Laws that they have to fill in? . . . If the Doctor had carried out his plan to suggest to the Minister to invite German rabbis to save us, as we had hoped, that would have been wise and just, and would have helped us greatly. But what good will these mute idols who cannot speak and are far from any knowledge do for us? . . . We have lost our faith in the Doctor, he is intent only on glorifying his own name to the ministers. . . .[172]

Lacking the support of the maskilim, Lilienthal was left with a frustrating, underpaid position instead of the bright future he had promised his family. When he returned to Munich, he could not claim to have undone the hesitation and opposition expressed by his father and father-in-law.

What actually happened during his stay in Germany is not known. It cannot be ascertained what the illness was that his father claimed to Uvarov necessitated additional leave at home or whether this extension—or even the abandonment of the Russian mission— was a precondition to the wedding between Lilienthal and Pepi Nettre. It is not even known if Lilienthal himself decided that it was best not to return to Russia or whether the decision was imposed on him by family pressure.

What is left, therefore, is a simple, if unprovable, hypothesis: realizing his failure in creating in Russia the future he envisioned, he submitted to the primary personal and familial demands of life and abandoned the Russian mission—through the back door.

Obviously, even if this theory were correct, it could not be expected that Lilienthal would cite such reasons for his decision. Therefore he later tried to connect his move with the fifty-verst law and never confirmed or denied the rumor of the conversion attempt. There is no reason to doubt that his later conclusions about the true designs of Nicholas's cultural and educational policies were anything but sincere; the evidence merely suggests that he did not reach these conclusions while in Russia.

4 · Enlightenment of the Jews

The New Schools

During Lilienthal's tenure at the Ministry of National Enlightenment, the number of private, Haskalah-based Jewish schools doubled in Russia—from four to eight. In 1841 two separate—and apparently competitive—schools were opened in Vilna. One, sponsored by Rosenthal, was headed by V. Zeiberling and staffed with Ḥaim Leib Katzenellenbogen, Mattias Strashun, Yeḥezkel Vidutskii, Wolf Tugendhold, and Sh. Y. Fin; the other was founded by Zvi Hirsh Kliaczko and employed Mordekhai Aaron Ginzburg and Shlomo Zalkind. Both schools had the same curriculum—Bible with Mendelssohn's translation and commentary, Hebrew grammar, Talmud, Jewish religion, Russian, German, arithmetic, and calligraphy. Together, they enrolled approximately eighty students.[1]

In Minsk a fascinating situation developed. A wealthy maskil, David Luria, gained control of the local Talmud Torah and transformed it into a modernized school teaching Russian and secular subjects in addition to Bible and Talmud. The traditionalist merchants who had opposed Luria but lost soon realized that their own sons were receiving an education inferior to that of the poor, orphaned pupils of the Talmud Torah. As a result, they attempted a compromise. Their children would continue to attend ḥeder from morning to mid-afternoon and then would take two hours of instruction in Russian, German, French, arithmetic, and geography in a separate supplementary school. The experiment was unsuccessful; it seemed that a choice had to be made between the old and new types of education. Apparently, most of the merchants chose the latter. In 1845, David Luria opened a second school, called Midrash 'Ezrahim (School for Citizens), which taught the same subjects as the Talmud Torah, with the addition of German, but had a more selective student body because of its annual fee of twelve rubles per student. Within a year this school flourished, enrolling over 100 students.[2]

The demand for modernized education was growing. No longer were the new schools restricted to the heterodox, peripheral communities such as Odessa and Riga. However, only in the large cities were there enough maskilim with sufficient funds and clout to launch their own schools. A sweeping modernized school system could only be established with the support of the government.

This began in 1847, when the first state-sponsored Jewish schools were founded. At the beginning, the ministry took over the private schools—only the Riga school was permitted to remain outside the direct jurisdiction of the government.[3] Within eight years, however, state-run schools were opened throughout the Pale, from Mitau in the north to Simferopol' in the south, from Brest-Litovsk on the Polish border to Vitebsk on the eastern frontier. No official listing of the schools is available; unofficial sources vary from 62 to 103 schools by the end of Nicholas's reign.[4] Table 1 lists 71 schools established by 1855.

TABLE 1

STATE-RUN SCHOOLS AND YEAR FOUNDED

Location	Year
Belaia-Tserkov'	1849
Berdichev—primary	1849
Berdichev—secondary	1850
Beshenkovichi	1855
Bratslav	1849–50
Bykhov	*
Cherikov	1852
Dinaburg	1851
Ekaterinoslav	1851
Elizavetgrad	1850
Gol'dingen	1850
Gomel'	1852
Grodno	*

Location	Year
Jacobstat	1850
Kamenets-Podol'sk—primary	1849
Kamenets-Podol'sk—secondary	1849
Kanev	1849
Kishinev—primary	1850
Kishinev—secondary	1850
Kovel'	*
Kovno	*
Lepel'	1855
Libava	1851
Liubavich	1852
Minsk—primary	1847
Minsk—secondary	1847
Mitau	1850
Mogilev—primary	1850
Mogilev—secondary	1852
Mstislavl'	1851
Nevel'	1852
Novgorod-Volynsk	1850
Odessa—primary	*
Odessa—2nd primary	*
Odessa—secondary	*
Ol'gopol'	1849–50
Orsha	1852
Pinsk	1853
Polotsk	1851
Ponievezh	*
Proskurov	1849–50
Rogachev	*
Shklov	1851
Simferopol'	1850
Slutsk	*
Starodub	*
Staryi-Konstantin	*
Tukum	1851
Vasil'kov	1849
Velizh	1852
Vilna—primary	1847
Vilna—secondary	1847
Vilna—rabbinical seminary	1847
Vilna province—11 primary	*

Location	Year
Vilna province—2 secondary	*
Vitebsk—primary	1848
Vitebsk—2nd primary	*
Vitebsk—secondary	1852
Zhitomir	1850
Zhitomir—rabbinical seminary	1847

*Date of founding unknown, but described by 1855. Cross-referencing every one of these schools would require a listing so long that it would be counterproductive. A separate card was kept on each school mentioned either in *KEY* or in a memoir of a teacher or student of one of the schools, as well as articles on the number of schools in various towns and provinces (see bibliography).

The *Journal of the Ministry of National Enlightenment* published detailed accounts of the opening ceremonies of many of these schools. The festivities in Ekaterinoslav, for example, were typical. The local authorities scheduled the opening of the school for the Coronation Day. At noon the director of the local gymnasium was host to all the officials and notables of the town and the leaders of the Jewish community. After a reading of the order charging the establishment of the school, the rabbi and a choir led in the singing of a hymn, a Mr. Shaporinskii spoke in Hebrew on "The Meaning, Purpose, and Importance of This Educational Institution," and a Mr. Sinaiskii delivered a talk on "The Advantages of Public over Private Education." Since a large part of the audience did not understand Hebrew, the speeches were translated into Russian by the local merchant Arshavskii. After this, the Jewish children sang the national anthem, "God Save the Tsar" in Russian, German, and Hebrew. After "listening with reverence to this cantata, which is precious to every Russian heart," the guests were invited to lunch sponsored by a Jewish merchant of the first guild, L. M. Krantsfel'd. "The kind host did not forget his coreligionists who could not share a meal with Christians: he prepared a beautiful meal for them in a separate room."[5]

Since no registration lists are extant, it is impossible to establish the number of students enrolled in these schools. Four scholars list enrollment figures, which vary only slightly: two cite 3,708, one 3,363, and one 3,487 students by 1855.[6] However, since there often was false reporting of attendance in order to please the authorities, these figures can be accepted only as rough estimates.[7]

The curriculum of the schools adhered strictly to the guidelines published by the ministry in 1844. In the archives at the YIVO Institute can be found the distribution of classroom hours for the Vilna primary school:[8]

Subject	Hours per week
Jewish religion	six
Hebrew language	two
Russian language	three
German language	two
arithmetic	three
geography	two
history	two
calligraphy	two

On Friday afternoon regular studies were suspended, and the pupils were prepared in the weekly portion of the Scriptures, taught from Mendelssohn's *Bi'ur*, which was reissued by the Vilna maskilim A. Lebenzon and Y. Ben-Ya'akov in the late 1840s and broadened to include new commentaries by the editors, as well as "old" ones by such diverse figures as the sixteenth-century exegete Obadiah Sforno, the late-eighteenth-century critic Wolf Heidenheim, the Gaon of Vilna, Samuele Davide Luzzatto, and Herz Homberg.[9]

The classes in Jewish religion—called *zakon bozhii* in Russian, or divine law—were taught from special textbooks edited by Leon Mandelshtam, Lilienthal's successor as "learned Jew" at the Ministry of National Enlightenment. In accord with Uvarov's instructions and the maskilim's ideological predilections, these textbooks were designed to supplement and, in time, replace the study of the Talmud in the new schools. They were issued in thousands of copies and sold—often under force—to the *melamdim* of the traditional schools, as well as to the directors of the government schools.[10]

The one such work which is extant provides a fascinating example of the intellectual politics of the Haskalah. In 1850 and 1851, Mandelshtam published a five-volume condensation of Maimonides' law code, *Yad ha-ḥazakah*, selecting the sections dealing with the study of Torah, relations with non-Jews, penitence, prayer and rituals, holiday observances, charity, and civil and criminal law.[11] Interspersed with the texts themselves are essays written by contemporary rabbis in Germany and Russia amplifying Maimonides' views on the obligation of loyalty to the secular monarch and his laws, the commandment to respect one's fellow citizens, and the exemption of Christians from the category of "idolators" with whom the Jews are forbidden a wide range of economic and social contacts.[12] These injunctions to loyalty and tolerance were fully compatible with the mainstream of traditional views on these subjects, which had evolved in response to economic pressures and the necessity of forging an alliance with the central authority.[13] However, Mandelshtam went far beyond the traditional viewpoint in a series of clarifying notes preceding several especially controversial passages. Explicating Maimonides' analysis that the talmudic dictum *dina de-malkhuta dina* (the law of the state is law) applies to all commercial transactions, Mandelshtam claims that this principle applies to all judgments of Russian civil and criminal courts, either in cases between two Jews or between a Jew and a non-Jew, and thus Jews are commanded by the Torah and Talmud to obey punctiliously all the laws of the Imperial Russian Code.[14] More radical than this idiosyncratic reading of Maimonides and the Talmud is Mandelshtam's conclusion from the rabbis' differentiation between contemporary gentiles and ancient idolators:

God forbid that we think that the nations under whose protection we live are included in the category "idolators" [*ᶜakum*], or do not believe as well that the Torah of Moses is true and given by God. On the contrary, they not only obey the seven Noachide laws, but also most of the commandments to which only the Jews are obligated, and therefore not only do they have a place in the World To Come, and are called "the righteous of the Gentiles" since they operate under law and are just and merciful to all subjects of the country, but also we are commanded and obligated to love them, to wish them well, and to thank them for their generosity and mercy with us, for we shall live forever in their country, and they are so endowed with knowledge and good qualities to so sublime an extent that, according to our Holy Torah we are obliged to regard them as our brothers in one nation, in addition to our duty as subjects to obey all the orders of our merciful Emperor just like all his other subjects, to follow his laws as written in the Law Code of Imperial Russia, since in our souls we know that it is as great a sin to disobey the word of the King as it is to transgress the commands of God, and Heaven forbid that we should be ingrates or desecrators of His Holy name and do so in public or in private.[15]

All Russian maskilim expressed complete loyalty to the emperor and patriotism to the state, but this unqualified equalization of the laws of the Torah and the tsar and statement of the eternity of Jewish life in Russia marked Mandelshtam as the most extreme maskil of his age.[16]

In most of the government schools such intellectual and even theological speculation was not engaged in. The point of the endeavor, after all, was not to turn the Jews into philosophers but to acculturate them to the Russian milieu. Especially after Uvarov was dismissed as minister in 1848 for being too liberal,[17] the direction of the schools became more practical and commercial. The Vilna secondary school, among others, was transformed into a *Realschule*, training its pupils for trade and industry by teaching them bookkeeping, geometry, mechanics, physics, and chemistry, in addition to the other subjects.[18]

The only schools that were encouraged to dwell on more spiritual—and Judaic—concerns were the two rabbinical seminaries founded in Vilna and Zhitomir in 1847. As a result of this specialization, the staff lists of these institutions read like a who's who of the Russian Haskalah. In Vilna the first inspector of the seminary was the writer and scholar Hirsh Katzenellenbogen. His son Ḥaim Leib taught Bible; the preeminent poet of the age, Adam Hakohen Lebenzon, taught Hebrew language; the Vilna censor Wolf Tugendhold, Jewish history; Sh. Y. Fin and Judah Behak, Jewish religion; I. Sh. Strashun, Hirsh Kliaczko, Shlomo Zalkind, and Judah Shereshevskii, Mishnah and Talmud; Jakob Naienburg, a graduate of the University of Berlin, German. The staff physician was Honorary Citizen Dr. M. Trachtenberg.[19] The Zhitomir list was shorter but equally influential. The inspector was the poet Ya°akov Eichenbaum. Talmud was taught by the scholars Bakst and Zweifel; history by the Brody maskil M. Sukhostaner; and Hebrew by Hirsh Segal.[20] Other prominent maskilim taught in the primary schools: Kalman Shulman in Vilna, Avraham Mapu in Kovno, Avraham Ber Gottlober in Kamenets-Podol'sk, and the most important of the later maskilim, Yehudah Leib Gordon, in Ponievezh.[21] The only notable maskilim of teaching age by 1855 who did not serve in the schools were Y. Ben-Ya°akov, who seems to have opposed them in principle, and I. B. Lebenzon, who was too ill to accept the post offered him.[22]

As these lists reveal, Lilienthal's and Uvarov's plan of staffing the new schools with West European Jews did not materialize. However, this does not imply—as many historians have assumed— that a specific decision was made on this. In fact, the reason that the policy was not implemented was unrelated to the Jews: it was a consequence of Nicholas's general panicked reaction to the revolutions of 1848. On March 18, 1848, he issued an order forbidding the importation into Russia of any foreign teachers, "in light of present seditious events and harmful intellectual trends beyond our frontiers."[23] Actually, three foreign Jews were indeed hired to teach in the new schools—Sukhostaner from Austria, Naienburg from Prussia, and an Austrian Jew named Malchiner who taught in the Kishinev elementary school—since they managed to accept their posts before the new law was enforced.[24]

Not all the other teachers were Russian Jews—two of the most influential staff members of the rabbinical seminaries were Polish Jews: Ya°akov Eichenbaum was born in Zamość, where he taught himself German and translated Euclid into Hebrew before coming to Uman' and Odessa and then to Zhitomir;[25] Wolf Tugendhold was born near Cracow and attended gymnasium and university in Breslau prior to appointment to the Vilna Censorship Committee.[26]

While a great deal is known about the staff of the new schools and seminaries, there is, unfortunately, far less information on their students. Nineteenth-century critics of the schools claimed that the vast majority of the pupils were from lower-class and poor families and came to the schools only to avoid the draft; only in later years did the more well-to-do elements of the population send their children to the state schools.[27] On the basis of these accounts, historians have asserted that only the poorest and most desperate Jews allowed their children to attend the schools—one frequently cited scholar even going so far as to say that no Jew ever voluntarily sent his children to the schools.[28]

The little available hard evidence on the students raises serious questions about these generalizations. The one extant attendance list is the class register of the Vilna Rabbinical Seminary in 1849. Of the 102 pupils, 4 are from wealthy, guild merchant families. The other 98 are listed only as *meshchane*, that is, townspeople, the social category of the vast majority of Russian Jews which has no economic significance; of these, 25 came from easily identifiable maskilic families, such as the Kliaczkos, Trachtenbergs, and Braudes, some of whom were of substantial means, though not in the merchant guilds.[29] An official report submitted to the authorities by the supervisor of the Grodno Jewish primary school detailed a situation similar to that in the private Minsk school of David Luria. At the beginning, the wealthy and traditional Jews of Grodno refused to send their children to the school and enrolled only the poorest and least intelligent of the local children. After a short while, however, many of the "reasonable and not-so-prejudiced" Jews noted that the unfortunates in the state school had achieved great progress in their studies and decided to send their own children to the school, raising the enrollment to 62 in 1853. Among the new students were children of prosperous families and even the son of the local rabbi. This changed situation led the "fanatics and *melamdim*" to use all sorts of force to dissuade the Grodno Jews from sending their children to the school, including the threat of military service and excommunication.[30] In other parts of the Pale, the student body seems to have been similar. M. Morgulis, a graduate of the Zhitomir Rabbinical Seminary, recalled that there was great tension in that institution in its early years between the scholarship students, who came from poor families, and those from wealthier portions of the population, who paid their own way.[31]

It is possible to conclude, therefore, that while a large percentage of the students in the new schools came from penurious families, a substantial number were from the more prosperous and "enlight-ened" parents. The latter supported the schools for clearly defined and articulated ideological reasons; the former, in the hope that their sons would escape the conscription system which—as ad-ministered by their own leaders—discriminated against the poor and the powerless.

This indicator of the new alignment of forces within the Jewish community was, by itself, a crucial consequence of the establish-ment of the new schools. A very common reaction to the abuses of the conscription system was a turning against the Jewish estab-lishment, not an increase in alienation from the Russian govern-ment. As a result of the opening of the state schools, a significant segment of the poorer elements of Russian Jewry who had no voice in the communal decision-making process protested against their leaders by ignoring threats and prohibitions and enrolling their children in the "heretical" schools. In the last years of Nicholas's reign, Haskalah became the ideology not only of an intellectual or economic elite but also of a vocal portion of the destitute and dispossessed.

In general, the standard view of historians that the new schools proved to be dismal failures with little influence on the course of Russian-Jewish history must be rejected. The critical question is not what did the schools fail to do—create a German-style Re-formed rabbinate, replace the heder, educate tens of thousands of Jews—but precisely what did they accomplish, even by 1855?

To begin with, the quantitative record was hardly so negligible as has been supposed. Even if the attendance figures cited above have been inflated by a third—most likely, a far too liberal cor-rection—it is apparent that within the first eight years after the founding of the first government schools, over twenty-five hundred Jewish children attended primary and secondary schools which instructed them in Russian, German, and secular subjects. While obviously still a tiny proportion of the total school-age population of the Jewish community, this figure represented an increase of at least 600 percent over the enrollment of the privately run mod-ernized schools and included children in every important Jewish center in the Pale. Given the resolute opposition to these schools on the part of the traditionalist leaders of the society, this was an impressive figure. In addition, the drawing power of the two rabbinical seminaries was staggering; reliable records attest to 251 students at the Vilna seminary and 271 in Zhitomir by 1855.[32] The significance of these numbers can easily be shown by comparing them to the attendance records of the most important contemporary nontraditional rabbinical seminary, the Jüdisch-Theologisches Seminar in Breslau. Founded in 1854, this seminary had only 48 students eight years later and throughout the first fifty years of its existence had an average enrollment of only 40.52 students.[33]

More important than this quantitative achievement was the qualitative effect that the schools had on their society. Without complete lists of students, it is impossible to determine what the vast majority did after finishing the schools, but a partial reconstruction of their student body shows that the first generation of graduates included the following famous and influential Russian Jews: N. I. Bakst, H. Barats, B. Bertenson, Y. Gershtein, A. Goldfaden, E. Kagan, S. Kaplan, S. Kovner, A. Landau, L. Levanda, A. Liberman, Z. Minor, M. Morgulis, A. Paperna, L. Pinsker, I. Soloveichik, and M. Veisbrod.[34] Together with the teachers listed above, these men constituted the literary, intellectual, and political elite of Russian Jewry from the 1840s through the 1870s and the creators of the new Russian-Jewish culture.

In fact, the only influential leader of nontraditionalist Russian Jewry who had no connection with the schools was Moshe Leib Lilienblum, who later bemoaned:

I was given over to ignorant teachers when I was fifteen years old. Now I know that while I wasted my strength and time in vanities, other boys my age were dealing with matters of true importance by studying in the Rabbinical Seminaries, gymnasiums, and merchant-schools. . . . I also know that many of these boys became happy and successful men, and I—a ne'er-do-well wretch. But how could I have known then what I know now?[35]

Moreover, by the end of Nicholas's reign, the new schools had already reached the stage of hiring their own graduates, thus reinforcing their position as important cultural forces within Russian Jewry.[36]

The most important accomplishment of the new school system, therefore, was its essential contribution to the institutionalization and consolidation of the Haskalah. Until the 1840s, the maskilim in Russia were an isolated, persecuted, and muzzled minority, often doomed to penury or exile. With the establishment of the new schools, they gained a power base and economic security, which relieved them of any dependence on the community leaders or even the consensus of Jewish society at large. As employees and allies of the government, they became a potent force within Russian Jewry and a grave threat to the traditional order.

At the same time, these maskilim were joined and reinforced by the growing number of Jews studying at the general educational institutions of the empire. In the early 1840s, there were 230 Jewish students attending Russian elementary schools, and between 100 and 120 were enrolled in regular, non-Jewish, gymnasiums. In addition, in the latter part of Nicholas's reign, some three dozen Jews attended Russian universities, mostly in the medical faculties.[37]

By the beginning of the 1850s, therefore, the new power of the maskilim was matched, for the first time, with the security of numbers. From a handful of disjointed individuals clustered in tiny enclaves on the borders of the Pale or in insulated anonymity in the largest cities, the maskilim grew to a well-coordinated movement of several hundred adherents, preaching their gospel to thousands of committed students throughout the Pale.[38]

From this new coherence and potency there emerged a new self-consciousness, or rather, a manifest reaffirmation of self-perception. As one of their most articulate spokesmen explained, even the youngest maskilim now sensed their mission. Every student in the state schools

regarded himself as no less than a future reformer, a new Mendelssohn, and therefore, in the quiet worked out a plan of action which he jealously guarded from his friends. [They] were thoroughly convinced that they were going to bring about a complete revolution in the world view of the Jewish people, and they impatiently awaited their moment of action. They were like military commanders standing at the ready for the approaching enemy attack, waiting only for the moment when they will be able to display the wonders of their courage and to distinguish themselves for their fatherland.[39]

This new sense of mission and power, this rejection of traditional society combined with a dedication to its restructuring on a new basis, transformed the maskilim from an amorphous set of intellectuals into a full-fledged intelligentsia. As Isaiah Berlin has taught, there is a fundamental difference between the concept of an intelligentsia and the notion of intellectuals. The former

thought of themselves as united by something more than mere interest in ideas; they conceived of themselves as being a dedicated order, almost a secular priesthood, devoted to the spreading of a specific attitude to life, something like a gospel.[40]

Thus, we can date the emergence of a coherent Russian-Jewish intelligentsia to the latter part of the rule of Nicholas I, in large part as a response to the stimulus provided by the Russian government itself.

The Ideology of the Russian-Jewish Intelligentsia

The members of the new intelligentsia all shared this sense of mission toward the common goal of reforming the Jews through education and self-regeneration. Yet from the beginning they did not adhere to one unified program but expressed a wide variety of conflicting views on its quality, substance, and methods.

This dissonance was not recorded by most historians of the era, who, blinded by the rays of hope that flickered in the 1860s, drew a sharp dividing line between the Haskalah before and after the accession of Alexander II. Some of these scholars allowed their sympathies for the generation of the Great Reforms to overwhelm their own evidence and consigned the pre-1855 maskilim to medieval oblivion. "From the darkness of the Middle Ages in which they were steeped until the time of Alexander II," begins the first book-length survey of the Russian Haskalah, the Russian Jews "emerged suddenly into the life and light of the West."[41] Other, more sober scholars described a subtler, but equally dramatic turning point. Until 1855 the Russian maskilim were naive, statist, germanizing autodidacts who adhered to the program formulated by Isaac Ber Levinsohn on the model of the Berlin Haskalah; after 1855 they were an educated, sophisticated, russified intelligentsia battling over the questions of assimilation, emancipation, and nationalism.[42]

This second view stems in large part from its authors' ideological opposition to the Haskalah—usually on nationalistic or socialistic grounds—compounded by a curious, if not uncommon, semantic transmutation. Like the terms Utopian Socialists in France and Populists in Russia, Berliners and Russifiers were epithets originally coined by the opponents of a specific ideology which soon became accepted in the political and scholarly jargon to refer to a broad range of positions all discredited and supplanted by a new truth.[43] A close examination of the views expressed by Russian maskilim *before* 1855, however, renders this terminology and time reference insupportable, as a comparison of the attitude of Isaac Ber Levinsohn and other contemporary maskilim toward three of the major issues of the Haskalah—the Jewish tradition and its reform, language policy, and the Russian government—will show.

Haskalah and Jewish Tradition   For Levinsohn, Haskalah was identical with the authentic Jewish tradition, correctly interpreted. Any seeming contradiction between it and the study of Hebrew, foreign languages, and productive trades, stemmed from a corruption of the true teachings of the rabbis on the part of the ignorant masses, particularly the Hasidim, and could be resolved through intelligent and informed study of the sources. This was the main goal of *Te'udah be-yisra'el,* which consisted mostly in an exposition of the correct meaning of rabbinical dicta and an enumeration of all the authorities throughout the ages who could qualify as true maskilim. The search for enlightenment, according to Levinsohn, had nothing in common with a rejection of the tradition or the authority of Jewish law. On the contrary, those who mock the Torah and insult the rabbis are obviously not deep thinkers or true philosophers.[44] Only those who combine Torah and secular knowledge can truly serve the Lord and reach happiness in this world and the next, for Torah and worldly wisdom are like Siamese twins who cannot be separated without mortal—and eternal—danger.[45] Levinsohn's purpose, therefore, was not to supplant the teachings of the Sages but to interpret them as they were intended, not to change the tradition but to restore it to its pure state before it was corrupted by the ignorant.

To this end, he enlisted the aid of the government for a series of practical measures: establishing new schools, appointing a chief rabbi and government-sponsored preachers, transforming at least a third of the Jews into agriculturists.[46] In advocating these reforms, he subjected his contemporary Jews, especially the Hasidim, to relentless criticism and even urged the government to prohibit the publication or importation of Hasidic works. However, he always believed that he was defending the tradition with his actions, not changing or subverting it.

Like Levinsohn, the majority of the Vilna maskilim were observant and believing Jews who were convinced that they were acting in accord with the tradition and only separating the wheat from the chaff. But in a petition submitted to the government in 1843, they went one step further than Levinsohn in advocating actual restrictions on Jewish behavior. Levinsohn had proposed merely that the government institute strict sumptuary laws prohibiting the wearing of luxurious clothes; the Vilna petitioners, led by Mordekhai Aaron Ginzburg and Mattias Strashun, asked for a complete outlawing of the traditional Jewish attire on the grounds that it had no basis in Jewish law and was merely a custom that now served only to separate the Jews from the gentiles.[47]

The differences between the signers of this petition and Levinsohn were essentially tactical and temperamental, not ideological. However, the next cohort of maskilim, those who reached maturity during the 1840s, approached tradition from an entirely different perspective. Often second-generation maskilim, they were far less steeped in rabbinical learning and outlook and were prepared to pick and choose those elements of the tradition that they deemed suitable for the new age and to reject the rest.

Some expression of this ideological generation gap was seen in the debate over Lilienthal and the redaction of Maimonides for the state schools. In the letters of the two Mandelshtam brothers, Leon and Benjamin, many more examples of the new approach are evident. For example, despite his hatred of the Hasidim, Levinsohn accepted the sanctity and authority of kabbalistic sources (although he seems to have expressed some doubts over the dating of the Zohar).[48] To Leon Mandelshtam, on the contrary, kabbalistic mysticism as a whole was an archaic system of superstition and nonsense. Not only were Hasidic masters practitioners of "the pernicious tricks of Luria and Vital," but the Kabbalah itself had served the Jews only

as an eggshell serves the metamorphosis of a chick; but Jews who raise themselves out of this chaos of superstition, sensing its narrow-mindedness and suffocating nature, begin to realize its superficiality. Through these slits there penetrate rays of enlightenment which prove that the Kabbalah, in relation to religion, is nothing but a shell.[49]

Not only the Kabbalah was an unnecessary and destructive anachronism but much of the rabbinical tradition was as well. Unlike Levinsohn and the Vilna maskilim, who restricted their criticisms to specific customs practiced by the Hasidim, the Mandelshtams indulged in sweeping condemnations of all the rituals and customs of contemporary Jewry, undistinguished by sect. To Leon, for example, these rites had served some purpose in preserving the Jews' existence throughout the ages—"if one can call that unsystematic insignificance an existence"[50]—but such utility was possible only when the world was devoid of wisdom and enlightenment.

But the time of fanaticism among the Christians has passed; the synagogue has nothing to fear from the church. But the Russian Jews retain their outdated customs, and continue to apply their antiquated habits and barbarous, gloomy mores.[51]

The rabbis—all rabbis, not just the Hasidic masters—cannot be expected to correct this situation and to prove the undesirability of the multitude of ceremonies canonized since the time of Maimonides, for they are too ignorant, spiritually degenerate, and dependent on their congregants. Only modern-educated teachers can lead the regeneration of the Jews. In this process the Talmud may be retained as a subject in the schools, but only if it is made to harmonize with and conform to present-day theology.[52]

This radical departure from Levinsohn's stance was penned in 1839 or 1840 and remained the ideology of the antitraditionalist wing of the Russian-Jewish intelligentsia until Moshe Leib Lilienblum began his more sophisticated polemic for religious reform in the late 1860s and early 1870s as part of his gradual rejection of the basic tenets of the Haskalah itself.[53]

Not only was such iconoclastic ideology expressed in Russia during the 1840s, but at the same time it was manifested in public violations of Jewish law. In the traditional society of Russian Jewry, such breaches of social discipline were more destabilizing and hence dangerous than private rejection of beliefs. Thus, the same maskilim who petitioned the government to ban the Polish-Jewish garb appeared before the ministers clad in that costume, explaining that they were not prepared to face the censure of their coreligionists without governmental support.[54] Yet already in the 1840s and 1850s the boldest of the maskilim publicly desecrated the most sacred of the commandments. Ya'akov Eichenbaum, the head of the Zhitomir Rabbinical Seminary, not only shaved his beard and wore European dress but ate nonkosher food, smoked on the Sabbath, and—even more public, and hence egregious—allowed the piano to be played in his house on Saturday.[55] The students of the Vilna Rabbinical Seminary, complained one of the more conservative maskilim,

realizing that the government would protect them, despised their nation to such an extent that they did not even deign to hide their evil actions, and committed all sorts of outrages openly and defiantly. Two of the rabbis spent their nights playing cards . . . on Tisha Be'av, one of the rabbinical students went to a much-frequented public house outside the city which was not owned by a Jew and ate and drank to his fill. . . . Another could not find kosher meat and so ate nonkosher food for several days. Several others defiled themselves with crab meat, and threw the shells into one of the stoves of the school.[56]

By 1855, not only had the Russian Haskalah split between moderate "restorers" and extreme "reformers," but it even numbered in its midst at least one penitent from extremism to moderation. Joachim Tarnopol, a graduate of the Odessa school, recalled in his history of the Odessa Jewish community—written in French in 1855—that he had grown up in a traditional family but, after enrolling in the secular school, had abandoned his previous piety and become a typical skeptical cosmopolitan. Upon reflection, however, he soon realized that the Oral Law did contain some elements worthy of the attention of modern moralists, just as modern civilization did not offer all the guarantees of the good life:

I retraced my steps and found my bearings in the golden mean, keeping myself at an equal distance from both extremes, trying to conserve what was good in each and rejecting the bad. . . . I came back to my coreligionists; finding them reformed, I became reconciled with them.[57]

While the Russian Jews retain some anachronistic and offensive customs, he argued, they are not devoid of virtues—outstanding family morality, patriotism, charity. They need only cleanse themselves of some unpleasant habits and rites and improve their physical circumstances by taking to agriculture and useful trades, and by studying science, discerning the wheat from the chaff.

Tarnopol's restatement of this wheat-and-chaff cliché, so dear to the maskilim, epitomized the degree to which he had proceeded along the road to a rather sophisticated commingling of tradition and modernity, a process usually dated only to the late 1860s or 1870s. Because of the strict censorship regulations of Nicholas's time, he could not detail in print his moderate recommendations for religious reform until 1868, but it is clear that he formulated his beliefs long before 1855, when, in words similar to those of the famous motto of the later Haskalah, "Be a Jew at home and a man in the streets," he enjoined his fellow Russian Jews, "However ardent Jews we may be inside our synagogues, let us be good citizens in our relations with the outside world."[58]

The Russian-Jewish intelligentsia under Nicholas I did not share one coherent attitude toward the Jewish tradition but contained several differing and opposing streams of thought, temperament, and behavior. These streams would rush more freely when the dams were thrown open during the next reign, but they clearly began to flow, and to cause waves, in the 1840s and early 1850s.

Haskalah and the Russian Language   Contrary to the claims of those who hold to the Berliner/Russifier taxonomy, no Russian maskil, even in Nicholas's time, actively advocated the use of German for its own sake among Russian Jews. On this question, Levinsohn's views were unanimously endorsed by all segments of the new intelligentsia: every Jew is obliged to learn at least one foreign language in order to be a civilized human being; while any pure tongue is permissible, including German, the most preferable language is that of the state in which one lives, hence Russian. This must be read, written, and spoken fluently, and taught to children in the schools.[59]

Beyond this ideological commitment to Russian, the maskilim frequently employed German for practical propagandistic purposes, because of its proximity to Yiddish, but it was always clearly regarded as merely a stepping-stone to Russian. The only contemporaries who were ideologically devoted to German were Uvarov and Lilienthal, who on this issue had no followers among the Russian maskilim. Even the most germanized of the Russian-Jewish maskilim, Wolf Tugendhold, composed a polemic tract encouraging the use of Russian among Jews by claiming that the Slavic and Semitic languages were etymologically related.[60]

While there was no serious debate over the place of Russian, the maskilim did express serious disagreements over the role of Hebrew and Yiddish in the education of the Jews. Levinsohn again was the standard-bearer of a major, but not the only, point of view. He repeated the standard maskilic claim that a thorough study of Hebrew grammar was essential for a correct understanding of the Scriptures but broadened his argument with a novel approach. Citing Fichte's dictum that languages determine nations and not the reverse, he maintained that it is impossible to be a true Hebrew without commanding the Hebrew language. Moreover, the Holy Tongue had preserved not only the Hebrewness of the individual

Jew but the national and religious character of the entire people. It alone has united the Jews over the centuries and throughout their far-flung Diaspora.[61]

Although this argument did contain the seed of a nationalistic appraisal of Hebrew, Levinsohn did not develop that line of thought. On the contrary, he clearly restricted the domain of Hebrew to the religious sphere of life and stated that Hebrew is no holier than any other language when used in secular contexts. And since it has ceased to be a spoken language and lacks the vocabulary necessary to a modern man, Hebrew cannot adequately fulfill the secular needs of the Jew; for this, he needs a pure, modern language.[62]

This last, quasi-utilitarian approach to Hebrew was rejected by the Vilna maskilim, led by Mordekhai Aaron Ginzburg and A. B. Lebenzon, who preached a secularized cult of the Holy Tongue. According to Lebenzon, for example, anyone who wrote in Hebrew, regardless of content, acted as "a priest of God";[63] dedicating his first book of poetry to the Hebrew language itself, he wrote,

You know my heart, you know that of all the joys of the world, of all human desires, I have chosen you alone. Only you do I long for all my days, my soul yearns for you. I love your lovers, and all those who seek and desire you are close to my heart.[64]

This devotion to form rather than content was rejected most vociferously by the younger and more radical maskilim, led by Benjamin Mandelshtam. Writing in excellent Hebrew—often better than his literary opponents—he subjected the poetry of Ginzburg and Lebenzon to savage criticism. They spend all their time fondling phrases, searching for metaphors, and completely miss the point of the endeavor:

Now the shepherds are multiplying, but each follows the love of his heart, rhetoric and poetry, and the sheep are being lost! Instead of leading their flocks by the horns, they sing them love songs, play their flutes, pluck their harps, without paying attention to the sheep themselves, who are straying into a region of enemies and distress, to the shadow of death, not order.[65]

The sacred task facing the maskilim is not idle literary production,

Mandelshtam insisted, but practical reform; not lyricism or, even worse, exegesis and grammar, but concrete acts of expunging the ignorance and superstition of the masses.[66]

This critique of the nascent renaissance of Hebrew letters foreshadowed the rejection of the aesthetic aspects and ideology of the Haskalah on the part of the foremost Hebrew and Yiddish writer of the second half of the nineteenth century, Shalom Yaʿakov Abramovich (Mendele Mokher Sefarim).[67] But yet another aspect of Abramovich's literary revolution was adumbrated in the 1840s: the turn to Yiddish as the most effective medium of mass persuasion. All of the maskilim so far considered despised Yiddish as a bastardized, corrupt jargon and placed its elimination on the top rung of their ladder of priorities. Even the few who secretly wrote creative works in Yiddish—including Levinsohn—never revealed their indulgence in public and never raised the question of how their intended audience could be enlightened if it did not understand the language of instruction. However, in 1841, the Odessa merchant Israel Aksenfeld posed precisely this question in a letter to Uvarov: Jewish writers have attempted to counteract the superstitions of the Hasidim through works full of patriotism and high morality, but how could these be successful, given the fact that the masses simply cannot read them?

It was therefore necessary to take a different tack: to write in a language understood by the simple Jewish folk, to describe both comic and instructive occurrences in real life, to attract the reader with a story, in order that truth should be exposed everywhere, but in a fine form of an interesting story. This difficult task I have taken upon myself.[68]

Although Uvarov approved this request, the work in question— Aksenfeld's *Sefer Ḥasidim*—was not published because of the refusal of the Vilna Hebrew printers to print a violently anti-Hasidic book in Yiddish.[69] But the strategy hitherto foreign to Russia (although widely adopted in Galicia) of swallowing one's aesthetic self-respect and spreading Haskalah through the hated jargon was adopted by a growing number of maskilim in the 1840s and 1850s and thus became an integral part of the arsenal of the intelligentsia already in Nicholas's reign.[70]

By 1855 the range of opinions on linguistic policy was as developed and diversified as it would be until the rise of modern political movements in the last quarter of the century. Naturally, the extent of russification gradually increased with every year, but this was the result not of ideological change but of pedagogic advance. Paradoxically, however, the constant spread of Russian as a spoken language among the Jews was not necessarily a measure of their roots in Russian culture and society, as has frequently been claimed.[71] It was not simply that the generations of the 1840s and 1850s were less familiar with the currents of Russian thought than their children and grandchildren. It was Russian thought itself that changed, from the polyglot cosmopolitanism of the first half of the century to the russified uniculturalism of the second. The Russian maskilim of Nicholas's reign who read and wrote French, German, even Italian,[72] in addition to Russian and Hebrew, were no more out of touch with their gentile compatriots than their successors two decades later. The fact that the latter read more Russian books and adopted more Russian attitudes was a consequence of the substantial transformation of the Russian intelligentsia itself in the interim: on the one hand, the turning inward to Russian sources and the Russian nation; on the other, the dissemination of the intelligentsia's new views from the rarified preserve of the capitals' salons to broad segments of society in the provinces. These changes were, to a large extent, an integral part of the new nihilist current in Russian thought. Eventually, this very same challenge would depose the Haskalah itself, subjecting its aesthetics, intellectual axioms, and politics to radical criticism. But until the advent of Avraham Uri Kovner and Moshe Leib Lilienblum, the Russian-Jewish intelligentsia persisted in the linguistic and cultural ideology it had developed under Nicholas I, periodically shifting its focus to reflect new facets of Russian life and thought.

Haskalah and the Russian Government   Throughout their Exile, the Jews forged a close and exclusive alliance with the central authorities of the states in which they lived. The objective stimuli to such a link soon gave way to what Yosef Yerushalmi has described as the "myth of the royal alliance" which endured long after it lost any grounding in reality.[73] Reinforced by the eighteenth-century ideal of the "enlightened despot," this myth became the keystone of the Haskalah throughout Europe and found its most startling expression in the ideology of the Russian maskilim.

Isaac Ber Levinsohn dedicated his *Te'udah be-yisra'el* to "God's anointed one [*mashiaḥ*], His Majesty Nicholas Pavlovich, for all the good he has done my nation,"[74] and went on to explain that all of the tsar's actions were motivated by an overwhelming love for the Jews and a desire for their happiness and success. All the evil decrees that befell the Jews stemmed from their own faults. The periodic expulsions from the border regions, for example, did not result from religious hatred or cruelty but from the acknowledged smuggling activity of the Jews.[75]

Even the harsh abuses of the conscription system were laid by Levinsohn to the sins of the Jews themselves. In a Hebrew satire on the conscription system, Levinsohn, speaking through the mouth of a Russian official, described the case of a woman whose son was drafted even though he was over the maximum age:

I know that the truth lies with you, unfortunate woman, but what can I do if twelve dogs of your people have sworn before God that your son is twenty-four years old? May God see this case and judge it, and I and the Russian throne are innocent.[76]

At the close of his play, "A Lawless World," Levinsohn's enlightened hero tells a group of villagers who have complained about their leaders' actions, "You seem to me to be like someone who thrashes himself in the bathhouse and screams, 'My God, it hurts!' Don't thrash yourselves and don't scream." The villagers reply, in Levinsohn's final, and poignant, statement on the subject, "My dear fellow, you are undoubtedly correct, but of what use is it? *Bog vysoko a pan daleko*—God is high up, and the emperor is far away."[77]

Such apologies for the tsar and his government were repeated by maskilim of all ages and circumstances, who firmly believed that the authorities were working only for the betterment of the

Jews, whose "civil amelioration," in Tarnopol's phrase, "depends on our social progress."[78]

The most effusive of the panegyrists were, once more, the Mandelshtam brothers. Benjamin compared Nicholas to Frederick the Great, Joseph II, even Bonaparte, and found him superior. The others merely responded to changes wrought by the Jews themselves, but Nicholas extended his arm to the Jews despite their benightedness, offering in his mercy to remold them into decent human beings. For this reason, "The thought of our king and master, the emperor, is much greater and more generous than that of all the kings of the East and West, and of all the islands of the sea."[79] Leon went even further: he could never love a wife so much as he loved Russia and her government.[80] Arriving in Moscow in 1840, he wrote that

if Fate has deprived me thus far of domestic bliss, but allows me to aid the government in the education and improvement of the Russian Jews, then I shall not complain of my lot as a son of [the Jewish] nation:

> My heart, my heart
> You cause me pain
> You drive me out
> Of my Father's house
> Your pride expelled
> Me from my love
> I, poor man,
> What remains for me
> The road to happiness?
> My fatherland![81]

This boundless patriotism and loyalty to the Russian autocracy was shared by the Russian maskilim until the late 1870s; even in retrospect, and under much more liberal censorship rules, the Cantonist system was viewed by the Russian-Jewish intelligentsia of the first half of Alexander II's reign as a benevolent idea vitiated by the actions of the Jewish leaders.

Alongside this near-jingoism of the vast majority of the Russian maskilim, however, there were rumblings, even before 1855, of profound dissatisfaction with the government's treatment of the Jews. In 1842 a group of Odessa Jewish leaders petitioned their governor-general, M. S. Vorontsov, for an extension of the civic rights of the Jews in Russia:

The Odessa Jewish community, which enjoys the rare privilege of living in a region governed by a wise and generous dignitary trusted by the Emperor, dares to hope that in this present moment, so important to more than a million loyal subjects, Your Excellency will not abdicate his humanitarianism, and will submit to the Monarch that, together with the moral regeneration of the Jews, he improve their civil status. Education will open up many roads for the attainment of useful citizenship on the part of the loyal subjects of the Russian Tsar. . . but without encouragement from the government, without material rights and privileges, such as those enjoyed by the sons of Russia, science, art, and enlightenment will ruin the descendants of Jacob.[82]

Seven years later, one of the first Jews to graduate from a Russian university, Reuben Kulisher, expressed even more bitter disillusionment with the basic axioms of the Haskalah's political ideology in his fascinating Russian poem *Otvet Slavianinu* (An answer to the Slav):

Naprasno-zhe vy menia korite	You wrongly reproach me
Chto mne protiven vash soiuz;	For opposing union with you;
Sebia samykh vy lish' vinite	You yourselves are to blame
V razryve greshnom bratskikh uz.	For the sinful rupture of fraternal ties.
. . . .	. . . .
O predrazsudke ne zheleiu	I do not excuse [my] prejudices,
Gotov ispravit' ia sebia,	I am ready to improve myself,
No uznaiu vrazhdebnyi golos	But I recognize a hostile voice
Khotia by sladko on zvuchal.	No matter how sweet it sounds.
I skol'ko-b vrag moi ni krichal,	How ever much my enemy shouts,
Ne tronus' dazhe i volos;	I shall not be moved a whit,
Plachu za nenavist' prezren'em	I shall repay hatred with contempt
Liubov' daiu vam za liubov';	Give you love for love;
Obidy vse snoshu s terpen'em,	I shall bear insults with patience
No i vo mne miatetsia krov'.	But inside, my blood will boil.
. . . .	. . . .

Skazhite-mne: chem nagradite	Tell me: how will you reward
Mne skol'ko prichinnykh bed,	All the misfortunes you have
Il' vy popravit' ne khotite	caused me?
Mne vami-zhe nanesennyi vred?	Or do you not want to correct
	All the harm you have inflicted
	on me?
Pora ostavit' eti ssory	It is time to abandon these
I nenavistnye slova	quarrels
I vashi obratite vzory	And hateful words
Vy luchshe na moi prava;	You should better turn
Togda vy sami ubedites'	Your attention to my rights;
Chto ia nichem ne khuzhe vas.	Then you yourselves will see
	That I am in no way worse than
	you.[83]

This appeal for emancipation was couched in the "Aesopian" language of the Russian intelligentsia and hence addressed the "Slavs" rather than the government. But it was still too subversive for Nicholas's censors, who banned the publication of this poem. Written in November 1849, it was not printed until 1911. As soon as the censorship laws were relaxed in the beginning of the next reign, however, the debate between the Kulishers and the Mandelshtams broke out in full force on the pages of the newborn Russian-Jewish press.[84]

The protagonists of the opposing positions did not suddenly choose their sides and develop their views in response to the liberalization of the new regime. They were all adult men, born in the first half of Nicholas's reign, who formulated their positions before they could articulate them freely. The political and ideological explosion of the 1860s was only triggered by the accession of Alexander II; the fuse, braided from many different strands, stretched far back into the previous reign. The Russian-Jewish intelligentsia, in all its multiformity, was a product of the transformation of Jewish society in Russia under Nicholas I.

New York Public Library

Tsar Nicholas I, early official portrait

New York Public Library

Tsar Nicholas I and entourage

New York Public Library

S. S. Uvarov,
Minister of National Enlightenment

P. D. Kiselev,
Minister of Court Domains

Max Lilienthal

ספר

תעודה בישראל

כולל

גדרי התורה והחכמה

עם

הערות מועילות וטובות

בדרך ארץ

סֹלּוּ־סֹלּוּ פַּנּוּ־דֶרֶךְ
הָרִימוּ מִכְשׁוֹל מִדֶּרֶךְ עַמִּי ·
(ישעיה נ״ז י״ד)

בדפוס השותפים דקק

ווילנא והוראדנא

ע״י המדפיסים , ר׳ מנחם מן ב״ר ברוך ז״ל , ור׳ שמחה זיסל ב״ר מנחם נחום ז״ל

בואו בשעריו לפ״ק

TEUDAH BEISRAEL

WILNIE i GRODNIE, w Drukarni Manesa i Zymela.

1828.

Title page of Isaac Ber Levinsohn, Te^cudah be-yisra'el, *1828*

СВИДѢТЕЛЬСТВО

Отъ *Минской* Город *ской* Думы Еврея *го*
что по 9 й народной переписи записанъ отъ *Минскаго* Уѣзда въ
Минскомъ Еврейскомъ обществѣ въ семействѣ подъ № *1*
показанъ имѣющимъ отъ роду *лѣтъ*, и что
Свидѣтельство это, какъ доказательство о записки его въ новую перепись,
не даетъ ему ни какого права жить внѣ мѣста приписки и отлучаться куда
либо далѣе 30 верстъ разстоянія, опредѣленнаго 104 Ст: XIV т: Св: Зак: уст.
о паспор: и бѣгл: (изд. 1842 года) безъ плакатнаго паспорта, или билета тогоже тома и устава по VI продл: 107 Ст: для временныхъ отлучекъ установленнаго. Свидѣтельство это должно находиться всегда при *немъ*
Дрейзину а въ случаѣ смерти его, отдачи въ рекруты или убыли другимъ
образомъ, начальникомъ семейства, или тѣмъ лицомъ у коего послѣднее время жилъ, оно имѣетъ быть представлено къ мѣстному Полицейскому Начальству,
или Раввину, или сборщику для немедленной отсылки онаго въ Губернское
Правленіе къ уничтоженію. При обнаруженіи же передачи сего свидѣтельства
другому лицу, виновный подвергается строжайшему взысканію, опредѣленному
за подлогъ *Села*
тысяча восемсотъ пятьдесятъ перваго года.

Городскій Голова

Гласный отъ Евреевъ

Секретарь

Internal pass of Russian Jew, 1850, issued by Minsk City Council

---

Curriculum of Judaic studies in state-sponsored Jewish schools, 1852

ПРОГРАММА

преподаванія Еврейскихъ предметовъ въ Еврейскихъ Училищахъ, утвержденная Г. Министромъ Народнаго Просвѣщенія 31 Декабря 1852 года.

Въ Казенныхъ Училищахъ Перваго Разряда.

I. КЛАССЪ.

1. Изъ Библіи, — 1-я и 2-я книги Моисея, — по 3 урока въ недѣлю.
2. Главнѣйшія Молитвы, съ Нѣмецкимъ переводомъ, — по Молитвеннику изданному Министерствомъ, — по 2 урока.
3. Изъ Маймонида, — статьи, назначенныя для сего класса въ особой программѣ, — и изъ Хаіе-Адамъ, о Заповѣдяхъ, — по 2 урока.
4. Первыя основанія Еврейской Грамматики, — по изданному Министерствомъ учебнику, подъ заглавіемъ «Азбука» и Краткой Еврейской Грамматикѣ, изданной Кандидатомъ Мандельштамомъ, съ упражненіемъ въ письмѣ, — по 2 урока.

II. КЛАССЪ.

1. Изъ Библіи, — начиная съ 3 кн. Моисея до книги Царствъ включительно, — по 3 урока въ недѣлю.
2. Изъ Маймонида, — статьи, назначенныя въ особой для сего программѣ, — по 2 урока.
3. Изъ Хаіе-Адамъ, — статьи: о Молитвѣ, о священныхъ повязкахъ и о воскрыліяхъ, — по 2 урока.
4. Еврейская Грамматика, по книгѣ Талмудъ Лешонъ-Иври, Виленскаго изданія 1847 г. изъ II части §§ 76-163 включительно; и изъ III части §§ 214-272 включительно, — по 2 урока.

YIVO Institute for Jewish Research

YIVO Institute for Jewish Research

*"The khappers," painting by unknown artist,
probably late nineteenth century*

*"The purse or the knout!"—caricature of Nicholas I's
treatment of the Jews by Honoré Daumier, 1854*

YIVO Institute for Jewish Research

New York Public Library

"Training recruits in Nicholas's Russia"
—drawing by the Russian artist A. Vasil'ev

"Convoy of recruits"
—1851 painting by the Ukrainian artist I. I. Sokolov

New York Public Library

New York Public Library

*"An inn on the Lithuanian frontier"—early nineteenth-century
genre painting by the Belorussian artist I. Trutnev,
depicting a Jewish innkeeper and his non-Jewish customers*

*"Sale of hay on the Dnieper"—early nineteenth-century
painting by the Ukrainian artist I. Soshenko*

New York Public Library

5 · Metamorphoses of Authority

This was the period known by that frightful and shocking name, the "time of the Cantonists," or more to the point, the "time of the sins of the kahal," for indeed our fathers, the leaders of our communities, committed a grave sin, a travesty inscribed in blood and tears . . . for which there is no expiation.

Rabbi Barukh Epstein

Kiselev's plan for the reform of the Jews laid heavy stress on their "enlightenment" and reeducation but also called for a radical restructuring of the very bases of their communal life—taxes and the kahal. Four weeks after the promulgation of the law establishing the state-school system, Kiselev's proposals regarding the power structure of Jewish society were put into force.

Abolition of the Kahal

First, the *korobka* tax was retained in a new tax law but was augmented and revised. The auxiliary levy, previously voluntary, was now obligatory in all Jewish communities; a special fine on all Sabbath candles was to be collected in order to fund the new schools; the duty on ritual baths and other religious rites was abolished, but the fee for wearing "Jewish garments" was raised. Most importantly, new tax agents were to be appointed by each

123

Jewish community to supervise the collection and administration of all taxes, under the complete control of the local authorities.[1]

This last provision was necessitated by the third legislative product of Kiselev's Committee for the Transformation of the Jews in Russia, the law issued on December 19, 1844, that abolished the kahal.[2] Under Russian law, the kahal and the Jewish community were two distinct and separate legal entities. All the Jews of a given locality were members of the Jewish community, the *evreiskoe obshchestvo*; the kahal was the executive agency of that community, composed of three to five commissioners who enjoyed broad jurisdiction over taxation, internal policing, and the administration of justice.[3] According to the new law, this executive agency was abolished, its powers transferred to the municipal self-government:

In all places where the Jews are permitted permanent residence, they shall, for police matters, be subject directly to the city or rural police, according to the area in which they live; for matters of estate law, economics, and taxation they shall be supervised by the Town Council or Assembly of the cities in which they are registered, even though many of the Jews live in townlets, settlements, and villages.[4]

Under the new order, the Jews would still not pay taxes directly to the government. The entire community would "participate in the apportionment of state and local duties" and would elect special agents to collect monies needed for the support of philanthropic and other communal services.[5] These new community officials would be called collectors (*sborshchiki*) and would bear the same responsibilities as the elders of the communes of artisans or townspeople.[6] They were to be served by elected assistants, and together with the officials independently elected (under the provisions of the Recruitment Statute of 1827) to supervise the fulfillment of the conscription laws, they would be under the direct authority of the local governing bodies.[7]

It is difficult to assess exactly what this law was intended to do. Kiselev's purpose in recommending the abolition of the kahal and the *korobka* was clearly to remove all vestiges of the legal obstacles separating the Jews from their neighbors, that is, subsuming the

Jews entirely into the legal and economic categories in which they already were inscribed. This the 1844 law did not do. The Jews retained their dual status as members of both an estate and a Jewish community. Moreover, the Jewish community was not divested of its autonomous character inherited from the Polish regime. While the juridical basis of this autonomy—the recognition of the corporate right to self-rule—was abrogated, the coherence of the community as a self-regulating tax entity remained intact, although its officials were now tied more closely to the state's supervision. Most important, the new law did not address the fundamental aspect of Jewish self-rule, the independence of the rabbinical courts and the integrity of Jewish law in the jurisprudence of civil and even criminal cases involving Jews—although these were specifically underscored by Kiselev as the main causes of the separateness of the Jews.[8]

With no information available on the drafting of the bill or on any intergovernmental debates which might have ensued, there is no way of knowing why Kiselev's proposals were not implemented in full. Unlike the situation in Western Europe, it would have been entirely possible for the Russian government to divest the Jews of their corporate status without granting them equal rights. Theoretically, they could have been absorbed into the estates in which they were registered but still have been subject to special restrictions—or even privileges. However, in practice, such a system would have been most difficult to administer, since the Russian estates were for the most part legal fictions that had no fiscal or even economic integrity. The basic taxation and recruitment unit was not the estate or the guild but the community or commune. To abolish the Jewish community would have necessitated including the Jews in the non-Jewish merchant, townspeople, artisan, and agricultural communes, which undoubtedly would have resulted in strenuous protests on the parts of their members and most probably in increased competition as well. Yet the Russian autocracy could have taken such a move—it hardly planned its legislation to comply with the economic needs or desires of its population. The dissolution of the Jewish communities, however, would have adversely affected the state's own interests, both fiscal and ideological. New taxes could have been collected from the Jews on the same level as before (if under a far more complex procedure), but, most likely, the tax arrears of the Jewish community, which were quite substantial, would have had to be written off.[9] In addition, the special recruitment provisions for the Jews would have been impossible to retain if the Jews were members of the general communities.

As always, the Russian government was far more interested in collecting its taxes and recruits than in the methods of obtaining them. Although Nicholas endorsed Kiselev's aims, he did not want to risk any tangible losses that they might entail, to pay the price for the rapprochement of the Jews.

This exclusive concern with taxes and soldiers also explains the absence of restrictions on the court system of the Jewish communities. Until 1864 the Russian government was not interested in regulating the lives of its subjects beyond their obligations to the state; thus, it made no separation between administration and justice, between the police and the courts. Although in theory the existence of private Jewish courts infringed on the monarchy's monopoly on power, so long as these courts were subjected to police control what concern was it of the government how Jews settled disputes among themselves? Kiselev's projected ban on rabbinical courts would only have made sense in a state which took its own courts seriously; Russia under Nicholas I did not.

What then were the results of the new law?

Most Jewish historians have correctly observed that to a large extent the abolition of the kahal was a paper reform since the kahal in fact persisted in its previous form at least until the last years of the nineteenth century.[10] Although called by a new name, the collector of recruits simply took over the responsibilities of the former kahal leaders. In the Jewish sources, moreover, as often as not even the titles remained the same, the *sborshchik* or *starosta* being referred to as the *rosh ha-kahal* or even the *parnas-ḥodesh*.[11] His assistants may now have been called deputies, but they fulfilled the same roles as the former "syndics" of the kahal. And, of course, the rabbinical courts continued to run smoothly without interruption or restriction and even seem to have issued the occasional writ of excommunication (*ḥerem*) long forbidden under Russian law.[12]

While the essential structure of the kahal remained intact even after its formal abolition, its function and status within Russian-Jewish society were significantly altered after 1844. This was due in large measure to the fact that at the time it was impossible to know that the Jewish community would survive in its established form. Indeed, both Russian Jews and their Western European sympathizers believed that the kahal and rabbinical courts had been substantially, perhaps fatally, debilitated by the new legislation. Thus, in a petition to Sir Moses Montefiore upon his visit to Russia in 1846, a Lithuanian rabbi wrote:

The honor of our life has been removed by the orders of His Imperial Majesty and his ministers that we may no longer judge cases between Jews in Jewish courts, and even that we may not have syndics and kahal officials [*parnasim ve-'alufei kahal*] as has been the custom in our country until now. . . .[13]

Montefiore himself repeated these claims to the Russian officials he met with.[14]

This perceived diminution of the authority of the kahal was of important historical consequence. Until 1844 the intense frustration that resulted from the hardships of the conscription system could only be vented through the time-honored avenues of passive protest; now, the trauma of the recruitment abuses could be manifested in entirely new, and active, forms.

Centrifugal Forces

The customary manner of calling the community's attention to the abuses of its leaders was through *ʿikuv ha-kriʾah*, the disruption of the synagogue service in order publicly to raise complaints. The power of this protest had always been its shock value, the dramatic disruption of the sacred service in order to right the most grievous wrongs. In Nicholas's Russia, however, such disruptions became so frequent that they virtually lost their effectiveness. One contemporary description of such a protest—and its futility—is particularly interesting in its reworking of one of the most central motifs of Jewish folk literature. In Minsk a poor widow whose son had been kidnapped by *khappers* burst into the synagogue and declared that she would not allow the Torah to be removed from the Ark until her son was released. The leaders of the community angrily ordered that the woman be pushed away and the service continued. Realizing her helplessness, the woman ran up to the Ark and cried:

Lord of the Universe! You took pride in the Patriarch Abraham who agreed to sacrifice his son. Order me to kill my son, and I will do so. But you hardly could have obtained Abraham's permission for the conversion of his son![15]

From the very beginning of the recruitment of the Jews, however, their anger and bitterness at the collusion of their leaders were not expressed solely through such passive channels of resistance. Several stories were told of Jews attacking convoys of recruits in order to liberate their children,[16] but a far more frequent object of violence were the kahal leaders and their deputies, the *khappers*. One memoirist recalled several cases of armed resistance against the latter:

[The Jews] struggled violently with the *khappers* and the police. They grabbed axes, knives, iron bars, or weapons that they had prepared in advance. And when [the *khappers*] entered, the whole household attacked them and beat them.
But the *khappers*, for their part, were not silent either. They brought with them crowbars and iron rods, and a real war was waged in the house. Blood flowed in the streets, they fought to their last strength, and whichever side was stronger won; of course, the *khappers* were victorious most often.[17]

More significant were the not uncommon mass riots against the kahal officials, which seem to have resulted from the belief held by the Jews that their leaders had the power to contravene edicts of the government. Thus, in the autumn of 1827, according to a local police report, the Jews of Bershad, Podolia, accused their kahal leaders of countersigning the conscription statute without calling a general meeting of the community. Crowds of Jews stormed the kahal building and the homes of its officials, smashing windows and breaking down doors.[18] Similar riots erupted in Starokonstantinov, Volhynia, and Minsk.[19] The Ministry of Internal Affairs investigated these attacks and ordered army units to patrol the Jewish quarters of cities every evening.

These precautions did not prevent the outbreak of other riots, which were at times even led by rabbis. In Grodno, for example, the noted Rabbi Eliyahu Shik condemned the collaboration of the communal leaders with the authorities' "passportless decree"[20] of 1853, and

called on everyone to revolt against the heads of the community, and to tear the kahal building to shreds. . . . With an axe in his hands he ran in front of the crowd that had gathered, each man armed with an axe; before they were stopped, they had broken the iron bolts on the door of the kahal building and freed the three prisoners incarcerated there.[21]

More frequent than such violent outbursts were the formal denunciations to the government of the violations of the law committed by kahal leaders. In most cases the implicated officials avoided punishment by bribing the Russian bureaucrats, and the informers were sent to military service or exiled to Siberia. The most famous such case concerned Benjamin Goldberg of Kletsk, known in the literature as "Benyominke moser," roughly translatable as Benjie the Snitch. He actively opposed the policies of the kahal leaders of his town and reported the conscription of a widow's only son to the authorities. The conscription official of the Kletsk community was arrested for this offense but allegedly bribed the judge, who promptly enlisted Goldberg instead. Appeals on both sides continued for years, with Benjamin and the official alternating time in custody. Finally, the kahal leader won and enlisted Goldberg into the army as an "undesirable."[22]

In rare cases, however, the communal leaders were indeed punished and imprisoned, most often when caught omitting names from the community registers—the only offense not encouraged or tolerated by the authorities. The most gruesome example of such a case—many details of which may have been exaggerated by legend and rumor—occurred in the town of Novo-Ushits, in the district of Kamenets-Podol'sk. Here two informers, Itsik Oksman and Shmuel Shvartsman, incurred the wrath of the kahal leaders with their constant denunciations of selective recruiting. Sometime in 1838 the communal and religious leaders allegedly called a secret meeting at which they sentenced the informers to death. Reportedly, two Hasidic leaders, the Rizhiner Rebbe Yisroel Friedman, later known as the Sadigorer Rebbe, and the Dunavitser Rebbe Mikhoel, gave their assent to this verdict. Thereafter, Shvartsman was murdered in the synagogue, his body cut into pieces and burned. Oksman tried to escape to Kamenets but was caught on the road and killed. Peasants discovered his body, and an investigation was launched by the local authorities. These officials had, however, also suffered from the denunciations of the informers and colluded with the Jewish leaders in covering up the affair.

Somehow a police official in Kamenets, who was an apostate Jew, learned about the murders and came to Novo-Ushits disguised as a Hasid. He soon became an intimate of the local rabbi, who disclosed to him the truth about the executions. The policeman made a full report to the governor-general of Podolia, who ordered a thorough investigation of the incident. Eighty Jews, mostly lay and religious leaders, were brought to trial. Twenty were sentenced to hard labor and forced to run the gauntlet; twenty more were exiled to Siberia; the rest were either freed or escaped.[23]

Apart from these individual denunciations, there were several cases of groups of poorer Jews banding together to appeal to the government for assistance against the abuses of the kahal authorities. Thus, for example, in 1839 a delegation of "the poor Jews of Vilna" appealed to the local magistracy to audit the communal records and disqualify the ruling officials on the grounds of dishonesty.[24] In 1843, thirty-eight Jewish artisans of the town of Dubrovno, Mogilev, under the leadership of one Itske Samsonkin, flooded the government offices in St. Petersburg with petitions attacking the taxation abuses of the leaders of their community and asking for support in electing one of the artisans to the communal posts.[25] Such appeals for justice and mercy were later penned by the artisans of several other communities, including Minsk.[26]

For the most part, however, opposition to the kahal leaders from within their communities was to no avail. And so, in the years following the 1844 abolition of the kahal, several groups of Jews felt empowered to take the next logical—if unprecedented—step of separating themselves from the Jewish community at large and applying for recognition as separate communities which could defend their own interests. In 1850 and 1851 the artisans of Dubno complained to the government that although they constituted only one-fifth of the local Jewish population, they had been forced to supply half the recruits and had been unable to obtain representation on the kahal boards. They therefore requested permission to elect their own representative to the (non-Jewish) town council and to be considered a separate conscription and taxation unit, apart from the rest of the Jews.[27] In 1852 the Jewish artisans of Belaia-Tserkov' organized their own guild, as was allowed by law; the next year they petitioned the authorities to consider their guild a distinct conscription and taxation unit

in order to throw off the yoke of the Jewish community which—according to its ancient traditions—looks with contempt upon artisans, and takes too large a share of taxes and recruits from them. If they will be permitted to constitute their own community [obshchestvo] the artisans will promptly and punctiliously pay all their duties, and will not be so oppressed.[28]

In the same year, the handworkers of Vladimir-Volynsk also petitioned the government for separate representation in the municipal self-government.[29]

Such separatist tendencies also appeared at the other end of the economic spectrum in the decade after the abolition of the kahal. According to the 1835 statute, Jewish merchants who joined the merchant's estate (kupechestvo) by enrolling in one of its guilds still had to bear responsibility for the tax debts of the Jewish community as a whole, although technically they were not registered in the community. This was parallel to the requirement that non-Jewish merchants be accountable for the arrears of the townspeople in the cities in which they lived. While the kahal was in existence in its traditional guise, no Jewish merchants dared to disclaim any obligation to the rest of the Jewish community. In the early 1850s, however, the tax debts of the Jews began to mount in geometric proportion as a result of increased draft quotas which often could not be filled and thus resulted in special fines.[30] Until 1827, one group of merchants pointed out, the tax arrears of the Jewish communities never exceeded 300,000 rubles; from 1827 to 1854, these debts rose to 8 million rubles.[31] The wealthier Jews, naturally, wished to avoid any responsibility for the repayment of these arrears, especially since they, as merchant guild members, were not subject to the draft at all. In addition, beginning in 1850, all merchants were required to pay special taxes for the members of their families who died while still—or again—in the ranks of the townspeople.[32]

Beginning in 1852 groups of Jewish merchants began to protest against such requirements. In Indur, Grodno Province, two Jewish merchants renounced any connection with the Jewish community and refused to contribute to its tax funds; in Minsk, thirty-seven guild merchant families disclaimed any responsibility for the tax arrears of the rest of the Jews; a similar situation arose in Kremenchug.[33] In 1854, eleven first-guild merchants and Honorary Citizens under the leadership of (the future Baron) Evsel Günzburg seem to have been attempting to obtain the same sort of tax status in a series of petitions supporting the government's policy of dividing the Jews into productive and nonproductive categories.[34]

Although these separatist tendencies were displayed by only a small proportion of Russian Jews and were for the most part not supported by the government, they were of critical importance since they were unparalleled in the history of the society. Rarely before had the Jewish community in Eastern Europe been subjected to such centrifugal pressures; never before had economic self-interest and self-definition so clearly overwhelmed the feelings of solidarity and allegiance as members of a united nation.

These requests for judicial independence from the Jewish community betokened a radical change in the function and status of the kahal. To an increasing extent, the kahal ceased to be the automatic representative of all the Jews, and submission to its authority became voluntary. This fundamental rift in Jewish society would only deepen as economic circumstances deteriorated in the ensuing decades and would in time lead to the emergence of class-based political parties and movements battling each other as much as the central authorities.

This would occur when the external political context was radically reformed at the end of the nineteenth century and beginning of the twentieth. Yet even in Nicholas's time, there were clear indications that the traditional guiding principle of Jewish life, its uncompromised unity in the face of outward attack, had given way to the pressures of the conscription system, the untenable tax burden, and the debilitation of the kahal itself. Although the Russian government was not willing to carry through its intention of reordering Jewish life to merge it with Russian society, it unconsciously effected an equally revolutionary destabilization of authority within the Jewish communities. No longer were the kahal officials regarded either implicitly or explicitly as the leaders of the Jewish people; the rich and the poor, the maskilim and the traditionalists shared a sense of distaste and distrust of their former officials. On this issue, Rabbi Barukh Epstein's description "the time of the sins of the kahal" reflected the same attitude of the maskil of Nicholas's time who wrote:

The leaders of the Jews were at that time in no way deserving of consideration as descendents of Abraham, for they were as far from the qualities of mercy as heaven is from earth. This was the "sin of the kahal" whose evil reached to the heavens and whose iniquity knew no bounds.[35]

Role of the Rabbis

One of the central paradoxes of Russian-Jewish history is that while the role of the lay leadership of the kahals in the administration of Jewish society and its relations with the state can be chronicled with reasonable surety, there is little precise information on the position of the rabbis in the government of the Jewish communities.

Part of the problem stems from the confused legal status of the rabbis. The 1804 statute on the Jews stipulated that from the beginning of 1812, no one may be elected or appointed to any position in the kahal or rabbinate without knowing Russian, Polish, or German; several subsequent ordinances required that all official registers maintained by the rabbis for the community be written in Russian or Polish.[36] The 1835 statute added the requirement that the rabbi take an oath of allegiance to the Russian state and its laws and the provision that if a rabbi could not fulfill all the functions of his position, the community or kahal could elect several learned Jews to assist him in his clerical and ritual duties.[37] As a result of these provisions, there evolved in Russia two distinct types of officials bearing the title "rabbi": the spiritual leader of the community, ordained according to the traditional rules, and the "government rabbi," often called the rabbiner, who represented the community to the government. In some communities, the same man held both positions; in others, the real rabbi refused to take on the burden and the dangers of the official post, ceding these to another, often less observant, Jew.[38]

In the second half of the nineteenth century this dual rabbinate became a source of great controversy and therefore can be studied with reasonable accuracy. In Nicholas's reign, however, the situation was so murky and the discussion so limited that it is simply impossible to distinguish between the two types of rabbis in many cases and circumstances.[39]

This confusion is exacerbated by the major documentary difficulty facing Russian-Jewish historians—the paucity of sources emanating from the traditionalist camp of Russian Jewry in the first three-quarters of the nineteenth century. The homiletic and legal literature of the period is substantial—though not nearly so abundant as that of other ages—but does not seem to contain much information on the extralegal problems and dilemmas of the time. Even when such subjects are raised, the discussion does not elucidate any concerns of the social or political historian. For example, only one responsum of the chief rabbi and president of the community of Vitebsk throughout most of the nineteenth century, Yiẓhak Aizik Bohorad, seems to touch upon the new social problems in Russian Jewry. It documents the case of a woman who was in grave danger of becoming an *ʿagunah* (perpetual grass widow) because the writ of divorce she obtained from her husband, a soldier who converted to Christianity, listed her father as a *kohen* when in fact he was not. The resolution of the case, however, deals not with the effects of recruitment on Jewish society or even with the problems of forced conversions but—as is proper in the context— with the legal standing of such a questionable document.[40]

Apart from a handful of comments in footnotes and introductions to such legal works, then, the only sources available from the traditional camp which describe the role of the rabbis in the decision-making of the Jewish communities and their reaction to the conscription system are two memoirs written later in the century and the hagiographic literature of Epstein, Lifshiẓ, and Schneersohn.

Undoubtedly, a major cause of the silence of the rabbis on contemporary issues was the effectiveness of the tsarist censorship apparatus, which quashed even the most veiled criticism of the regime in obscure, apolitical works and led to a cautious self-censorship on the part of authors legitimately fearing the wrath of the police.[41] Yet this is only a partial explanation for the lack of evidence from the traditionalists. It does not account for the almost complete absence of memoirs, later collections of unpublished letters, or even polemic tracts published abroad. The latter two could not have been affected by the Russian censors' power. The imperial censorship procedure was hardly so efficient as its successor and never succeeded in intercepting the private correspondence of nonpolitical subjects. In fact it never really even attempted to do so.

A more satisfactory explanation must be found in the very culture of Russian rabbinic Judaism. Historical writing, whether autobiographical or scholarly, was not regarded as a suitable enterprise for the learned, and even the traditional genre of chronicle writing was not actively encouraged in Eastern European Jewish intellectual and literary society. This eschewal of historiography resulted not only in the lack of histories written from the traditionalist perspective but also in the loss of contemporary letters and other unpublished sources: archive-keeping, like the rest of the historian's craft, was abandoned to the nonbelievers.

Without more information from the participants themselves, the role of the rabbis in the selection of recruits for Nicholas's army and the apportionment of taxes to his treasury cannot be determined with any precision. It does seem safe to conclude, however, that an overwhelming majority of the rabbis refrained from any public criticism of these matters, either in word or in deed. Only one rabbi was reported to have resigned his post in protest against the selective draft—the elusive Menashe of Ilya, who in 1828 quit his position in Smorgon', according to his grandson, when the local kahal leaders demanded his acquiescence in the work of the *khappers*.[42]

Five other rabbis are recorded as having taken a public stance against the kahal authorities: (1) In Grodno, the noted Rabbi Eliyahu Shik of Driechin condemned the collaboration of the kahal leaders with the passportless decree of 1853 and led the riot in Grodno;[43] (2) Rabbi Ya°akov Berlin, the father of Naphtali Zvi Berlin, the future head of the Volozhin yeshivah, led a similar attack in the town of Mir;[44] (3) The head of the Minsk yeshivah, Rabbi Gershon Tanḥum complained against the registration omissions of the local kahal;[45] (4) Rabbi Israel Lipkin of Salant shamed the leaders of his community into releasing an orphan from an illegal draft;[46] and (5) Rabbi Ya°akov Boisker of Zhagory also instigated the release of an improperly conscripted recruit.[47]

One can only speculate on the reasons for the silence of the majority of the rabbis. Apart from fear of retribution, it may well be that an element of rational calculation was involved. There was a covert educational deferment given to rabbinical students by the kahal leaders with the encouragement of the rabbis; it stands to reason that the rabbinical authorities may therefore have preferred the economically discriminatory selection procedures to a more random and equitable system that could have seriously depleted the cohort of future spiritual and scholarly leaders.

Despite this overwhelming silence about the treacheries of the conscription and taxation systems, the rabbis did not share in the fate of their lay counterparts in the communal officialdom. Even the most radical maskilim were forced to concede, on the contrary, that the status of the rabbis, the extent of their influence, and the allegiance of their supporters increased markedly in the last half of Nicholas's reign.[48]

One historian has attempted to explain this phenomenon by positing that the debilitation of the authority of the kahal leaders which stemmed from the 1844 law effected a separation between the religious and lay leaders of the communities and allowed the former to exercise greater independence once they were released from the financial and political control of the lay officials.[49] This theory confuses cause and effect. The legislation that abolished the kahal did not address the role of the rabbis or weaken the control of the collectors over the communal treasury; the separation between the rabbis and the lay leaders was not a cause but an effect of their augmented authority.

That increase in power and prestige can only be explained as part of a far broader and more complex phenomenon: the unique way in which Russian Jewry responded to the pressures of the modern era. Like its Western European counterpart, Russian Jewry underwent a thoroughgoing religious realignment in the course of the nineteenth century. The forms that this realignment took, however, were very different in Russia. The three separate processes in this development, in ascending order of importance, are the movement for religious reform, the increase in conversions, and the emergence of an "Orthodox Judaism."

Movement for Religious Reform

One memoirist of Nicholas's time recalled meeting a Cantonist who believed that "no God could exist, if He could permit so much suffering and pain. And if there is indeed a God, He is solely the god of Evil . . ."[50]

This, however, was hardly a common response to the vicissitudes of the age. From the mid-1820s on, although the number of Jews in Russia who questioned the traditional order and its theological and ritual proscriptions grew from year to year, for most of the new skeptics, only minor changes in the customs of the Jews were necessary. Even those who called for wholesale reforms of both rituals and theology never expressed—at least in print—doubt about the existence of God or even the veracity of his Scriptures. Moreover, in the first half of Nicholas's reign, the maskilim refrained from reifying their skepticism in any active religious reforms; the farthest any of them went was to lapse into private nonobservance.

In 1840 the first ritual reforms were instituted in a Russian synagogue. In Riga, Max Lilienthal regularly preached in German, introduced a confirmation ceremony, and replaced the customary wedding ritual with one imported from Germany.[51] In the same year, the influence of the growing Reform movement in the West was manifested in Odessa; the progressive elements of the community left the main synagogue and organized their own congregation, which came to be known as the Brody Temple after the provenance of most of its members.[52] Although its adherents claimed that the temple did not change any rituals and conducted the service according to the tradition, it is clear from their own testimony that this was not the case. Not only did the new temple insist on absolute silence during the prayers and introduce a choir to lead the services—major innovations in custom—but also its members shaved their beards and wore European clothes.[53] A similar regime was instituted in the New Synagogue that opened in Odessa in March 1847.[54]

Riga and Odessa were, of course, westernized cities on the frontiers of the empire, with a mixed Jewish, as well as non-Jewish, population. Consequently, such reforming trends might well be relegated to foreign influences at work there. An analogous development occurred, however, in the center of the Pale, in Vilna. In the early 1840s the Vilna maskilim organized their own congregation, called Toharat ha-kodesh (Purification of the Sacred), which first met in the home of Hirsh Zvi Katzenellenbogen and then moved to its own quarters. It is not clear precisely what stimulated the maskilim to establish their own synagogue. One writer claimed that the traditionalists refused to permit the maskilim to pray in their midst, but there is no independent corroboration of this statement. Several maskilim asserted that the new congregation was founded after a serious dispute occurred between the enlightened and the traditionalists at the funeral of the Hebrew writer Mordekhai Aaron Ginzburg, but the sources are contradictory on the nature and extent of this dispute.[55] In any case, the traditional community reacted with anger and vengeance to the establishment of Toharat ha-kodesh: all the members of its boys' choir were reported to have been conscripted into the army as Cantonists.[56]

The liturgical reforms of the new congregation were similar to those of the Odessa temples. The major innovation was an insistence on decorum; the spontaneous, loud, unsynchronized praying of traditional synagogues was deemed unaesthetic and an affront to the Lord. A choir was introduced, and the ʿaliyot to the Torah were assigned not orally or by auction, as in the typical Eastern European service, but by passing out cards for each honor to the appropriate congregant.[57] One writer noted that the parishioners had abandoned the wearing of phylacteries on the intermediate days of festivals—a custom of the Hasidim—but hinted that this was an easy reform, since they did not don their tefillin on weekdays either.[58]

To some of the local intelligentsia, these innovations were not enough. Benjamin Mandelshtam complained that traditional hymns were still sung, even if their meaning was obscure, and that the new preacher, A. Lebenzon, did not deliver his sermons in a modern European tongue.[59] In Odessa some of the members of the temples criticized the musical quality of the service, suggesting the traditional cantillation be replaced with singing that was "more in harmony with the progress of contemporary music," more in unison with what they claim is their religious sentiment—in short, a melopoeia taken from the beautiful works of Mozart and Haydn or the masterpieces of other musical celebrities.[60]

But beyond these discordant voices, the new synagogues satisfied a growing need in Russian Jewry, insuring the continued allegiance of a large number of even its radical skeptics to some form of religious observance. From their own testimony, we know that many maskilim had ceased attending synagogue after their enlightenment. Osip Rabinovich wrote in 1847,

. . . the very format of the prayers, with violent cries, hand clapping, convulsive movements, without any system, as if in the forest, evoked in us not reverence but horror. A secret voice whispered to us that this was not the way to worship the blessed Creator; some unclear flash of lightning appeared in our immature minds. . . . Later, having attained adolescence, we began to become acquainted with the writings of the great thinkers and poets, and our inner eyes matured, and God appeared to us in all his grandeur in the beauty of Nature, which we began to understand and love, and these outrageous crowds in the synagogues became unbearable, and we deprived ourselves—May the merciful God forgive us—of the sweet consolations of prayer, since we tried to appear as rarely as possible in these dens of slovenliness and anarchy. . . .[61]

With the establishment of the new congregations, however,

the sweetness of the present overwhelms the agony of the past. . . . What a pleasure now, when fatigued by the necessities of life, we once more can feel the need for prayer, and come into a beautiful temple, where we can freely and silently pour out the travails of our soul to the All-knowing heart.[62]

It is not clear what proportion of the Russian-Jewish intelligentsia shared such views—the history of religious reform among Russian Jews has yet to be approached seriously by any scholar.[63] What is clear is that these trends in worship and belief never developed into a full-fledged Reform movement on the German or American model. The denationalized ideology of western Reform was predicated on the myth of religious pluralism within national unity that was profoundly alien to Russia as a whole. The notion that there could be Russians of the Mosaic persuasion comparable to Russians of the Christian persuasion seemed preposterous—indeed, semantically unfeasible—to virtually all subjects of the tsar, gentile or Jew; the national and religious integrity of each group was so palpable and inescapable a reality.[64]

But even if relegated to a small segment of the society, religious reform was an important and longevous force in Russian-Jewish life from Nicholas I's time on. Staffed either by rabbis from abroad or by graduates of the state-sponsored rabbinical seminaries,[65] the progressive congregations of Odessa, just as those later established in Moscow and St. Petersburg, survived into the Soviet period, and those in Vilna and Riga until the Nazi occupation.[66]

Increase in Conversions

Another possible response to the traumas of the age was the complete abandonment of the Jewish faith and people. And, indeed, the rate of conversions to Christianity increased substantially during the reign of Nicholas I. The exact number of converts is difficult to determine, however, because the vast numbers of Jewish Cantonists forcibly baptized all but obscured the voluntary apostates in the available statistics.[67] Approximately thirty thousand Jews were converted to some denomination of Christianity between 1825 and 1855. Even if it is assumed that a full half of the Cantonists were baptized, it would appear that at least five thousand Jews voluntarily became Christians during this time.[68]

Unfortunately, the entire question of apostasy in Russia has not yet received sufficient scholarly scrutiny. There is no serious study of the problem in any period, even where archival materials are ample and accessible.[69]

For the period under consideration here, there is only one extant archive, that of the Lithuanian Consistory of the Russian-Orthodox Church, based in Vilna, which contains fifty-three files detailing the conversion of eighty-three Russian Jews to Russian Orthodoxy between 1825 and 1855.[70] Since the population of Lithuania was (and remains) overwhelmingly Catholic, with an important Evangelical-Lutheran contingent, these materials obviously reflect only a partial picture of apostasy even within this region. Nonetheless, they offer an interesting sample which elucidates phenomena previously undocumented.

Of the eighty-three converts, sixty-two were males, sixteen females, and five children of unrecorded gender. Of the forty-five whose ages are recorded, thirty were between eighteen and thirty years old, seven were either sixteen or seventeen years old, and eight were over thirty. Six were soldiers recruited as Cantonists but baptized after attaining majority; two men were drafted by their communities, they claimed, because they expressed the desire to convert to Christianity and were subsequently released from service.[71] One woman was the wife of a Jewish soldier in the St. Petersburg battalion who was discharged due to poor health and sent back home to Vilna; she decided to remain and converted.[72] Another woman was the wife of a Jewish noncommissioned officer. She converted and was divorced from her husband, who remained a Jew. Their child was given to her custody at the divorce, but the husband refused to allow the child to be baptized. The case went to the courts but ended when the rabbi of the husband's community reported that the child had died.[73] Four men and two women apparently took advantage of the law that alleviated criminal sentences upon baptism in the Orthodox faith: two were convicted of trading in contraband, two for vagrancy, and one each for libel and fraud.[74] Most of the converts did not have any steady employment; only one was a guild merchant; one was an army doctor; one each a dentist, a tailor, a farmer, and a trader; two were students in Russian gymnasiums.[75] Most of the converts were single or divorced; only sixteen acknowledged being married, and twenty-one converted along with another member of their family. Thirty-two files contain interesting information on the literacy of their subjects: sixteen could not sign their names in any script, eight signed in Hebrew, five in Russian, and two in Polish, as well as Russian and Hebrew; two scrawled signatures in Hebrew betokened semiliteracy.[76] Although all of the files contained confessions of a revelation of the superiority of Russian Orthodoxy to all other faiths, only one departed from the formulas of the others and seems to have been made out of an unquestionable religious conviction: Esther Izabelinskaia of Grodno, an eighteen-year-old woman literate in Russian, studied for her baptism at the Rozhdestvo-

Bogorodianskaia Women's Monastery, where she remained after her conversion.[77]

One case raises intriguing questions about the receptivity of the church officials to Jewish converts. Kasper Berman, an eighteen-year-old student in the fifth grade of the Vilna gymnasium in 1834, applied for baptism on the grounds that he "was enlightened by his studies and convinced of the fallacy of Judaism and the veracity of Christianity." He asked to be accepted into the true Orthodox faith and allowed to study medicine. The archimandrite, however, was not convinced. Kasper did not study the dogma of the church and never appeared in catechism class; his petition, therefore, was denied. He applied again, but the abbot was steadfast: "Knowing his inconstancy and poor character, which will not be of honor to our religion, I see no good in him"; he must remain a Jew until he finishes gymnasium, and then he may convert. The file ends without a resolution.[78] How many other Russian Orthodox priests were so fastidious about whom they would admit into the state of grace is not known.

It is clear, however, that Nicholas did place some limits on the conversion of the Jews. The archives of the London Society for the Promotion of Christianity among the Jews, now kept in the Bodleian Library, establish that Nicholas repeatedly refused to permit foreign missionaries to evangelize to the Jews of Russia, restricting them to the Kingdom of Poland.[79] Apparently, the risk of losing Orthodox believers to the Protestants outweighed the benefits of saving a few Jews; in Poland, the worst that could happen was the conversion of Catholics.

From archival data, it is possible to posit a tentative typology of Jewish apostates in Nicholas's Russia. Apart from the Cantonists, there were three distinct categories of voluntary converts: (1) the true believers, (2) the poor and criminal, and (3) those seeking educational and professional advancement. In the next reign, another category was added: the renegade, bent on destroying the Jewish religion.[80]

Melodramatic biographies of the last two types abound in the quasi-historical moralistic literature on converts published in the Yiddish press in the 1920s and 1930s by extremely talented raconteurs.[81] The other two categories are not dwelled upon: the "laboring classes and dangerous classes" of Russian Jewry could only be apotheosized as the vanguard of the revolution, never studied critically; the believing Christians were better left unmentioned.

Two of the most interesting of these biographies can be reconstructed on the basis of reliable evidence and used to point out the changes that occurred within the category of converts for educational gain during Nicholas's reign. Ḥaim Grinboim was born in 1814 in a small town in Volhynia. Orphaned at a young age, he supported himself by wandering from one yeshivah to another, until he reached Dubno in 1830. He studied Talmud in Dubno in the famous Marshalkovich *bet midrash* and soon met the maskil Wolf Adelson, who brought him to enlightenment. Shortly thereafter, Adelson was chased out of town by the traditionalists, and Grinboim left with him, settling in Kamenets-Podol'sk, where he divorced his wife and attended the local gymnasium. At the same time, probably under the influence of Isaac Ber Levinsohn, who lived in the area, Grinboim translated Moses Mendelssohn's *Jerusalem* into Hebrew and then the tractate *Sanhedrin* into Russian. He finished gymnasium in 1842 and wrote to Lilienthal asking for a job in the new schools funded by the government. After receiving no reply to several letters, Grinboim decided to convert. Baptized in the Russian Orthodox Church, he was now named Vladimir Fedorov. He then entered the philological faculty at the University of Kiev, from which he graduated in 1847, to become a professor of Greek in a Kiev gymnasium, and, in 1852, the local censor of Hebrew and Yiddish books.[82]

In 1843, Grinboim/Fedorov wrote to his friend, the Hebrew writer Avraham Ber Gottlober, explaining the circumstances of his conversion. This letter is the most detailed testimony of an apostate that we possess and merits citation in full:

Kiev, 25 December 1843
(Please forgive me if you will find some errors in this letter of mine, for it is being written in haste, as today is a holiday and I must go to the House of Worship.) My name today is Vladimir Fedorov, my work is the labor of the Lord, my nation that of the great,

courageous, and awesome Russians; and now that I have told you that, let me answer your letter point by point; but before I do this, let me describe to you my condition before I lowered my body— and perhaps my soul—in water, the waters of forgiveness to expiate all my sins, for I am a Hebrew by birth, a sin which I inherited from my ancestors by the very act of being born. While I was still in Kamenets, I wrote a first letter in Hebrew to the scoundrel Lilienthal, asking him to fulfill his promise to me to inform me if there is any hope for people like me to obtain employment in the schools that will be built under his authority. I also sent him an abridgement of my translation of *Jerusalem* for his advice, and for his permission to dedicate it to his name, so revered among the Jews. Even though he did not reply, I did not give up and wrote a second letter, saying: "here I have already finished the gymnasium a year ago, and still cannot find any sustenance that will assure me of never going hungry; therefore, I decided to go to Kiev to enroll in the University, but I was not interested in studying medicine, and decided on another field of study; however, I am afraid that I shall leave the faith of my fathers to follow a God whom I have not yet known. Since I know your [i.e. Lilienthal's] fear of the Lord and love of your people, I appeal to you to harken to the voice of a man standing at the crossroads of two paths, not knowing which way to turn; in your great wisdom, please point out which road I should take to reach temporal and eternal bliss."

However, even this letter was not honored with a reply, although he wrote all sorts of unimportant things to the rich men of Kamenets, ignoramuses who don't know their left hands from their right. When I saw that he wasn't answering, I decided that he had nothing to tell me, that all his desires and actions were empty, that he was rushing after wind; in addition, I saw your bitter fate among the Jews, and that of many others like you, although you are not inferior to me in knowledge and wisdom, and perhaps even greater than me; *I decided that I have no choice but to abandon this lowly nation, which has no share of the benefits of this world and no heritage in those of the eternal world,* for its actions are every evil, *and I joined the ruling nation,* whose name is respected among the nations, and to whom everyone bows.

Even then, I did not act quickly, but even after making this decision, and hearing from the local important people that they "would gladly bring me to enjoy the delicacies of the king if only I were not a Hebrew," I still wrote to you and asked you about Lilienthal, if there was any basis to his actions, and also sent two or three letters to Berdichev.

But when I saw that all hope was lost, that help would be forthcoming only if I was baptized, I said so be it: I have no father or mother, brother or sister to pain with an action that they would consider evil; they are all in the world of truth and know that I am righteous, that I am estranged, despised by the Jews even more than if I were a Christian, so what more could I lose? I shall go and join people who have power and strength, honor and glory in this world and eternal bliss in the next. I prepared myself for this step—and was baptized. And praise to the Lord who has not taken His mercy and truth from me, and led me this far. May God grant me a pure heart and proper spirit to love all mankind, to love God revealed in the Trinity, and to love the Jews as well, for as Jesus said, "Forgive them, Lord, for they know not what they do." And tell me in truth, why should the Jews suffer eternal torment even after their deaths, if it is so easy for them to be saved and released from suffering by [changing] only their religion they would be able to lead pleasant lives and eternal life, but they are a stiff-necked people, hated and despised! Their blood is on their own heads, and who could complain about us, I have saved my own soul.

Your Friend,
Vladimir Fedorov[83]

Ironically, had Grinboim been able to hold out for just a few years, he would have discovered that his despair was unjustified. The government schools would indeed be opened, even without Max Lilienthal; Grinboim undoubtedly would have found a position in these institutions, as did his friend Gottlober.[84]

Grinboim's conversion was hardly typical of the maskilim of his time, but it was symptomatic of the dilemma facing many "enlightened" Jews before the establishment of the state-sponsored school system. From the late 1840s on, there was a secure, if modest, place for maskilim within Russian-Jewish society. This does not mean that none of them converted to Christianity after this time. But now it was not sustenance that was sought in the baptismal font, but fame and fortune.

The most famous Russian-Jewish apostate of all time, Professor Daniel Khvolson (Chwolson) perhaps exemplifies best this later type of maskilic convert. Born in Vilna in 1819, he studied with the renowned Rabbi Israel Salanter but soon taught himself German from Mendelssohn's *Bi'ur* and Luther's translation of the Bible and resolved to become "enlightened." In 1841 he traveled to Riga to appeal to Max Lilienthal for help in obtaining an education; Lilienthal provided him with an introduction to Abraham Geiger in Breslau, where Khvolson took private lessons in various subjects— including German classes from Friedrich Lasalle. In 1845, Khvolson entered the Breslau University, graduating in 1850 from the faculty of Semitics with a dissertation on the Sabaeans. In 1851 he returned to Russia to work as a censor of Hebrew books in St. Petersburg. Four years later he was offered a chair at the University of St. Petersburg on the condition that he convert to Russian Orthodoxy. Apparently without much internal struggle, he consented to baptism and entered the Orthodox Church along with his wife and two sons in 1855. Later, when asked what he believed in that compelled him to convert, Khvolson responded with perhaps the most famous epigram of a Russian-Jewish convert: "I believe that it is better to be a professor in St. Petersburg than a *melamed* in Eishishok."[85]

In the course of his lifetime, Khvolson became somewhat of a legendary hero to traditional Russian Jewry. He was renowned for his defense of the Jews against the repeated charges of ritual murder and was cordially received by the most respected rabbis of the Pale. Rumor had it that he had converted solely in order to help the Jewish people in the "high places." In retrospect, it is clear that the latter was far from the case. It is uncertain, however, precisely what Khvolson's motivations were in defending the Jews and cultivating the rabbis; at least one writer claims that Khvolson did so only for pecuniary gains from his patrons, the barons Günzburg.[86] At all times, Khvolson's worst relations were with the maskilim. After helping to found the Society for the Promotion of Enlightenment among Russian Jews early in the reign of Alexander II, Khvolson resigned from the society in a bitter dispute.[87] His hatred of the Russian-Jewish intelligentsia seems to have been motivated not by an attachment to traditional Judaism but by a simple need for self-justification. For Khvolson to have acknowledged the legitimacy of the maskilim would have required him to admit the speciousness of his witty dichotomy. By 1855 there was, after all, a middle ground between the professor in the capital and the *melamed* in the provinces—the maskil in Vilna or Odessa.

Khvolson's conversion did bring him fame and glory, but this was not the case for all apostates. Even during the first surge of conversions in Russia, there were signs that baptism could not obliterate the stigma of Jewishness in the eyes of important segments of Russian society. At times, the abuse was merely verbal; for example, one Cantonist recalled that for years after their conversions, former Jewish soldiers would be attacked by their comrades as "dirty Jews."[88] Often, the residue of Jewishness was more problematic; in 1842 the convert Joachim Tsimmerman, a graduate of the University of Kiev, was passed over by the faculty of that school for a post he had been promised. The explanation was fascinating: "despite the fact that both [Tsimmerman and his wife] have accepted the Orthodox faith, stemming from Jews, and being married to a person of that origin, he might in the future have connections or acquaintances of that origin."[89] In 1850 the problem of Jewish origins was even addressed in law. From then on, a Jew who converted to Christianity was permitted only to change his first name; he was never to change the family name that he bore prior to his baptism.[90] In Russia alone in Christendom, the state required that the descendants of Jews bear their Jewish surnames as a mark of their tainted origin forever.

Needless to say, this law was not always faithfully observed. Most children of converted Jews disappeared without a trace into their Orthodox or Lutheran or even Catholic families. For several thousand Jews of diverse origin—poor and rich, illiterate and professorial, criminal and spiritual—in Nicholas's Russia, and tens of thousands thereafter, the baptismal font did provide the means of escaping the travails of their people, not to mention the authority of the rabbis. Yet even in Nicholas's time, there were foreboding omens, prophesied later in the century by the town fool of Slutsk who once ran to the front of the synagogue and shouted:

Yidelekh, briderlekh, khapt arayn un shmadt zikh op vos gikher— s'vet nokh kumen a tsayt, az m'vet afile dos aykh nit farginen [Jews, brothers, hurry and get converted as quickly as possible; a time will come, when they won't permit you even that!][91]

Emergence of an Orthodox Judaism

In Western Europe the combined pressure of the dissolution of the Jewish community by the state, the spread of Haskalah, the emergence of a Reform movement, and the increase in conversions toppled traditional Jewish society. As the eminent sociologist of religion Yehezkel Kaufmann put it, for Western Jewry, the century after Moses Mendelssohn constituted "the end of the era of the Torah."[92] As part of the pan-European process of secularization, masses of Jews abandoned the Oral Law, the great yeshivot were closed for lack of students, the heder was replaced by the state school, Jewish learning by secular books, newspapers, theater.

> This was not the process of "forgetting the Torah" which our forefathers talked about and which was found in various countries at all times. That was a matter of ignorance, not deracination. . . . The neglect of the study of Torah was not merely a change in the way of life of the Jews, but a profound and all-embracing transmutation, an absolute substitution of values, the beginning of a new era.[93]

In Russia, too, traditional Jewish society ceased to exist during the course of the nineteenth century under the weight of all the same factors, but it was replaced by a religious and social complex that did not follow any ostensibly universal pattern of development. Here, the abandonment of ritual and learning—of "Torah" in Kaufmann's sense—was restricted to a small, if increasingly influential and vocal, minority of the Jews. The vast majority responded to the appearance of heterodoxy by gradually consolidating itself into an "Orthodoxy": a self-conscious traditionalist society battling its enemies on their own ground, often with their own tools, organized by leaders armed with a vigilant new strategy and militant new ideology.[94]

Ironically, much of the stimulus to this new stance of the traditionalists was supplied by the Russian government itself. Even the most radical of the maskilim were forced to concede that the recruitment policy, in particular, had strengthened the hold of the Torah on Russian Jews:

> . . . the nation that took this decree as a punishment from God for its sins, resolved in its heart to do full penance to Him, to strengthen the position of the Torah and Talmud; the old societies of Bible, Mishnah, Midrash, and Gemara study were reinforced and en-

larged, and were joined by new societies; many stools were added to the yeshivot and more academies were founded with much zeal, for the numbers of philanthropists grew, particularly from among the poor, eager to gird themselves and educate their children. . . . Since the community leaders protected the children of the rich and the learned and refused to enlist them, and with the assent of the rabbis in their assemblies laid the burden of the decree on the poor and ignorant, many of the poor were moved to pay more attention to the education of their young, to teach them Torah in the safety of the yeshivot . . . and so the number of students studying the Torah for its own sake, and not for its own sake, has flourished, like grass on the field.[95]

The impetus was then taken up by the rabbis themselves. When Menahem Mendel of Liubavich returned from the rabbinical commission in St. Petersburg, he called together the most influential spiritual leaders of Russian Jewry to plan a covert campaign against the schools, the government, and the maskilim. According to the Liubavich family account, attending this meeting were Rabbi David Lurie of Bykhov, Rabbi Shlomo Lifshits of Minsk, and Rabbi Yehezel Beinenson of Slutsk.[96] After the conference, these three rabbis later met with the other rabbinical lights of the Pale in Vilna, Kovno, and Brest-Litovsk and coordinated strategy against the Haskalah. Rabbi Lurie—who had five years previously been arrested by the government on a false charge of treason trumped up by jealous relatives[97]—reportedly personally went to Vilna where he held a public assembly calling for the boycott of the schools, to which he applied the traditional curse "May their names be damned!" to the maskilim, causing ripples throughout Lithuanian Jewry.[98]

Apart from the actual battle against the schools, this meeting was notable in three respects. First (if the Liubavich account is accurate), one rabbinical leader was conspicuously absent—Yizhak ben Haim of Volozhin. In the new Orthodoxy that was emerging in Russia there would be no room for Yizhak's "collaborationist" politics, now clearly discredited. It may be that Yizhak's public position on the schools even lost him support among his own followers and students. One traditionalist spokesman put it very delicately,

His extensive public work did not permit him to concentrate sufficiently on matters concerning the yeshivah. . . . This caused a group of the students to lose their attachment to him, although they still held him in great respect, and to leave the yeshivah for other academies. Yiẓḥak himself realized that he was too occupied in political matters to dedicate himself properly to the yeshivah, and he left the actual running of the yeshivah to his son-in-law, Eli'ezer Yiẓḥak.[99]

Another former student reported that the number of Yiẓḥak's students was halved during his years of political activism.[100] Only after his demise did Volozhin regain, and then surpass, its previous status as the most prestigious academy in Eastern Europe.[101]

Second, even discounting the obvious bias of the materials emanating from the court of the Schneersohn family, it does appear that the status and power of the Liubavich dynasty of Hasidim rose considerably as the battle against Haskalah and the disintegration of traditional Jewish society intensified. The first Liubavich yeshivah was founded in the home seat in 1841–42, consciously as a weapon against the spread of "enlightenment": "[Rabbi Menaḥem Mendel] viewed the establishment of the yeshivah as a beneficial act and a necessary precaution, a barrier against the rising tide of the iniquity of Haskalah that was then storming through our land. . . ."[102] Within a few years, additional academies were opened in some twenty towns throughout the Pale, and those in the important towns of Gomel and Bobruisk were enlarged.[103] This prodigious spread of Liubavich Hasidism well beyond its native Belorussian territories to all parts of the Pale was doubtless a function of its popular ideology, combining intellectual rigor with mysticism, but it was reinforced by the militant and aggressive anti-Haskalah strategy of its leaders. Again according to the family history, Menaḥem Mendel issued the following public missive "of an urgent nature":

To all Rabbis, especially in the Hassidic communities: organize a yeshivah with a *rosh yeshivah* wherever there is a sizable group of lads requiring instruction; where the number does not warrant a yeshivah, engage a capable melamed, or preferably, send the youths to a yeshivah elsewhere.

To all Hassidic melamdim: endeavor to enroll every single child and youth in a heder, leaving no one without instruction; enlarge heder schools; refrain, when possible, from sending children to Talmud Torah.

To all *shokhtim* [ritual slaughterers] and melamdim in Chassidic communities, charged with conducting public Torah study groups for adults in the synagogues: explain clearly to your groups the reason for the Petersburg Commission, that, at the instigation of the *Berlinchikes*—corrupters of Israel and notorious atheists—in order to uproot from the hearts of Jewish children any vestige of faith and religion and to assimilate them with Gentiles, Rabbis were called to agree to an abridgement of the *siddur* [prayerbook] and *humash* [Pentateuch], to organize public schools for secular studies to wean Jewish children from their faith. It is to be made clear that the first victims would be children receiving no education, and that pupils of private melamdim would be more secure than Talmud Torah pupils.[104]

The *rebbe* also counseled more practical resistance. He advised Jewish communities to "avoid finding sources of revenue for the maintenance of the public schools"; in his own town he tried appealing to the authorities' central concern, warning that opening a school would detract from the communities' ability to fulfill their recruitment and taxation duties.[105] With the help of such offensive tactics, Liubavich acceded to a position of greater importance within Russian Jewry, foreshadowing its later prominence among the Hasidic courts in the twentieth century.

The third and most important facet of the 1843 meeting was its signaling of a definite end to the feud between the Hasidim and the mitnagdim that had waged for nearly a century, often leading to denunciations and even mutual bans of excommunication. From now on, the two sects of traditional—or rather Orthodox—Judaism joined in an overt alliance against their common enemies, the heterodox maskilim. Again, this fusion was partially determined by internal forces—by this time Hasidism had largely won its battles and become as much "establishment" as its opponents, owing in no small measure to its increasing emphasis on talmudic study, exemplified by the Liubavich wing—but the existence of a clear enemy on the outside, threatening the very foundations of their common beliefs, greatly facilitated and accelerated the reconciliation.[106] The cynical outsider might observe that by the end of Nicholas's reign, Bludov's dismissal of the sectarian differences between the Hasidim and their opponents was closer to the mark than the minister could have known.

Even within the Orthodox camp, however, there arose at this time serious doubts over whether the battle against the new era could be won without radical changes in the institutions and ideology of traditional Jewry. As the Israeli scholar Emanuel Etkes has most recently demonstrated, the emergence in the 1840s of the new religious trend known as the *musar* movement, developed by a coterie of rabbis led by Israel Lipkin of Salant, was directly linked to the spread of the Haskalah. Lipkin and his disciples argued that the debilitation of authority and belief had gone so far within Russian Jewry that the only way to save the tradition was to shift the emphasis from communal and political agitation to the strengthening of every individual Jew's moral and ethical resolve. In the new *musar* yeshivot, talmudic study would be supplemented with readings from Jewish ethical literature; outside the academy, groups of Jews, even women, were encouraged to gather together to study morals, to learn how to resist the new temptations of the age.[107]

During Nicholas's reign, this movement had only modest success; its greatest gains would come later in the century, when Lipkin's predictions about the weaknesses of the traditional order were patently corroborated by the massive gains of the Haskalah. By 1855, however, the decomposition of traditional Jewish society in Russia had gone so far that one of Lipkin's associates, Rabbi Yeḥiel Heller of Suvalki—ironically, one of the authorities cited by Mandelshtam in his edition of Maimonides—would preface his collection of responsa with one of the most dire descriptions of the power of the maskilim and the plight of the tradition ever penned by a Russian rabbi:

In this bleak generation to which we have deteriorated, we must protest against the debasement of the Torah. Its traducers have gained the upper hand: they boast that the Lord's Torah lies trampled under foot, they spread malicious mockeries of the most exalted and revered matters. We who hope in the Lord must renew our strength in the coming days to support our crumbling edifice [the Torah]. She shall speak from the humble ground and say: have pity on me, Children of Truth, for I am your mother, drowning in blood; the children of iniquity have rejected me and wounded me, and an impudent woman now rules so high, for the foolish have spread their folly, the evil-doers have built up coarse haughtiness, making my soul sick with loathing. I pray that your righteousness will bind my fatal wounds, that you will hearken to my words for I am distressed, my soul oppressed, lest the wicked brand me barren and bereaved. They shall see that I have wise sons, and together we shall rejoice when they beg God for mercy, for He is our protector, He shall cause us to be joyful and the sinners to fall.[108]

To the distress of the rabbis, the sinners did not fall, the "children of iniquity" continued to spread their gospel and to prosper. At the same time, however, masses of Jews did respond in new ways to the defense of Torah. The traditional authority structure of Jewish society in Russia was thoroughly transformed during Nicholas's rule, but in a complex and subtle manner, which neither the government nor any of the protagonists had presaged.

6 · Economic
Transformations

Loyf tsu Romanovsken,
zog—du bist a vaser-treger,
zog—du bist a holtsenzeger,
zog, zog, ver du bist,
nor nit blayb a prazdnoshataiushchiisia.

(Run to Romanovsky
Say you are a water-carrier
Say you are a wood-cutter
Say, say, whoever you are
Only don't remain an "idler.")
                                    Yiddish folk song[1]

One week after the publication of the law abolishing the kahal, a
new statute on Jewish agricultural settlement appeared, again increasing the financial inducements to colonization without providing sufficient means or land to transform a significant number of
Jews into farmers.[2]

With the passing of this law, most of the major recommendations
of Kiselev's Committee on the Transformation of the Jews were
addressed: the new schools, taxation system, communal structure,
and agricultural incentives. But the most far-reaching of Kiselev's
proposals, the reclassification of the estate allegiance of the Jews,
was not acted upon along with the other reforms.

The Reclassification of the Jews

The delay resulted from a serious difference of opinion within the
ruling circles of Russia over the appropriateness of the "sorting"

scheme, known in Russia as the *razbor* of the Jews. Kiselev had recognized the irrationality of subsuming most of Russia's Jews into the amorphous category of townspeople, when in fact a large number of them neither lived in towns or cities nor engaged in the sort of occupation traditionally associated with the Russian *meshchantsvo*. Influenced by previous governmental studies that blamed the Jews for the economic plight of their neighbors, Kiselev determined that it was necessary to restrict entry into the townspeople estate to urban Jewish traders of substantial property and to force the rest of the Jews to become artisans, agriculturists, or guild merchants. He therefore advised Nicholas that Russia should emulate Prussia in distinguishing between "useful" and "nonuseful" Jews. The former would consist of all guild merchants, licensed artisans, farmers, and true townspeople with a permanent urban residence. All other Jews would be deemed nonuseful and given five years to join one of the other estates and to leave their rural homes; those who failed to meet the deadline would be subjected to severe punishment, including extraordinary conscription duties.

The tsar found this proposal most satisfactory, raising it from fifth to third position on his list of priority legislation on the Jews. But some of his advisers and ministers disagreed and managed to thwart his designs. The leader of the opposition was Count M. S. Vorontsov, the governor-general of New Russia, who strenuously objected to both the tone and the content of the *razbor* proposal. Interrupting his vacation in London in 1843—Vorontsov was one of the most anglophilic of Russians—he wrote a sharp letter to the minister of the interior after receiving a copy of Kiselev's memorandum. He began by refuting the very categorization of petty Jewish traders as nonuseful:

The project calls "nonuseful" all those numerous Jews who either purchase small amounts of products from their primary producers in order to sell them to wholesalers, or engage in the useful sale of consumer goods purchased in large quantities from other wholesale agents. Impartially considered, it is shocking to call these numerous traders "nonuseful" and harmful, when through their petty but much maligned trade they undoubtedly aid both the agricultural sector and commerce in the Polish provinces, where no native small merchant class has ever existed, or exists at this time.[3]

Apart from the terminology, Vorontsov argued, the entire *razbor* policy was ill conceived. The extreme measures called for by Kiselev would only be acceptable if they could succeed in turning a large number of Jews to more productive occupations, "like a prudent doctor who decides on a bloody operation since he is convinced that a short-term but forceful pain will cure a chronic and painful illness."[4] But in this case, the diagnosis was fundamentally mistaken. Most of the Jews who would be affected by the reclassification were extremely poor and would have no means of learning a new trade, not to speak of accumulating enough capital to acquire a house or to buy their way into the merchant guilds. A painful operation like the one suggested by Kiselev would be counterproductive, if not fatal. The illness of the Jews, their poverty and exploitation of the peasants, would only be exacerbated by crowding them into the big cities without sufficient means of support. In conclusion, Vorontsov noted, "I daresay that these negative consequences would be inevitable if the measures are applied in all their severity; I dare think that they would be harmful to the state's own interests and cruel as well."[5]

Apparently, Vorontsov's objections were shared by members of the committee itself. They replaced the term "nonuseful" with "those lacking productive occupation," deleted the most extreme recommendation, the expulsion of the Jews from the villages, and were able to delay the execution of the plan for several years.[6]

Only in 1846 was the *razbor* of the Jews finally announced by the government, couched in surprisingly conciliatory and sophisticated terms. The announcement, extant only in an official German translation published at the time in the *Allgemeine Zeitung des Judentums*, began with a fascinating restatement of the government's perception of its generosity toward the Jews. In his exalted solicitude for the welfare of his Jewish subjects, Nicholas commissioned a special committee to analyze the sources of the current unsatisfactory situation and to propose suitable solutions. The committee found that as a result of the former Polish government's refusal to grant them any civic or property rights, the Jews of the

Western Provinces were forced into complete dependence on the landowners and into petty trade and the liquor industry. The "return" of the Polish territories to Russia, however, changed the Jews' circumstances entirely:

The Imperial Government permitted them to enjoy the benefit of civil rights on an equal basis as all other subjects, and granted them not only the permission to enroll in merchant guild estates, but also the right to participate in elections and office-holding of the city councils and various other urban governing boards.[7]

Moreover, they were allowed to acquire real estate and to settle as farmers, either on their own land or on tracts provided to them by the government. In addition, "in order to open to them all possible paths to Civilization," they were permitted to attend all public educational institutions, including the academies and the universities. Most importantly, they were allowed to settle not only in the former Polish provinces, but also in New Russia and the Ukraine.

Thus, the Jews were granted the right to settle in seventeen provinces, in a territory with a surface area of 17,000 square miles and a population of twenty million, an area which through the ports of the Black Sea and in part, the Baltic, has a lively internal and foreign trade. [The Jews] have had at their disposal all possible means to turn to useful activities and to establish for themselves a secure prosperity.

Unfortunately, however, they have not been willing to avail themselves of the opportunities presented to them, and have persisted in avoiding any amalgamation [Verschmelzung] with the society under whose protection they live, existing, as before, for the most part, off the work of the rest of the population, which justifiably continually complains of this.[8]

In order to counter the Jews' obstinacy, the government has heeded the advice of the best-educated Jews and abolished the kahals, established special Jewish schools, extended the opportunities for Jews to engage in agriculture, and presently will forbid the wearing of traditional Jewish costumes.

Since the Government has provided all the means for the moral and material well-being of the Jews, it is justified in hoping that the Jews will finally abandon any undertaking that endangers the interests of the rest of the population, and will choose for themselves, like their compatriots, more sound modes of living. It is absolutely correct that the refractory and disobedient be punished as idlers who are a burden to the society of which they are a part. Therefore, in order to make a just distinction between those Jews who have already sought to make themselves useful and those who have no trade or other legal occupation, the Government shall require the latter to declare themselves in one of the following categories: (1) one of the three merchant guilds, (2) the ranks of townspeople of any city or town who own a residence, (3) any artisan guild to which they bring the requisite knowledge of a craft, and (4) agriculturists.[9]

The government shall provide monetary support to defray the costs of the transition to agriculture and exempt all colonists from taxation and conscription duties. All Jews must reregister themselves according to these rules by January 1, 1850. After that date, any Jew who has not done so or who has not attained an academic degree or the rank of Honorary Citizen will be listed in a special category and subjected to punitive measures which the government will elaborate at a later date. "So warned in advance, the Jews have the choice of taking up the means offered to them to conduct an honest and secure life, or to suffer the unpleasant consequences which their persistence on the path of evil must lead to."[10]

This announcement, naturally, led to panic in the Pale, but it is unclear how many Jews actually changed their estate classification in direct response to the threats of the government. Indeed, Vorontsov was correct in asserting that for the vast majority of the Jewish townspeople there was no possible way to improve their economic status or to learn a new trade. The government must have been aware of this fact. January 1, 1850, came and went without the *razbor* of the Jews being effectuated. Only on November 23, 1851, did the administration issue an edict on the subject, in the form of Temporary Regulations on the Reclassification of the Jews, which reiterated the categories and threats enumerated by Kiselev and extended the term for registration to July 1, 1852.[11] On May 21, 1852, the minister of the interior reported to the Senate that this deadline, too, could not be met and applied for another extension; this was granted in a decree passed on May 30, postponing the *razbor* of the Jews until November 1, 1852.[12]

This was the last mention of the reclassification scheme in any official Russian publication. Clearly, the expenditure of effort that would have been required to supervise the registration of the Jews was enormous. The local authorities throughout the Western Provinces had to be mobilized to interview every Jew in the realm, to determine his occupation and economic status, and to decide whether he fit into the general categories established as useful by the temporary regulations. Such a rallying of organization would be extraordinary for the Russian bureaucracy at any time. In late 1852 and 1853 the focus of the government's attention was well beyond the Pale, on the growing tensions with the Turks. Soon, mobilization for war rendered any large-scale domestic enterprise completely impossible. The inventories of the Jews were never completed, and the entire subject was quickly forgotten.

Although Kiselev's plans for the reordering of the economic structure of Russian Jewry were abandoned, the government of Nicholas I did indeed effect a radical shift in the occupational and demographic organization of Russian Jewry. This was a complex, and often unconscious, consequence of the entire range of economic and social policies regarding the Jews. To understand this phenomenon, it is necessary to digress from a neat chronological course and to examine the biological and economic development of Russian Jewry throughout Nicholas's rule. This requires delving rather deeply into an arcane and convoluted nightmare—the statistical and financial reports of the Russian state.

The Demographic Shifts

It was hardly a secret in tsarist Russia that the periodic "revisions of souls" taken by the government in lieu of a census had only tenuous connections with reality. Pavel Ivanovich Chichikov's famous scheme in Gogol's *Dead Souls* was only ingenious in that it dealt with dead peasants. Everyone tampered with the tax rolls in order to evade monetary or conscription duties. Peasants and landowners had a harder time concealing their existence, but urban traders and the nationalities with whom the government had little business and less communication quite easily hid themselves from the government's lists in massive numbers. Of course, the authorities collaborated in the open game of distorting the tax rolls for a price, since the only reason to take on the job of a tax assessor was to reap the benefits of not assessing taxes. There were clearly defined rules and wage-price guidelines for this enterprise—the payments were not considered bribes, merely part of the assessor's salary.

Descriptions of the intricate shadow-boxing rituals of revision-time abound in Hebrew and Yiddish, as well as Russian, literature. One memoirist of Nicholas's time, Yeḥezkel Kotik, recalled how his grandfather, the kahal official, kept his annual appointment with the tax assessor:

> . . . no one in town could handle one matter as he could. This was the "reviser" who used to come to audit the tax rolls of Kamenets, to see if it didn't have more than the 450 souls who were listed. Grandfather was a master of "speaking" with the reviser, no one could be better. This "conversation" always ended with the official quickly pocketing 200 rubles. On the day of the revision, many houses would be shut, the inhabitants would leave town, going wherever they chose, and the town seemed dead, like a cemetery. You could almost not see one living creature on the streets, while the reviser would walk through them with the entire local police force at his side, counting the souls. They always found around 400 persons. Fifty were missing; they were said to be away on business. Every year the reviser would leave, writing in his protocol that everything was in order.[13]

Actually, Kotik claimed, there were 250 Jewish families in Kamenets at this time, but two-thirds of them were not registered until universal conscription was introduced in 1874.[14]

Some government officials feigned outrage in discussing this overt evasion. Reviewing the statistics on Russian Jewry in 1861, one demographer wrote:

> It is no less difficult to ascertain the number of Jews today than in the time of King David. Given the concealment of Jews during the revisions and the unity of the kahals and their members, any statistics are far from accurate. The Jewish kahal is some sort of

void, in which people disappear without a trace. The number of births began to fall especially steadily since a thirty-kopek fee was introduced for the registration of new births.[15]

According to this bureaucrat, the Vilna communal rolls showed that from 1850 to 1856, 9,244 Jews died and 5,619 were born, a loss of 3,625 persons. "If this should, God forbid, continue, in 1875, Vilna will have no Jews."[16]

More honest officials recognized that the fault lay with the government as much as with the Jews. The first analyst of the vital statistics of Russian Jewry, B. Miliutin, noted that the figures taken from the Ministry of the Interior's tax rolls did not correspond with those accumulated by the ministry's own Department of Foreign Creeds nor with the numbers submitted to the ministry by the Jewish communities themselves.[17]

Recognizing the chaotic nature of Russian-Jewish statistics (as well as those of Western European Jewry), the founder of Jewish demographic studies, Jacob Lestchinsky, attempted to devise a suitable formula for correcting official data supplied by the Russian government. Unfortunately, Lestchinsky's corrected figures seem in retrospect to be as unreliable as those he rejected. He never detailed his calculations (although he admitted that they were indispensable to serious study),[18] neglected to document the sources of most of his data, and made some serious errors of transcription and analysis regarding the figures for our period.[19] Most importantly, he failed to distinguish between the different sorts of statistics compiled by the Russian authorities, only some of which are acceptable.

Since there is insufficient information to posit a reliable formula for the percentage of Jews who were missing from the official registers, it seems counterproductive to posit new "corrected" figures for the actual Jewish population of Nicholas's Russia. However, important demographic and economic trends, if not absolute numbers, can be deduced from the official data, if it is assumed that the rate of concealment remained constant. This assumption would be problematic if statistics were available either on the years before the introduction of compulsory military service or on the last three years of Nicholas's reign, when the conscription rates were raised significantly and the passportless decree caused a much higher degree of evasion of the draft. Official revision statistics, however, are extant only for the period from 1830 to 1851, for which the assumption of a constant rate of concealment seems irreproachable.

Use of the revision data is further complicated by the fact that the four sets of figures that are extant—for 1830, 1838, 1847, and 1851[20]—do not cover identical territories. The 1830 figures include Belostok Oblast but not Bessarabia; the 1847 survey for some reason omitted the provinces of Kurland and Lifland; the 1851 revision, by far the most complete, added territories outside of the Pale not computed in the other calculations. This asymmetry led even sophisticated historians like Lestchinsky and Ben Zion Dinur astray. They refuted the official data on grounds of inexactitude without realizing that the total figures for different years could not be compared without taking into account the territories omitted.[21] To avoid this dilemma, calculations here shall be limited to those regions covered in all the surveys—the fourteen provinces of the

TABLE 2

MALE JEWISH POPULATION OF THE PALE OF SETTLEMENT, 1830–51

Province	1830	1838	1847	1851
Chernigov	6,823	9,721	9,674	13,525
Ekaterinoslav	1,709	2,759	2,516	5,846
Grodno	31,813	33,918	45,403	43,178
Kherson*	8,851	13,187	8,804	20,996
Kiev	45,006	55,863	65,757	78,182
Minsk	36,947	48,918	43,470	45,760
Mogilev	36,681	45,989	44,496	49,479
Podolia	69,882	82,342	80,726	84,910
Poltava	4,555	7,713	7,872	10,829
Taurida (Crimea)	2,507	2,076**	1,502	5,010
Vilna/Kovno	46,559	68,729	72,968	64,043
Vitebsk	18,878	21,848	24,988	27,410
Volhynia	94,098	101,349	83,403	86,502
Total	404,309	494,412	491,579	535,670

SOURCE: See n. 20, pp. 215–16.
*Includes Odessa
**Published figure is 4,110 for both genders, which has been broken down according to the average male-female ratio for this year, 100:97.9

TABLE 3
GROWTH RATE BY PROVINCE, 1830–51

Province	Percentage
Volhynia	− 8
Podolia	21
Minsk	24
Mogilev	35
Grodno	36
Vilna/Kovno	38
Vitebsk	45
Kiev	74
Chernigov	98
Taurida	100
Kherson	137
Poltava	138
Ekaterinoslav	242

SOURCE: See n. 20, pp. 215–16.

Pale (actually, thirteen until 1842, when the Vilna *guberniia* was subdivided into the Vilna and Kovno provinces).

An additional problem is posed by the absence of statistics for the female Jewish population in the 1830 and 1851 figures. Since the exact ratio of males to females in these years is not known, it seems prudent to avoid the dangers of compounding inaccuracy and to restrict comments to the male population—the only group, after all, which concerned the government and thus more likely to be registered with some care.

Table 2 lists the official figures compiled by the Russian government for each of the provinces of the Pale in the four years surveyed. Table 3 calculates the rate of growth in each of these provinces from 1830 to 1851, ranked from lowest to highest.

It must be stressed again that these figures constitute only approximations based on reported population alone. Nevertheless, it is possible to posit some relevant generalizations. Within the twenty-two years surveyed, the reported male Jewish population of the Pale of Settlement increased by approximately 32.5 percent. The largest increase was between 1830 and 1838, in which the reported population rose by some 22 percent.

More important than this apparent impressive rise in population is the clear shift in geographic distribution. While the largest populations remain in the traditional centers of Russian-Jewish life—Volhynia, Podolia, Vilna, and Minsk provinces—the rate of growth is far greater in the new territories of the south—Chernigov, Ekaterinoslav, Kherson, and Poltava provinces and the Crimea. Clearly, this indicates a substantial migration from north to south and west to east, caused by a variety of factors: the relative prosperity of the new territories, the absence of established kahals—and thus the likelihood of a more egalitarian draft system—the availability of agricultural plots, and even the receptivity to Haskalah.

While available sources do not permit establishing these two trends with any degree of exactitude, they do allow two other trends to be documented with substantially greater certainty. There can be little question that the data given in the 1851 Ninth Revision of the Russian Empire on the number of Jewish guild merchants and agriculturists is accurate. Unlike the *meshchane*, who had every reason not to register with the authorities, the guild merchants and agriculturists had to be listed by the government in order to claim their status and conscription and taxation exemptions. Since the 1851 revision was the only full-scale population survey of the period, its figures can be accepted as reflecting the actual number of Jewish members of these estates.[22] The 1830 figures are subject to more doubt, but for purposes of comparison they can be presumed to indicate the approximate total of merchants and farmers in that year.

Table 4 presents the revision statistics on guild merchants in 1830 and 1851 in the provinces of the Pale, in ascending order of rate of growth. Within twenty-two years, the number of Jewish guild merchants more than quintupled, from 4,853 to 27,469. Interestingly, although the ranks of this estate grew in every province, the largest increases were, once more, in the south. The phenomenal growth of the merchant estates of Chernigov, Kherson, Poltava, Kiev, and Ekaterinoslav provinces cannot have been due solely to the migration noted above; it must have been caused, to some degree, by the rise in importance of the southern grain trade, especially in Odessa, in this period.[23] Yet the strictly economic factors in this growth must not be exaggerated, as many historians of a materialist bent have done. For as can be seen in table 5, fully 95.6 percent of the Jewish guild merchants in 1851 belonged to the third guild, that is, reported relatively modest capital holdings.[24] It is safe to assume that a large number of Jews who joined the third guild did so in order to avoid the conscription duty and tax burden of the townspeople estate, while in fact their business activity was in no way different from that of *meshchane*. Indeed, one of the most significant characteristics of Russian-Jewish demography in this and later periods is the drive to join the third guild on the part of traders who did not really have the capital to engage in large-scale enterprise. The pressure to leave the ranks of the *meshchantsvo*, even without direct governmental intervention on the order of Kiselev's *razbor* project, was an unintended consequence of Nicholas's military policies.

There were, of course, two directions to take when leaving the townspeople estate: into the merchant guilds or into the agricultural

TABLE 4

JEWISH GUILD MERCHANTS IN THE PALE OF SETTLEMENT, 1830 AND 1851

Province	1830	1851	Ratio
Vilna/Kovno	510	1,015	100 : 199
Mogilev	575	1,209	100 : 210
Grodno	270	613	100 : 227
Vitebsk	270	677	100 : 251
Minsk	338	1,126	100 : 333
Volhynia	863	3,640	100 : 422
Taurida	249	1,215	100 : 488
Podolia	746	5,879	100 : 788
Chernigov	82	767	100 : 935
Kherson	294	3,061	100 : 1041
Poltava	129	1,381	100 : 1070
Kiev	494	5,910	100 : 1196
Ekaterinoslav	43	976	100 : 2270
Total	4,863	27,469	100 : 565

SOURCE: See n. 20, pp. 215–16.

TABLE 5
JEWISH MERCHANTS BY GUILD, 1851

Province	Guild I	Guild II	Guild III	Total
Chernigov	59	15	693	767
Ekaterinoslav	11	7	958	976
Grodno	34	12	567	613
Kherson	35	93	2,933	3,061
Kiev	24	145	5,741	5,910
Minsk	55	64	1,007	1,126
Mogilev	20	39	1,150	1,209
Podolia	7	125	5,747	5,849
Poltava	6	22	1,353	1,381
Taurida	98	63	1,054	1,215
Vilna/Kovno	40	34	941	1,015
Vitebsk	52	18	607	677
Volhynia	25	117	3,498	3,640
Total	466	754	26,249	27,469

SOURCE: See n. 20, pp. 215–16.

colonies established by the government for the Jews. Russian Jews always reacted enthusiastically to any governmental proposal to settle them on the land, despite the dislocation involved—this was as true in the reign of Alexander I as during the 1920s and 1930s. Yet consistently the Russian (and Soviet) governments preferred fulminating against the "unproductive" economic activities of the Jews to taking coordinated and constructive measures toward increasing their productivity. Thus, as table 6 indicates, while the number of Jewish farmers quadrupled from 1830 to 1851, the increase was just over half as large as that of Jewish guild merchants in the same period.[25]

Unfortunately, the revision statistics do not contain data that would permit confirmation of another important demographic phenomenon which paralleled the movement from the *meshchantsvo*— the steady urbanization of the Jews of Russia. This process was noted by Russian officials already in the 1840s, and Lestchinsky attempted to corroborate their impressions with seemingly convincing figures.[26] Again, however, he did not detail the sources for his numbers.

The only reliable statistics available are for the overall growth of the urban population of the Western Provinces documented from archival sources by the Soviet historian P. G. Ryndziunskii.

TABLE 6

JEWISH AGRICULTURISTS IN THE PALE OF SETTLEMENT,
1830 AND 1851

Province	1830	1851
Poltava	—	—
Taurida	—	128
Vitebsk	—	228
Volhynia	—	355
Chernigov	3	380
Vilna/Kovno	132	441
Podolia	52	532
Kiev	745	597
Grodno	—	899
Mogilev	—	1,310
Minsk	—	1,493
Ekaterinoslav	—	1,834
Kherson	2,674	7,272
Total	3,606	15,429

SOURCE: See n. 20, pp. 215–16.

TABLE 7

URBAN POPULATION IN THE WESTERN PROVINCES,
1825 AND 1856

Province	1825	1856
Vitebsk	46,613	78,232
Minsk	49,669	91,544
Mogilev	37,232	67,381
Grodno	60,594	108,754
Vilna	68,485	69,674
Kovno	—	57,329
Volhynia	98,907	103,569
Podolia	55,663	103,494
Kiev	74,083	196,548
Total	491,246	876,728

SOURCE: See n. 20, p. 216.

These are reproduced in table 7.[27] Since it is known from Ryn-dziunskii—and every other contemporary and later student of the economy of the former Polish territories—that the overwhelming majority of the urban population of these provinces was Jewish, these statistics allow tentative acceptance of the hypothesis of a substantial movement from rural to urban settlements within the Pale.

Obviously, no statistics could document another trend—the illegal migration of Jews from the Pale of Settlement to other parts of the Russian Empire. Official reports from Bessarabia and the Kingdom of Poland—where the conscription duties were much less onerous—continually complained about the influx of Jews from the Pale hoping to avoid the draft and requested guidance on whether to subject these Jews to the local recruitment ordinances.[28] At the same time, the first significant numbers of Russian Jews began stealing across the western frontiers of the empire itself into neighboring Prussia and Austria.[29]

The only Jews who were allowed to reside permanently outside the Pale of Settlement were, of course, Jewish soldiers posted in various parts of the empire. Ironically, these soldiers, who were permitted to bring their families to live with them, often constituted the nucleus of Jewish communities that would grow during the reign of Alexander II—hardly a consequence presaged by the Russian government. In Moscow and St. Petersburg, for example, the wives of Jewish soldiers took an active part in the local economy, opening stores and boardinghouses—the latter, incidentally, serving to conceal civilian Jews illegally doing business in the capitals.[30] Those Jewish soldiers who had not married prior to their recruitment were faced with a grievous problem if they wanted to find a Jewish wife. As a result, there arose in Nicholas's Russia perhaps the most inventive trade ever engaged in by Jews, the transport of single women from the Pale to the interior of Russia.

Some enterprising entrepreneur would organize a transport of girl-brides and set off with them traveling around Russian cities and towns, disposing of his live "wares" along the way. In compensation for their fares and keep, he was promised the entire purchase price: the girls, voluntarily submitting to his command, were satisfied with the prospect of finding a fiancé and getting married. Moscow was the most remunerative market for brides: the local soldiers were more prosperous than their provincial comrades, and their number there was relatively high. The entrepreneur would first head for Moscow . . . and sell his best "wares," and then take the rest to other cities. In this way, the male Jewish population of the interior of Russia was forced—as they ironically put it—to acquire their wives "from carts."[31]

It would be difficult to find a more compelling metaphor for Russian Jewry's response to the policies of the government—a combination of ingenuity and tragedy.

The Economic Shifts

The study of the economic history of Russian Jewry in Nicholas's reign is attended by the same source problems that limit demographic analysis. Nonetheless, several historians have attempted to weave together comprehensive accounts of the economy of Russian Jewry in this period, relying on their faith in infallible schemes of historical development to supplement—if not to supplant—the meager hard data at their disposal. To the nonbeliever, the results are most discouraging. The bulk of these studies, written by Soviet scholars in the 1920s and early 1930s, bury some illuminating insights under mounds of Stalinist cant; the two Western analyses, motivated by a less rigorous but still pervasive materialist determinism, shroud their own observations in the jargon elaborated by their more orthodox colleagues.[32]

Without access to new archival materials, it is impossible to detail the entire range of economic activities of the Jews of Russia in the first half of the nineteenth century. But a careful sifting of the facts presented by the previous studies and a survey of the policies of the government as expressed in its legislation and official reports make it possible at least to discern various important trends and developments.

The Liquor Trade Perhaps the most vital domestic industry in nineteenth-century Russia (as it is in the Soviet Union today) was the manufacture and distribution of liquor. Revenues accruing to the state treasury from vodka distilling and sale equaled, and sometimes surpassed, income from direct taxation throughout Nicholas's reign.[33] As a result, the government would have preferred to control this industry as a state monopoly but found that it could not do so efficiently, given the scope of the demand for vodka and the entrenched rights of the nobility of several occupied regions. Instead, a compromise was arrived at: the empire was divided into "nonprivileged" provinces, in which vodka production and sale was the monopoly of the state and farmed out to large-scale entrepreneurs, and "privileged" provinces, including the former Polish territories, in which the landlords were allowed to continue their command of distilling and trade in liquor in their properties, leasing their rights to whomever they chose—almost exclusively Jews.[34]

From the late eighteenth century on, numerous imperial officials protested this situation most vigorously, blaming the Jews for the poverty and drunkness of the peasantry. In the statute of 1804 the government acted on these complaints: Jews were to be prohibited from leasing any stills, taverns, or inns as part of the overarching policy of their removal from all villages and rural settlements.[35] Although several thousand Jews were in fact displaced from their homes in the early 1820s in line with this policy, the government itself was forced to concede that the expulsions, in general, and the forced closing of Jewish taverns, in particular, were counterproductive in that they deprived the treasury of large amounts of income and had a seriously detrimental effect on the entire economy of the Western Provinces. The government of Nicholas I quickly moved first to limit, and then altogether to abandon, the expulsion policy. Although the ban on Jewish participation in the sale and production of vodka in the countryside remained on the books, it was universally disregarded in practice and soon in law. The 1835 statute on the Jews specifically permitted all Jews in the Pale of Settlement to lease taverns and inns throughout the countryside, in addition to lands, mills, postal stations, et cetera. Only the leasing of estates settled with peasants was prohibited.[36]

Almost immediately after the promulgation of this statute, the government realized that it had gone too far in legalizing the Jews' role in the vodka industry. The problem now was not the effect of the Jews on the peasantry—rather a duplicitous concern on the part of a regime based on serfdom—but rather the chaotic situation that obtained on the borders of the privileged and nonprivileged provinces. Since the free competition in the former resulted in vodka prices significantly lower than those set by the government in the latter, there was a massive amount of smuggling of cheap vodka into the interior of Russia. The dilemma facing the government was how to reduce the amount of contraband without lowering revenues. After much debate, a novel solution was hit upon. Instead of introducing free trade into the nonprivileged provinces, as recommended by several of the more westernized officials, the government would attempt to replace the many small-scale liquor traders with large-scale commercial distillers and distributors. In accord with this decision, gradual restrictions on the participation of Jews in the distilling and sale of vodka in the countryside were reintroduced, while at the same time Jewish businessmen were encouraged to enter the ranks of the large-scale *otkupshchiki*, or leasers, even controlling areas in which they were not permitted to live.[37]

This new compromise was codified by a special codex on Jewish liquor rights published on August 15, 1845.[38] Here a clear distinction was drawn between Jewish guild merchants who were permitted to engage in vodka sale anywhere they chose and Jewish *meshchane* who were allowed to lease only enterprises that had no connection with liquor. In addition, a new provision was introduced: no Jew of any estate was henceforth to live in any tavern, inn, or establishment where liquor was served outside of cities and towns, to engage in the sale of any alcoholic beverage directly to consumers, or to distill liquor on his own. Large monetary penalties would be imposed on any landowner contravening these provisions, and the Jews concerned would be subject to fines for first offenses and then deprived of all rights and privileges and sentenced to forced labor for subsequent offenses.[39]

This distinction between Jewish liquor entrepreneurs and rural tavern keepers was retained even after the farming-out system itself was significantly altered by the introduction of a new excise tax (*aktsiz*) order in the Western Provinces in 1849.[40] But Jews apparently found ways of retaining their role in the sale of vodka in the countryside by selling vodka on the sly from other establishments that they leased from landlords. In response to this persistence, in June 1853 the government ordered that all Jewish leaseholders must hold formal contracts stipulating that no alcohol is involved in their ventures; in addition, the law prohibited Jews from residing permanently in villages and rural settlements.[41] This last provision seemed to be a reinstatement of the old expulsion policy, and indeed various local officials began to expel the Jews from the villages in their domains.[42] Only with the accession of Alexander II did the cycle start again: realizing the impracticality of such expulsions, the government again suspended them, until the next time that the prospect seemed feasible, the problems forgotten.

The new vodka policy did not succeed in abolishing the Jewish tavern keepers in the Western Provinces. Even after 1853, Jews continued to produce and sell liquor of all sorts throughout the countryside. But the 1845 and 1853 laws did begin to achieve their goals of reversing the trends in Jewish participation in the vodka industry, gradually diverting the bulk of business from the small-scale rural brewer and trader to the wealthy Jewish liquor entrepreneurs. No reliable statistics on the numbers of Jewish stills or taverns are extant; obviously forbidden in law, they could not be included in the periodic economic surveys of the government.[43] However, despite the rise in liquor production in the Russian Empire over the course of the century, the number of distilleries decreased from 2,489 in 1801 to 723 in 1860, with large-scale commercial enterprises overtaking the local stills on estates.[44] And in 1860, when the first report on excise duties owed by *otkupshchiki* was published, fourteen Jewish Honorary Citizens and guild merchants were liable for a total of 6,667,610 rubles per annum as the treasury's share in their vodka sales; Honorary Citizen—later Baron—Evzel Günzburg alone paid to the government 3,777,440 rubles per year.[45] Nicholas's government had, therefore, succeeded where his brother Alexander's had failed: Jewish *meshchane* were gradually driven out of the vodka industry and the countryside, in general, while the state's revenues from liquor continued to mount.

Trade and Commerce   A similar process of differentiation occurred in the most important realm of Russian-Jewish economics, domestic and foreign trade. Although specific figures are lacking on the percentage of Jewish traders and merchants in pre-Nicholaevan Russia, it is a well-established fact that under Polish rule the Jews dominated the commerce of the regions later forming the Pale— that was, after all, their historic reason for being in Poland in the first place. From the time of the first Partition, every Russian official who discussed the question noted and bemoaned the role of the Jews in trade. Writing in the *Journal of the Ministry of the Interior* in 1844, for example, one bureaucrat acidly complained,

One might say that every Jew is born a merchant. Anytime something comes into his hands, he is ready to sell it, to speculate on anything. In this regard, the women in no way yield to the men: they buy and sell on their own, sit in the markets and drag themselves through the streets and homes with various goods or supplies. . . .[46]

He failed to note, however, that in the period he was describing a major shift had taken place in the commercial activities of the Jews. While the Jewish guild merchant continued to dominate both foreign and domestic trade in the Western Provinces—particularly the crucial grain trade in the south[47]—the middling and petty Jewish trader was gradually being displaced by his wealthier co-religionists and by non-Jewish petty traders.

Part of this displacement resulted from the general transformation of the "fair economy" of the Russian Empire. During the course of the first half of the nineteenth century, the traditional fairs in the interior of Russia declined substantially as factory owners began to sell their products directly to consumers at permanent markets rather than at seasonal fairs, causing the near-disappearance of the old-fashioned itinerant trader, both Jewish and gentile.[48] Only in the Ukraine did the fairs grow during this period, but there, too, the wholesale merchant played a steadily declining role, losing ground to industrialists distributing their own products.[49]

The Jews, in addition, were affected by the government's war against contraband. The long-established cupidity of Russian border guards was compounded by the high tariffs imposed by the state to create an enormous incentive for smuggling Prussian and Austrian goods into the Western Provinces. The Jews, as the predominant mercantile element in the frontier regions, quite naturally played a major role in this extralegal trade. Although various Jewish communities attempted to restrain their members from yielding to the temptations of contraband by imposing bans of excommunication on smugglers,[50] the yields were too high, the risks too low to be ignored. Although the government deplored this activity, it was unable to find a solution that would work without adversely affecting its own revenues—until Nicholas himself took unilateral action in this regard.

In 1843, Minister of Justice V. N. Panin submitted a judgment on a standard lawsuit between a Jew and a noble to the emperor's approval. Since the Jew concerned lived on the western frontier of the empire, Nicholas was reminded of the problem of smuggling. Instead of accepting Panin's verdict, Nicholas ordered that all Jews living within fifty versts of the western borders be expelled to the interior of the provinces.[51] Although the ministers shared the tsar's concern with the problem of contraband, they expressed grave hesitation over the appropriateness of so extreme a measure. The Senate and the Committee of Ministers discussed the problem, called on Panin's legal advice, and sought some way diplomatically to dissuade Nicholas of his decision. The imperial will was steadfast; Nicholas insisted on the exact implementation of his order, permitting only an extension from two years to four for the evacuation of the Jews and the sale of their property.[52]

No precise information is available on the number of Jews expelled from the border territories after 1843, but indirect evidence points to a substantial reduction of smuggling activities in the years following the edict. Thus, the Berdichev fair, one of the main points of exchange of Western contraband, suffered a serious reduction in trade volume, from a turnover of 2,598,000 rubles in 1836 to merely 232,900 in 1843.[53] Of course, part of this was a reflection of the general decline of the fair caused by other economic factors, but it is clear that the precipitous fall was a direct consequence of the removal of Jews from the frontier territories. In 1846 the volume of trade climbed back to 600,000 rubles, but it dropped to 566,400 in 1856. Similarly, the number of Russian Jews trading at the Leipzig fair, the source of much of the contraband that made its way into Russia, declined dramatically throughout Nicholas's reign, particularly in its last decade.[54]

This did not mean, of course, that the petty Jewish traders disappeared from the Pale—only that the amount of business was substantially reduced, making it more and more difficult for the Jewish *meshchane* to make their living through trade. The wealthy Jewish merchants—whose income rose steadily throughout this period as the result of the expansion of the grain trade, the money market, and government orders of military and civilian supplies— were besieged by thousands of Jews yearning for some part of the commercial activity. As the Slavophile Ivan Aksakov put it in his description of the Ukrainian fairs of the 1850s, "around each Jewish wholesale merchant a hundred petty, poor Jews crowd, who secure goods from the wholesale store to sell . . . lending commerce a certain feverish vitality. . . ."[55] What seemed exotic and rather quaint to a nostalgic noble like Aksakov was the beginning of a crisis of major proportions in Russian-Jewry: the emergence of an increasingly pauperized *lumpenproletariat*, unable to find work in commerce, banned from their traditional occupations in the coun- tryside, gathering in the cities and towns of the Pale desperately chasing after every kopek. The Russian government did not have to institute a special *razbor* of the Jews in order to dissuade them from engaging in petty trade; Nicholas's other economic policies were persuasive enough. The problem was the lack of a reasonable alternative.

Factory Industry All of the studies on Russian-Jewish economic history of the period claim that a partial solution to this problem was the employment of several thousand Jews in newly established factories—the beginning of a Jewish proletariat in the Pale.[56] This is the most grievous example of the ideologically motivated distortions that beset the study of Russian-Jewish economic life. Aided by the tsarist government's careless use of the terms "factory" and "plant" to describe any manufacturing enterprise, however primitive and based on serf labor, Marxist historians, desperately seeking data to fill categories essential to their analyses, applied terms such as "capitalist factories" and "proletariat" to phenomena which clearly did not qualify for these appellations.

During the first half of the nineteenth century, Jewish businessmen, generally of the first merchant guild, began to invest quite extensively in two fields of manufacturing that were growing in the Russian Empire at this time, textiles and beet sugar. These were the two least "capitalistic" of industries, both developed by landlords on their estates primarily with the use of serf laborers. The textiles were for the most part woven by peasants in their homes; the sugar beets were so perishable and difficult to transport that they had to be processed as close as possible to the fields in which they were grown.[57] Owing to the protectionist policies of the Russian government—especially the high tariffs on Polish goods—the market for textiles and sugar grew considerably in Russia at this time, and Jewish leaseholders steadily moved to extend their leases from mills and stills to looms and sugar processors. The landowners in the Western Provinces were more than happy to farm out these rights to their Jewish leaseholders, particularly after the price of Russian (and Ukrainian) grain fell on the world market in the late 1820s, causing the landlords to seek new sources of capital.

Quite naturally, the Jewish "manufacturers" attempted whenever possible to hire their coreligionists in the new enterprises. This was generally impossible in the sugar plants, especially with the rising prohibitions on Jewish residence in the villages and rural settlements. But Jewish owners of textile manufacturies most often did hire Jews, and a few non-Jewish manufacturers did the same when they established plants in areas largely inhabited by Jews.

Dozens of pages have been devoted by scholars to meaningless statistical analyses of these Jewish hired laborers. The only reliable figures establish that some 2,185 Jews were employed in 673 enterprises in 1828.[58] No figures from the end of Nicholas's reign are available. Even the figure of 2,185 workers is not very informative, since the exact number of workers per "factory" is not known. There do seem to have been a very small number of plants of substantial size owned or run by Jewish capitalists, employing several hundred Jewish laborers at the beginning of Nicholas's reign. One in Ruzhin, Kiev Province, owned by Count Potocki-Kalinowski and leased to the Berdichev Jew Lislianskii, employed 276 workers, Jews and non-Jews. Another, which appears to have been owned directly by the second guild merchant Orel'(?) Fain-zil'berg, employed 259 workers, all but 4 of whom were Jews.[59] But these were exceptions. The majority of the factories seem to have been no more than conglomerations of at most a few dozen, mostly serf, spinners, weavers, and finishers. Tabulations of "average" number of workers per factory, compared between various provinces, are obvious statistical illusions that prove nothing.[60]

Far from an incipient proletariat, the Jews employed in textile manufactures of Nicholas's Russia were artisans of indeterminate skills who were hired by owners or leasers of peasant-based enterprises for a combination of economic and philanthropic motives. A true Jewish proletariat only developed in the Pale of Settlement in the last decades of the nineteenth century, when new factories producing hosiery, bristles, cigarettes, and matches were established and hired large numbers of unskilled Jews.[61] In Nicholas's time, even the mixed blessing of the proletarian life was unavailable to Russian Jews.

Artisans   Driven from trade, commerce, and the liquor industry, the Jewish *meshchane* flocked to the one branch of the economy that was not closed to them—crafts and handwork. The number of Jewish artisans seems to have risen steadily in the first half of the nineteenth century—although, here, too, there are only partial and unconfirmable statistics. For example, in 1789, 15.3 percent of the Jews in Berdichev were reported to be artisans, and in 1849, 29.6 percent; in Minsk the proportion rose from 13.1 percent in 1812 to 22.8 percent in 1851.[62]

The legal status of Jewish artisans was rather complex. In the backward economy of the Russian Empire, most craftsmen were peasants supplementing their field work with modest handwork; there were very small craft guilds consisting of full-time artisans, but membership in these guilds was only required of those wishing to hire assistants or take on apprentices. There were, therefore, no restrictions on Jews engaging in crafts on their own, and the statute of 1804, as well as that of 1835, permitted Jews to join any craft guild so long as this did not contravene local privileges.[63] In addition, various laws culminating in provision 63 of the 1835 statute allowed Jews to live outside the Pale while studying or training in a craft, and in a few cases Jews were kept on as full-fledged artisans in areas outside the Pale where there were no Christians to do the work.[64]

Such exceptions always elicited the passionate protest of the non-Jewish artisans of the areas concerned. For example, in 1844 a group of Christian artisans of Staraia-Rusa complained that Jewish tailors had moved into their territory and taken business away from them. The government investigated and found that there was only one Jewish tailor in town, who supplied the local army units with uniforms—a service that could not be provided by the non-Jewish craftsmen. Although the military authorities requested that the tailor be permitted to remain in town, upon repeated protests from the local *meshchane*, he was sent back to the Pale.[65] But the government had no standard policy on how to resolve such controversies; in several other cases affecting the Caucasus and Black Sea settlements, among others, the authorities ruled in favor of the Jews.[66] The decisions seem to have been made on the basis of who lobbied harder—or, possibly—contributed more.

In general, the Christian guild artisans resented the competition of the Jewish artisans, who were often better trained, and uniformly refused to enroll any Jews in their guilds. As a result, beginning in Nicholas's reign, groups of Jewish artisans petitioned the government for permission to establish their own guilds.[67] This, too, evoked the opposition of the established artisans, and very few Jewish guilds were officially licensed by the state. This situation led to serious problems when the *razbor* legislation was finally introduced in 1851: article 5 provided that the only Jewish craftsmen who would not be considered "nonproductive" were those who belonged to guilds.[68] In response, large numbers of Jews joined the craft guilds. Official figures show that 2,653 Jews in the province of Vitebsk belonged to guilds, as did 7,446 in Podolia and 4,234 in Kiev *guberniia*.[69] The government soon realized that it had gone too far. The Jews were now taking over the guilds in the Western Provinces, constituting some 70 percent of the licensed artisans in Podolia and 80 percent in Kiev. On April 16, 1852, the State Council sought to undo its own work by providing that the officials of craft guilds must be Christians no matter how many of their members were Jews, that the Jews could only be enrolled in the guilds if they were certified as artisans by guilds in major cities and towns, and that the authorities should take strict precautions to control the registration of unqualified Jews in the guilds.[70] In order to provide some other outlet for the masses of Jews seeking to avoid the harsh consequences of the *razbor*, the government created special "nonartisan" guilds *(neremeslennye tsekhi)* for urban Jewish workers who could not be accommodated by the established guilds—masons, carpenters, plasterers, draymen, et cetera. No information is available on whether these organizations were ever actually established; the government abandoned the entire *razbor* scheme as entirely impractical and overambitious.

By the end of Nicholas's reign, therefore, another significant shift had taken place in Russian-Jewish economic life: the flight from trade and commerce to crafts. Had the Jews been able to organize themselves into guilds and establish a regulated order of masters, journeymen, and apprentices, dividing the available work in some rational system, this shift might have been most beneficial. In the chaos of Russian law and the economy of the Western Provinces, however, the increase in Jewish craftsmen merely led to heightened competition, the dividing of an ever-dwindling cake into smaller and smaller pieces.

At the end of Nicholas's reign, as at its beginning, the Russian Jews were concentrated in one branch of the economy of the empire, trade and commerce, which they continued to dominate, at least in the areas in which they were permitted to live. But, as Simon Kuznets has demonstrated,

a high proportion to the total engaged in a specific field, in and of itself, is no special advantage. The specialization is partly a result of lack of antecedent experience, partly a result of restrictions. Relative complete domination by a minority of an industry means that it occupies both the high and the low position; i.e. profits from the well-managed and successful units and suffers from the poorly managed and economically less productive ones. . . . Any consideration of dominance of Jews must be related to the proportions of their numbers in the economic activities that absorb the masses of mankind; and in that sense dominance can be achieved only in narrow segments where it is an inevitable result of cohesion and specialization—and carries with it not only economic advantages but also disadvantages. The economic balance is uncertain, but it is likely to be negative as noneconomic factors propel Jews toward pursuits different from those that would normally follow from an economic calculation of potential returns to given ability and resources.[71]

During the years of Nicholas's rule, that balance swung sharply to the negative. The policies of the government, in part consciously, in part inadvertently, led to a dangerous new stratification of Russian-Jewish society along economic lines. While a small number of Jews were able to take advantage of the opportunities offered by these policies to amass great fortunes and to begin to replace the traditional aristocracy of wealth, learning, and communal power as the leaders of the community, much of their growth resulted from the displacement of large masses of Jews from their traditional occupations. At the same time, the government restricted the options available to these displaced Jews and forced them to congregate in cities and towns already overcrowded with impoverished Jews. The resultant differentiation between the rich and the poor only aggravated the forces set in motion by noneconomic factors which were threatening to pull Russian-Jewry apart.

In 1825 the economic life of the Jews in Russia was unhealthy but viable; in 1855 the disease had metastasized to the point where only radical new cures could prevent utter disaster. Although it

correctly diagnosed the problem, the Russian government stead-
fastly refused to alleviate the symptoms and soon abandoned the
one, impractical remedy which it had proposed, the *razbor* of the
Jews. The consequences of this obstinacy would soon prove to be
as detrimental to the tsarist regime as to Russian-Jewish society.

Conclusion

The 1843 expulsion of the Jews from the fifty-verst border region was Nicholas's only direct intervention into Jewish policy in the whole decade. However, the events of 1848 in Western Europe convinced him of the need to reassert his authority in all aspects of his administration and to distrust any advisers whose absolute subservience was questionable. Therefore, from 1848, Kiselev lost much of his influence with the emperor, although he remained in the upper ranks of ministerial advisers. Uvarov, on the other hand, was dismissed for being dangerously liberal and was replaced as minister of education by the primitive Prince P. A. Shirinskii-Shikhmatov, noted only for his statement, "I have neither my own thought nor will: I am only the blind tool of the Sovereign's will."[1] After dealing with several problems far more central than the Jews, Nicholas again turned his attention to them at the beginning of the 1850s.

As a result of the emperor's personal involvement in Jewish policy, none of the measures recommended by Kiselev's Committee for the Transformation of the Jews that were introduced after 1850 actually took hold as they were intended. For example, although there were isolated cases of violent attacks by police on Jews in traditional dress, outlawed by a law passed in May 1850, this prohibition was never enforced in full in any part of the Pale.[2] Nicholas was more interested in other questions—that is, the military. Beginning in December 1850 he turned his attention again to the conscription of the Jews and ordered that all Jewish communities be required to present three additional recruits as a penalty for every one missing from their quota. In addition, he introduced a fine of one additional conscript per every 2,000-ruble debt accrued by any Jewish community in the payment of its taxes.[3]

183

These unrealistic penalties caused the tax and conscription arrears of the Jewish communities to mount in intractable geometric progression. But Nicholas continued to demand more Jews. In June 1851 he decided to subject the Jews to the increased quotas that had been in effect since 1841 for the *grazhdane* and *odnodvortsy* of the Western Provinces, under which ten recruits were to be presented annually for every thousand members of the community, instead of the five to seven in biennial drafts as was the case for the rest of the population.[4] Such a raising of conscription quotas had been called for in the *razbor* proposal but was intended only for the "nonproductive" Jews. Under this law, all Jews subject to the draft were to be recruited at the higher norms—a change protested to no avail by a group of first-guild merchants, headed by Evzel Günzburg, who supported the *razbor* scheme.[5]

Obviously, the new quota put an unprecedented amount of pressure on the Jewish communities. There were simply not enough bodies to dress in uniforms and present to the authorities. This elementary demographic truth was not recognized by the tsar, who was certain that the crafty Jews were hiding their able-bodied men. In February 1853, Nicholas tried a new approach. The recruiting officials of the Jewish communities would themselves be drafted into penal battalions if they failed to meet their quotas.[6] This measure, too, was unsuccessful. Finally, Nicholas hit on the most radical solution to the problem of Jewish conscription arrears. He decreed that any Jewish community could arrest any Jew found traveling without a passport and present him as a recruit under its own quota; in this way an individual Jew could catch a passportless Jew and substitute him for a family member eligible for the draft.[7]

Even the extraordinarily cohesive Jewish community could not survive so socially disruptive a situation, particularly in a time of intense economic disarray. And so the Jews of Russia entered into a period of confusion and havoc that lasted almost three years. Their lives were completely dominated by the conscription crisis— just as the actions of the government in their regard were dominated by recruitment regulations. By the middle of 1854, Nicholas himself recognized that the crisis he had created in Jewish society was intolerable, and he granted a series of concessions to the Jews in their draft duties.[8]

The palliative was administered by Nicholas far too late to effect a cure; this would come only after the cause of the illness had passed from the scene. On February 18, 1855, Jews gathered together throughout the Pale and jubilantly celebrated their good fortune: Tsar Nicholas I was dead.

At the end of Nicholas's reign, as at its beginning, the overwhelming majority of Russian Jews lived traditional Jewish lives in autonomous communities insulated and isolated from Russian culture and mores. But the thirty years between 1825 and 1855 had witnessed an unprecedented obtrusion of Russian politics into Jewish society.

This intervention was motivated less by the deep-seated anti-Semitism of the tsar and his underlings than by their myopic perception of raison d'état, compounded by the inefficiency and essential conservatism of the imperial bureaucracy. Even when some of the more Western-oriented ministers to the emperor introduced a plan for the reform of Russia's Jews along the lines of the "civic betterment" of Western European Jewry, their naive hopes were frustrated by the institutional physiology of the Russian state. "Jewish policy" throughout Nicholas's reign remained shortsighted, repressive, and discriminatory. But it was not anomalous. On the contrary, it can only be understood as one part of Nicholas's overall approach to governing his subjects, especially those in the troublesome Western Provinces.

Whatever the context, Nicholas's government forcefully and regularly intervened in the internal workings of Jewish society in ways entirely novel; the consequence of this intrusion was the transformation of the very foundations of Russian-Jewish life.

It all started and ended with conscription. In thirty years, some seventy thousand Jewish males, most of them children, were drafted into an army that swore to eradicate the Jewishness of any of its soldiers who managed to survive. Few returned to their families; most either converted or died. But the loss to the Jewish community was not only, or even essentially, demographic. The true trauma resulted from the idiosyncratic nature of the recruitment system in Russia which left the choice of conscripts up to the officials of each Jewish community. The lay leaders of Russian Jewry were thus faced with a gruesome task, surpassed in its moral agony only in the boundless brutality of our own century: selecting which Jews should be sacrificed for the benefit of the community at large.

The dislocation that resulted from this ordeal was unprecedented. The previous psychological and institutional solidarity of Jewish society in Eastern Europe was shattered, the authority of the communal leaders was subverted—never, it seems, to be regained. This debilitation of the structural bases of Russian-Jewish life was aggravated by yet another plank of the government's policy for the Jews—the formal abolition of the kahal. Although the autonomous Jewish community persisted in fact as well as in law, it lost much of its former élan as the traditionalists and the enlightened, the rich and the poor, all increasingly looked to new sources of allegiance, organization, and power.

At the same time as the conscription and kahal policies eroded the social stability of Russian-Jewish society, its frail economic order was ravaged by other agencies and actions of the government. Convinced that Jewish peddlers and taverners—and not serfdom—caused the penury and misery of the Russian peasantry, Nicholas and his officials hounded the Jews out of their traditional occupations and homes in the villages but refrained from providing them with any practical alternative sources of livelihood in the towns and cities. Only the wealthiest strata of Jewish entrepreneurs were supported by the government, encouraged to fill the vacuum left by their coreligionists. The government claimed that it wanted to rationalize the economic order and status of the Jews; all it accomplished was to spawn more poverty, as well as competition among the Jews. The consequent rift only deepened the erosion of cohesiveness and solidarity which resulted from the other policies of the administration.

Ultimately, however, most destabilizing and disruptive of Jewish unity was the cultural and educational policy of Nicholas's regime. In the first decades of the nineteenth century, currents of Jewish enlightenment thought and practice had infiltrated into Russia. A few small pockets of maskilim appeared in the Pale; a larger number of Jews seem to have been attracted to the Haskalah but were unable or unwilling to join forces openly with the combative new movement. Soon, Nicholas's government—or rather, his minister of national enlightenment—began to support the purveyors and purposes of Haskalah. This alliance intensified the predisposition of Russian Jews to view the maskilim as powerful, well-connected friends of the authorities and hence a grave danger to traditional Jewish life. Although these fears quite probably were exaggerated, the intervention of the government was decisive. It led, on the one hand, to strengthening the Haskalah in Russia in size and in prestige and, on the other, to intensifying the opposition to enlightenment on the part of the bulk of Russian Jewry. Compromise and moderation became more and more difficult as the government increased its interest and activism. By the 1840s Russian Jewry was split into two new groups—the traditionalists and the enlightened.

The former remained by far the majority but increasingly felt themselves endangered by the minority. Those elements of traditionalist society, which for a combination of theoretical and practical reasons favored some collaboration with the government and the maskilim, were outvoted. At the same time, the old antagonisms between the Hasidim and their opponents, already mitigated by internal forces, steadily dissipated as the new enemy appeared on the horizon. Traditionalist Jewry in Russia began to transform itself into an Orthodoxy, united in a new militant defense against the dangers it perceived from the outside.

The maskilim, on the other hand, were convinced that the march of history was on their side. And so they solidified their alliance with and dependence on the government, which they identified with the beneficent and progressive forces of modernity and civilization. The most important arena of cooperation was education, specifically the network of state-sponsored schools for Jewish children, planned and regulated by the Ministry of National Enlightenment and staffed with maskilim. Despite the intense opposition of the Orthodox and hence the modest enrollments, the schools had a significant impact on Russian Jewry. They educated a large part of the next cohort of the Russian-Jewish intellectual elite and provided the maskilim with employment opportunities and financial security. Confident of their eventual victory and the inevitable liberation, the maskilim became, by the end of Nicholas's rule, a self-conscious and self-confident intelligentsia, dedicated to creating a new life and culture for Russia's Jews.

All the members of this intelligentsia believed that the evils plaguing the Jews would disappear if they would only shed some superstitions and outmoded customs and behave like decent, modern, educated Europeans and useful subjects of the tsar. But beyond this basic credo, the maskilim did not adhere to one view of Judaism or one strategy for its reform. Even on the fundamental question of relations with the government there was some diversity of opinion, some questioning of the axiomatic support of the paternalism of the regime—but open debate was hardly feasible, given the rigors of Nicholas's censors. Still, the issues were all raised and many of the future responses presaged; in the decades to come, these varying approaches and solutions would be elaborated and reworked as the deep-rooted pathology of Jewish life in Russia became more and more apparent.

Nicholas's censor A. V. Nikitenko wrote in his diary that "the main failing of the reign of Nicholas I consisted in the fact that it was all a mistake."[9] Certainly in regard to the Jews, Nicholas's policies were both ill-conceived and unsuccessful. But they did transform the context and much of the content of the lives of the Russian Jews. From their insular existence on the margins of Russian society, in Nicholas's time the Jews were thrust into the maelstrom of Russian life and politics. They have yet to emerge.

Notes
Bibliography
Index

LIST OF ABBREVIATIONS

AZJ   *Allgemeine Zeitung des Judentums* (Leipzig, 1837–)

Baron   Salo W. Baron, *The Russian Jew under Tsars and Soviets* (New York, 1964)

Dubnov   S. M. Dubnow [Dubnov], *History of the Jews in Russia and Poland*, 3 vols. (Philadelphia, 1916–20)

ES   *Evreiskaia starina* [Jewish antiquity], 13 vols. (St. Petersburg/Leningrad, 1909–30)

Gessen   Iulii Gessen, *Istoriia evreiskogo naroda v Rossii* [History of the Jewish people in Russia], 2 vols. (Leningrad, 1927)

Ginzburg   Shaul Ginzburg, *Historishe verk* [Historical works], 3 vols. (New York, 1937)

HLM   Binyamin Mandelshtam, *Ḥazon la-moʿeid* [A prophecy for our time], pt. 2 (Vienna, 1866–67)

KEY   S. G. Lozinskii, ed., *Kazennye evreiskie uchilishcha. Opisanie del byvshego arkhiva Ministerstva narodnogo prosveshcheniia* [Government Jewish schools: a description of the files of the former Ministry of National Enlightenment] (Peterburg [*sic*], 1920)

Lev   V. O. Levanda, *Polnyi khronologicheskii sbornik zakonov i polozhenii kasaiushchikhsia evreev* [A complete chronological collection of laws concerning Jews] (St. Petersburg, 1874)

MB   Barukh Halevi Epstein, *Sefer Mekor Barukh* [Spring of Barukh], 4 pts. in 3 vols. (New York, 1954)

PSZ   *Polnoe sobranie zakonov rossiskoi imperii* [Complete collection of laws of the Russian Empire], 2nd collection, 1825–55 in 30 vols. (St. Petersburg, 1830–56), cited by vol. no. followed by law no. (*PSZ* 2:2157)

TB   Isaac Ber Levinsohn, *Teʿudah be-yisraʾel* [Testimony in Israel], photo-offset of Vilna and Grodno edition of 1828 (Jerusalem, 1977)

ZMNP   *Zhurnal Ministerstva narodnago prosveshcheniia* [Journal of the Ministry of National Enlightenment] (St. Petersburg, 1834–)

Notes

Foreword

1. For the best survey of the history of the Jews in Russia before 1825, see Gessen, vol. 1. The standard survey of this subject in English is Dubnov, vol. 1, pp. 306–413.

Introduction

1. See the secret minutes of the Council of Ministers of Nicholas II, reproduced in Michael Cherniavsky, *Prologue to Revolution* (Englewood Cliffs, N. J., 1967), and Hans Rogger "Russian Ministers and the Jewish Question," *California Slavic Studies* 8 (1975):15–76.

2. On Russian anti-Semitism, see Shemu'el Ettinger, *Ha-'antishemiut ba-ʿet ha-ḥadashah* [Anti-Semitism in the modern age] (Tel Aviv, 1978), pp. 99–190.

3. I. G. Orshanskii, *Russkoe zakonodatel'stvo o evreiakh* [Russian legislation on the Jews] (St. Petersburg, 1877), pp. 3–6.

4. On Orshanskii, see Iulii Gessen, *Galleria evreiskikh deiatelei* [A gallery of Jewish activists] (St. Petersburg, 1898), pt. 2, for his career as a Jewish historian; and V. Nechaev, "Orshanskii, Il'ia Grigor'evich," *Entsiklopedicheskii slovar'* 42, pp. 230–31, on his career as a general Russian legal historian. All the other major historians of Russian Jewry, except for Dubnov, were trained as lawyers as well. For the connection between the professional study of Russian-Jewish history and the legal circles of St. Petersburg, see the fascinating article by M. M. Vinaver, "Kak my zanimalis' istoriei" [How we studied history], *ES* 1 (1909):41–54.

5. See Richard Pipes, *Russia under the Old Regime* (New York, 1974), pp. 288–90, and his article "Catherine II and the Jews: The Origins of the Pale of Settlement," *Soviet Jewish Affairs* 5 (1975), 2:14–15.

6. First provision of 1835 statute on the Jews, *PSZ* 10:8167. For the sake of convenience, every citation from *PSZ* has been cross-referenced with the appropriate number of the law in Levanda's compilation. Thus, the 1835 statute is Lev 304. On Jews distinguished from foreigners, see *PSZ* 1: 52/Lev 134.

7. Of all the historians of Russian Jewry, only Salo Baron remarked on this relativity, caused by the special nature of Russian society. See his "Newer Ap-

proaches to Jewish Emancipation," *Diogenes* 29 (1960):64. Throughout this study, an attempt has been made to pursue such a comparative approach. For the sake of clarity, at times the details of laws and policies which did not affect the Jews directly have been omitted, although consideration of these is implicit in the conclusions.

8. In this study the term "townspeople" as the English translation of *meshchane* is used. The more precise "burghers" is misleading, as it implies *Bürgerrecht* which did not obtain.

9. First collection of the *PSZ* 28:21,547. For a recent analysis of the statute and its background, see Shemu'el Ettinger, "Takanat 1804" [The Statute of 1804], *He-ᶜavar* 22 (1977):87–110.

10. *PSZ* 11:8924/Lev 321.

11. *KEY*, p. 6.

12. S. M. Seredonin et. al., *Istoricheskii obzor deiatel'nosti Komiteta ministrov* [Historical survey of the work of the Committee of Ministers] (St. Petersburg, 1902), vol. 2, pt. 1, p. 58.

13. *KEY*, p. 64.

14. Interesting, though sketchy details of the State Council's deliberations on the Jewish problem can be discerned from the brief descriptions of its archives published as *Opis' del arkhiva Gosudarstvennago soveta*, 16 vols. (St. Petersburg, 1908–10).

15. See, for example, W. Bruce Lincoln, *Nicholas I* (Bloomington and London, 1978), p. 289, and S. Beilin, "Iz istoricheskikh zhurnalov" [From historical journals], *ES* 6 (1913):542.

16. Gessen, vol. 2, pp. 16–17.

17. See pp. 59–69, for an explanation of this rather controversial classification of Uvarov.

18. *PSZ* 1: 403/Lev 143.

19. *PSZ* 2: 1582/Lev 164.

20. *PSZ* 2: 1583/Lev 165.

21. *PSZ* 2: 2884/Lev 190.

Chapter 1

1. See Sh. Ginzburg and P. Marek, *Evreiskie narodnye pesni v Rossii* [Jewish folk songs in Russia] (St. Petersburg, 1901), p. 42. The second line is censored in this edition.

2. Y. Slutsky and M. Kaplan, eds., *Hayalim yehudim be-ẓiv'ot 'Eiropah* [Jewish soldiers in the armies of Europe] (Israel Defense Force, 1967). See chapters on each of these countries.

3. Unfortunately, the literature on the conscription system of Imperial Russia is surprisingly scant, and no adequate scholarly account of the subject exists. The best, if outdated, analysis is Auguste de Haxthausen, *Les forces militaires de la Russie* (Berlin, 1853), pp. 66–90; see also John Shelton Curtiss, *The Russian Army under Nicholas I, 1825–1855* (Durham, 1965), pp. 233–36, for a sketchy account.

4. First collection of *PSZ* 17,249/Lev 44.

5. *PSZ* 17 432/Lev 47.

6. Gessen, vol. 2, p. 32. The first mention of the possibility of drafting Jews into the Russian army was made in Senator G. R. Derzhavin's 1800 Report on the Jews, published in his *Sochineniia* [Works] (St. Petersburg, 1868–78), vol. 7, p. 330.

7. See, for example, Sidney Monas, *The Third Section: Police and Society in Russia under Nicholas I* (Cambridge, Mass., 1961), pp. 11–12, and Roderick E. McGrew, *Russia and the Cholera, 1823–1832* (Madison, 1965), pp. 62–63.

8. Marquis de Custine, *La Russie en 1839* (Brussels, 1843), vol. 2, p. 50.

9. Kh. Korobkov, "Evreiskaia rekrutchina v tsartsvovanie Nikolaia I" [The recruitment of Jews in the reign of Nicholas I], *ES* 6 (1913): 70.

10. Translated in Nicholas V. Riasanovsky, *Nicholas I and Official Nationality in Russia, 1825–1855* (Berkeley and Los Angeles, 1969), p. 1.

11. Ginzburg, vol. 2, p. 78.

12. S. Dubnov, "Kak byla vvedena rekrutskaia povinnost' dlia evreev v 1827g." [How the recruit duty was introduced for the Jews in 1827], *ES* 2 (1909): 257.

13. Dubnov, "Recruit Duty," *ES* 2 (1909): 258.

14. Ibid., pp. 262–65.

15. *PSZ* 2: 1330/Lev 154.

16. *PSZ* 2: 1329/Lev 153.

17. In the 1832 Russian Legal Code, the *Svod zakonov rossiiskoi imperii*, vol. 4, bk. 1, sec. 12, only three groups—the inhabitants of the Baltic provinces, the Jews, and the *odnodvortsy* and *grazhdane* of the Western Provinces—had special recruitment regulations. In the 1842 *Svod*, vol. 4, bk. 1, sec. 11, twelve groups were listed as being governed by special statutes.

18. For the sake of comparison, both the 1832 and the 1842 redactions of the "Obshchii ustav rekrutskoi"—the General Recruitment Regulations—contained in the section of the *Svod* cited in note 17 have been referred to.

19. See, for example, the official history of the Ministry of War, *Stoletie Voennago ministerstva: glavnyi shtab*, vol. 4, pt. 2, bk. 1, sec. 2, pp. 329ff.

20. See I. G. Orshanskii, *Russian Legislation on the Jews* (St. Petersburg, 1877), p. 413; Gessen, vol. 2, p. 116; Ginzburg in *KEY*, p. xxvii.

21. A summary table of the draft quotas can be found in the official history of the Ministry of War, cited in note 19, as table 1 at the end of section 2.

22. See p. 184 for further discussion.

23. For the sake of convenience, only the article number of provisions of the 1827 Statute on the Recruitment of Jews has been cited. This provision was found in art. nos. 8, 10, and 74.

24. Art. no. 175 of the General Recruitment Regulations, 1832 version; see note 17.

25. Ibid., point 5. It is unclear if this provision was ever implemented.

26. *Svod voennykh postanovlenii* [Code of military orders] (St. Petersburg, 1838), pt. 2, bk. 1, sec. 2, no. 65.

27. 1827 statute, art. 68; *PSZ* 19: 18,240. Compare the situation in France after 1808 where "young Jews planning to enter the rabbinate could not enjoy the exemptions from military service granted to the clergy." (S. Posener, "The Immediate Economic and Social Effect of the Emancipation of the Jews in France," *Jewish Social Studies* 1 [1939]: 317.)

28. 1827 statute, art. 48.

29. Ibid., arts. 32 and 33.

30. Ibid., supplementary instructions, 3: 16.

31. 1827 statute, art. 49.

32. *PSZ* 3: 2045.

33. 1827 statute, app. D. There is an interesting discrepancy between this text of the Jewish Oath and that of a Hebrew translation of the time reproduced from archival sources by Shaul Ginzburg in Ginzburg, vol. 3, p. 10. In the Russian text, the last words of the first paragraph read *dlia zashchity zakonov zemli Izrail'skoi*—for the defense of the laws of the Land of Israel; the Hebrew translation reads *le-maʿan haẓalat 'arẓenu ve-toratenu ha-kedoshah*—for the defense of our land and Holy Torah. Was this a case of a censor-translator changing the text to comply with his own ideology? Of course, this oath is but one more in the long history of the *more judaico* since the Theodosian Code; see Salo W. Baron, *The Jewish Community* (New York, 1942), vol. 3, index.

34. 1827 statute, supplementary instructions, 2: 19–42.

35. Ibid., additional instructions to military authorities, nos. 1–14.

36. Ibid., nos. 91–95.

37. Ibid., nos. 88–90.

38. See, for example, the moving speech by Rabbi Yeḥezkel Landau of Prague to the first group of Jewish conscripts from that city, reproduced in Z. Von Weisel, "Yehudim be-ẓeva ha-keisarut ha-'ostrit-hungarit" [Jews in the army of the Austro-Hungarian Empire] in Slutsky and Kaplan, *Jewish Soldiers*, p. 20.

39. *PSZ* 4: 3052/Lev 193.

40. Ginzburg, vol. 3, p. 62.

41. Ibid., pp. 62–65.

42. Ibid., pp. 68–69.

43. Ibid., pp. 65–66.

44. Ibid., pp. 357–69.

45. M. Merimzon, "Razskaz starago soldata" [The study of an old soldier], *ES* 5 (1912): 407; I. Itskovich, "Vospominaniia arkhangel'skago kantonista" [Memoirs of an Arkhangel'sk Cantonist], *ES* 5 (1912): 56–57; M. Shpigel', "Iz zapisok kantonista" [From the notes of a Cantonist], *ES* 5 (1912): 251–54. Although written decades after the fact, and thus subject to some possible inaccuracies, these memoirs can be used as unquestionable sources since they all agree on major points and paint the same picture of the horrors of life in the Cantonist battalions.

46. Ginzburg, vol. 3, p. 89.

47. Ibid., pp. 95–99.

48. Ibid., pp. 99–102.

49. Ibid., p. 68.

50. Ibid., p. 69.

51. In his study on the conversion of Jews in the nineteenth century, N. Samter claimed that a majority of the 69,400 Jews who converted to Christianity during the century were Cantonists; see his *Judentaufen im 19ten Jahrhundert* (Berlin, 1906), p. 42. See also pp. 141–48.

52. See table cited in note 21. These figures have been cross-checked with the yearly recruit levies as published in the *PSZ*, and there is no significant deviation. The only official figures ever published can be found in the history of the Ministry of War, pt. 2, bk. 1, sec. 2, p. 209, which lists sporadic figures that correspond to these calculations, but refer only to Cantonists not to the total number of recruits. These figures are cited without reference to their source in Ginzburg, vol. 3, p. 36. The usually careful I. Levitats, *The Jewish Community*

in *Russia* (New York, 1943), p. 68 and Baron, p. 31, cite the same figures from Ginzburg as representing all recruits drafted in these years, not merely the Cantonists.

53. Itskovich, "Arkhangel'sk Cantonist," *ES* 5 (1912): 55; Shpigel', "Notes of a Cantonist," *ES* 5 (1912): 250; Ginzburg, 3: 19.

54. A. Fridberg, "Zikhronot mi-yemei neᶜurai" [Memoirs of my youth], *Sefer ha-shanah* 3 (1901): 86.

55. D. Brodskii, "Iak do Khresta privodili kantonistiv zhidiv" [How Jewish Cantonists were converted], *Zapiski istorichno-filologiches'koho vidilly Ukrains'koi Akademii Nauk* 12 (1927): 303, n. 1.

56. Alexander Herzen, *My Past and Thoughts*, trans. Constance Garnett, abr. ed. (New York, 1974), p. 169.

57. Ibid., p. 170.

58. Levitats, *Jewish Community in Russia*, p. 64.

59. O. Margolis, *Geshikhte fun yidn in rusland* [History of the Jews in Russia] (Moscow, 1930), pp. 328–29.

60. Ibid., pp. 330–33. Levitats, *Jewish Community in Russia*, p. 63, discusses this list but presents inaccurate statistics from it.

61. YIVO Institute for Jewish Research, Archives of the Kehillah of Minsk, Group RG 12, box 1, file 4/197.

62. In the most accurate listing of demographic data of this period, B. Miliutin, "Khoziaistvennoe ustroistvo i sostoianie evreiskikh obshchestv v Rossii" [The economic order and state of the Jewish community in Russia], *Zhurnal Ministerstva vnutrennikh del* 5 (1850): 262, the male population of the Jewish communities of Minsk and affiliated towns was officially put at 6,445. It can be assumed, therefore, the population one generation earlier was approximately 6,000.

63. See table cited in note 21.

64. A. B. Gottlober, "Zikhronot mi-yemei neᶜurai" [Memoirs of my youth], in his *Zikhronot u-masaᶜot*, ed. R. Goldberg (Jerusalem, 1976), p. 206.

65. D. Pines, "Bor'ba s khaperami" [Battle with the *khappers*], *ES* 8 (1915): 396–97.

66. Y. D. Dereviansky, "Di batsiung fun der gezelshaft un di regirungs-krayzn tsu der rabiner-shul" [The attitude of society and the authorities to the rabbinical seminary], *YIVO-Bleter* 10 (1936): 14–19.

67. Yeḥezkel Kotik, *Mayne zikhroynes* [My memoirs] (Berlin, 1922), pt. 1, pp. 177–80.

68. Y. L. Levin, "Zikhronot ve-raᶜayanot" [Memoirs and thoughts], *Sefer ha-yovel li-khvod Naḥum Sokolov* (Warsaw, 1904), p. 357.

69. See p. 184 for further discussion.

70. Yekutie'l Berman, "Shenot ra'inu raᶜah" [Years of evil], *Ha-meliz* (1861), p. 209.

71. Ibid.

72. Fridberg, "My Youth," pp. 94–95.

73. A. M. Dik, *Der erster (sic) nabor* [The first levy] (Vilna, 1871), p. 18.

74. Gottlober, "Memoirs," pp. 157–59. Professor Gerson D. Cohen informed me of fascinating parallels and precedents to such a letter-prayer—for example, in ancient Sumerian religion. On the latter, see William W. Hallo, "Individual Prayer in Sumerian: The Continuity of a Tradition," *Journal of the American Oriental Society* 88 (1968): 71–89.

75. For examples of folk songs recording these tactics, see S. Ginzburg and

P. Marek, *Evreiskie narodnye pesni v Rossii* [Jewish folk songs in Russia] (St. Petersburg, 1901), pp. 42–46.

76. S. Y. Fin, "Dor ve-doreshav" [A generation and its seekers], *Ha-karmel* 4 (1879): 193–96. See also pp. 148–54.

77. See, most importantly, the differing views on the social effects of Hasidism in Jacob Katz, *Tradition and Crisis* (New York, 1961), chaps. 21 and 22, and Shmuel Ettinger, "The Hassidic Movement—Reality and Ideals," in H. H. Ben Sasson, ed., *Jewish Society Through the Ages* (New York, 1972) pp. 251–66.

78. See his memoirs *Mah she-ra'u ʿeinai ve-shamʿu 'ozenai* [What my eyes saw and my ears heard] (Jerusalem, 1947), p. 14.

79. See pp. 124–27 for further discussion.

Chapter 2

1. Dubnov, vol. 2, pp. 34–37; Gessen, vol. 2, p. 47.

2. Unfortunately, no primary sources on these discussions can be located, and reliance has been placed on the secondary works which are not sufficiently detailed.

3. Gessen, vol. 2, p. 47.

4. The statute is *PSZ* 10: 8054/Lev 304. For the sake of clarity, the article nos. are noted in the text itself.

5. Contrary to the claims of many textbooks and maps, the Kingdom of Poland (more commonly known as Congress Poland) was never part of the Pale of Settlement. In general, the political and legal status of the Jews in the kingdom was substantially different from that of the "Russian" Jews, paralleling the divergent political, legal, and social structure of their host societies.

6. *PSZ* 10: 8052/Lev 303.

7. Rumors about such a provision swept through the Pale periodically, resulting in fascinating demographic and social abnormalities. See, on this question, Y. Halperin, "Nisu'ei behalah be-mizraḥ 'eiropah" [Panic marriages in Eastern Europe], *Zion* 27 (1962): 36–58. Restrictions on Jewish marriage age were not, of course, unique to Russia. On the restrictions in Germany and Austria, see, for example, Jacob Katz, *Out of the Ghetto* (Cambridge, Mass., 1973), pp. 10, 163–64, 194.

8. *PSZ* 10: 8192/Lev 307. No reference to this decree can be found in any of the standard histories of Russian Jewry.

9. *PSZ* 11: 9226/Lev 328.

10. *PSZ* 11: 12,486/Lev 404; Gessen, vol. 2, p. 52.

11. *PSZ* 11: 9722/Lev 336.

12. *PSZ* 2: 9843/Lev 338.

13. V. N. Nikitin, *Evrei zemledel'tsy* [Jewish farmers] (St. Petersburg, 1887), pp. 191–221.

14. *PSZ* 12: 10,242/Lev 345.

15. *PSZ* 14: 12,940/Lev 409; see I. Levitats, *The Jewish Community in Russia* (New York, 1943) pp. 52–56.

16. An interesting correspondence on this subject between Uvarov and

Bludov has been preserved in the Saul Ginzburg Materials, Rivkind Archive, The Hebrew University, File 22/3, no. 2, items i–v. Excerpts of this correspondence were published in the anonymous article "Tsenzura v tsarstvovanii Nikolaia I" [Censorship in the reign of Nicholas I], *Russkaia starina* 107 (1903): 658–63. A description of the denunciations of the maskilim can be found in Ginzburg, vol. 1, pp. 50–53, and in Y. Tsinberg, *Geshikhte fun der literatur bay yidn* [History of Jewish literature] (New York, 1966), vol. 10, pp. 67–69. One of the most interesting denunciations was written by I. B. Levinsohn, reprinted in his *Bet ha-'ozar (Shoreshei levanon)* [Treasurehouse: the rocks of Lebanon] (Vilna, 1871), p. 295.

17. See pp. 52–54 for further discussion.

18. Correspondence cited in note 16.

19. *PSZ* 11: 9649/Lev 334.

20. See "Censorship in the Reign of Nicholas I."

21. See Sidney Monas, *The Third Section: Police and Society in Russia under Nicholas I* (Cambridge, Mass., 1961), pp. 133–96.

22. Isaiah Berlin, "A Marvelous Decade," pt. 2, *Encounter* 26 (1955): 28.

23. On Hebrew and Yiddish publishing in Russia in this period, see the articles cited in S. Shunami, *Bibliography of Jewish Bibliographies* (Jerusalem, 1969), nos. 2979–86, and the relevant items regarding Poland, nos. 2951–74.

24. Gessen, vol. 2, p. 78.

25. The memorandum was published from archival sources by S. Dubnov in his "Istoricheskie soobshcheniia" [Historical notices], *Voskhod* (1901), iv: 29–40 and v: 3–9. For some reason, Dubnov left in question the actual author of the memorandum, stating that he knew for certain only that Kiselev supervised its editing and delivery. However, the chronology of the drafting of the memorandum and the appointment of the committee, established by Gessen from the archives of the Jewish Committee itself and available in part in *KEY*, seems to dispel all doubts regarding Kiselev's role in the writing of the memorandum. See Gessen, vol. 2, p. 78.

26. Memorandum, pp. 30–35. Unfortunately, all the sources of these spurious, and often curious, views cannot be traced. The only published work cited in the original notes to the memorandum is the *Histoire philosophique des Juifs depuis la décadence des Machabées*, published in Brussels in 1834 by the obscure French historian Jean-Baptiste Capefigue, from which Kiselev extracted only accurate factual data. The spurious "evidence" cited by Kiselev consisted of reports made to the various Jewish committees by pseudoscholars and converts denouncing Judaism and letters by naive maskilim taken out of context by the authorities. Until the archives of the Jewish committees are made available to scholars, this question, as so many others, will remain unresolved. It is clear, nonetheless, that a large part of this report is based on perceptions of Jews' moral degradation and potential utility to the state which were common in Western Europe at the time and formed the basis of much of "Jewish policy" in the West. See the discussion of Christian Wilhelm von Dohm's *Ueber die bürgerliche Verbesserung der Juden* and the various contributions to the Metz essay contest of 1788 in Jacob Katz, *Out of the Ghetto*, pp. 57–79.

27. Ibid., p. 3. Some of the specific recommendations made by Kiselev were reminiscent of those put forward by the governor-general of Lithuania, Frisel, in 1800, summarized recently by Ettinger, "The Statute of 1804."

28. Memorandum, pp. 3–5.

29. Ibid., pp. 4–7.

30. Ibid., pp. 8–9.
31. Several sections of Kiselev's report bear remarkable resemblance to Uvarov's report of 1841. See pp. 64–69 for further discussion.
32. Memorandum, pp. 37–40.
33. Max Lilienthal, "My Travels in Russia," in David Philipson, *Max Lilienthal, American Rabbi* (New York, 1915), p. 194.
34. Jacob Katz, *Out of the Ghetto*, p. 42–56.
35. Memorandum, pp. 39–40.
36. The Russian title was Komitet dlia opredeleniia mer korennogo preobrazovaniia evreev.
37. *KEY*, p. 44.
38. Gessen, vol. 2, pp. 81–82.
39. *PSZ* 6: 4369; *PSZ* 10: 7957; *PSZ* 15: 13,591. Also D. Doroshenko, *Narys istorii Ukrainy* [Outline of the history of the Ukraine] (Warsaw, 1933), vol. 2, p. 296.
40. *PSZ* 10: 4869; Doroshenko, *Outline of History*, p. 298; A. Romanovich-Slavatinskii, *Dvorianstvo v Rossii* [The nobility in Russia] (St. Petersburg, 1870), p. 94; on the conscription of these ex-nobles, see *PSZ* 10: 4869. See also p. 184.

Chapter 3

1. There is still no acceptable study of the Haskalah in any country in Europe. The best accounts are the standard textbooks on Hebrew (and in part, Yiddish) literature, Yosef Klausner, *Historiah shel ha-sifrut ha-ʿivrit ha-hadashah* [History of modern Hebrew literature] (Jerusalem, 1953–56), 6 vols., and Y. Tsinberg, *History of Jewish Literature* (New York, 1966), which are limited since they approach the subject purely from the vantage point of literary history and do not treat Haskalah writings in non-Jewish languages in any depth. Important, too, are the several studies on the Haskalah by Isaac Eisenstein-Barzilai; Shalom Spiegel, *Hebrew Reborn* (Cleveland, 1957); and the chapters on Haskalah in Jacob Katz, *Tradition and Crisis* (New York, 1961) and *Out of the Ghetto* (Cambridge, Mass., 1973).
2. A sketchy account of these men (except for Horowitz) can be found in the first English work on the Haskalah, Jacob S. Raisin, *The Haskalah Movement in Russia* (Philadelphia, 1913); on Zalkind Horowitz, see Arthur Hertzberg, *The French Enlightenment and the Jews* (New York, 1968), pp. 298–99, 334–35, 338; also Klausner, *Historiah*, vol. 3, pp. 20–25, on Nevakhovich.
3. See Efra'im Kupfer, "Li-demutah ha-tarbutit shel yahadut 'ashkenaz ve-hahameha be-me'ot ha-14–15" [To the cultural characteristics of Ashkenazic Jewry in the 14th–15th centuries], *Tarbiz* 42 (1972–75): 113–47; Haim Hillel Ben Sasson, *Hagut ve-hanhagah* [Thought and leadership] (Jerusalem, 1959), pt. 1; Simha Assaf, *Mekorot lo-toledot ha-hinukh be-yisra'el* [Sources on the history of Jewish education] (Tel Aviv, 1925), vol. 1, pp. 40–73; see also the provocative essay by Emanuel Etkes, "Ha-Gr" a ve-ha-haskalah: tadmit u-mezi'ut" [The Gaon of Vilna and the Haskalah: image and reality], *Perakim be-toledot ha-hevrah ha-yehudit be-yimei ha-beinayim u-veʿet ha-hadashah mukdashim le-profʾ Yaʿakov Kaz* (Jerusalem, 1980), pp. 192–217.

4. See, for example, Klausner, *Historiah*, vol. 3, pp. 25–32, who provides a bibliography on this figure.

5. Cited in M. Peikazh, *Ḥasidut Braẓlav* [Bratslav Hasidism] (Jerusalem, 1972), p. 30.

6. S. Stanislavskii, "Iz istorii i zhizni odnoi evreiskoi shkoly (1826–1853gg), kul'turno-biograficheskii ocherk" [From the history of one Jewish school (1826–1853), a cultural biographical note], *Voskhod* 4 (1884): 132; *KEY*, p. 91n.

7. B. Natanson, *Sefer ha-zikhronot, divre yemei ḥayai Riba"l* [Book of memoirs. Biography of Isaac Ber Levinsohn] (Warsaw, 1878), pp. 3–9.

8. This grammar, *Yesodei leshon Rusiah*, was never published, and its manuscript was lost during Levinsohn's own lifetime. Klausner remarked sarcastically that this was not a great loss, since Levinsohn did not know Russian well enough to teach it to others (Klausner, *Historiah*, vol. 3, p. 40). Of course, this very ignorance would make the work very interesting to historians and linguists.

9. Levinsohn's letter to Shishkov was published along with comments by Iulii Gessen in *Perezhitoe* 1 (1908), documentary section, pp. 23–27.

10. Joseph I. Schneersohn, *The "Tzemach Tzedek" and the Haskalah Movement* (Brooklyn, 1969), p. 15.

11. Levinsohn letter to Shishkov.

12. Natanson, *Isaac Ber Levinsohn*, p. 49.

13. Klausner, *Historiah*, vol. 3, pp. 47–48.

14. Sh. Y. Fin, "Safah le-ne'emanim" [Words to the faithful], *Ha-karmel* 4 (1880): 671. The story of the Society of Seekers after Enlightenment is a curious one: first mentioned by Ze'ev Jawetz in *Kenesset* (1867): 139, and picked up by Yaʿakov Halevi Lifshiẓ, *Zikhron Ya'akov*, vol. 1, pp. 74–75, it came to be thought of as a true society, functioning throughout the Pale, although there is no indication whatever that it ever existed. In Schneersohn, *The "Tzemach Tzedek,"* p. 35, it is described as a veritable conspiracy coordinating heresy across Europe.

15. The most reasonable of these determinists was Raphael Mahler, *Divrei yemei yisra'el* [History of the Jews] (Merḥaviah, 1962), vol. 2, bk. 1, pp. 13–48; more radical was O. Margolis, *History of the Jews in Russia* (Moscow, 1930), representative of the Soviet scholarship on the Haskalah of the 1920s and 1930s.

16. See pp. 170–80.

17. On Levinsohn's poverty and strategems to escape from it, see Natanson, *Isaac Ber Levinsohn*, and Klausner, *Historiah*, vol. 3, p. 59.

18. See Joachim Tarnopol, *Notices historiques et caractéristiques sur les israélites d'Odessa* (Odessa, 1855), pp. 64–66, 137–66. On the doctors, see Gessen, "K sud'be evreev-vrachei v Rossii" [On the fate of Jewish doctors in Russia], *ES* 3 (1910): pp. 612–23.

19. Iulii Gessen, "Smena obshchestvennykh techenii, I. B. Levinsohn i d-r M. Liliental' " [The shift in social trends: I. B. Levinsohn and Dr. M. Lilienthal], *Perezhitoe* 3 (1911): 15–18. In 1847, Uvarov granted Levinsohn a sum of fifty rubles for his efforts. Ibid., p. 45.

20. Of the eleven original works, five were by Levinsohn, one by M. A. Ginzburg, one by Yaʿakov Kaplan, one by A. B. Gottlober, and three by H. S. Slonimskii, an accomplished mathematician whose works provide an interesting case of the gradual suspension of rabbinical approbations to Haskalah works. Slonimskii's first mathematic tract, *Mosedei ḥokhmah*, did receive the approval of a rabbi, since it appeared to be part of the traditional genre of religiously neutral arithmetic and algebra textbooks published in Hebrew. His next work,

Kokhva de-shavit, delved into the more problematic area of astronomy and contained some corrections of the Hebrew calendar; it was not approved by a rabbi, nor were any of Slonimskii's subsequent books. An interesting memoir on Slonimskii was recently published by his grandson, the noted composer Nicholas Slonimsky—"My Grandfather Invented the Telegraph," *Commentary* 63 (1977): 56–60.

21. *Pirḥei ẓafon* [Flowers of the north] (Vilna, 1841–44).

22. Tarnopol, *Notices historiques*, pp. 81–91; Report in *ZMNP* (1835), sec. 8, pp. 608–12.

23. Ibid.

24. *KEY*, pp. 33–34. On Stern, see the very laudatory obituary in *Odesskii vestnik*, republished in *Russkii invalid* 40 (September 21, 1853): 40; and *ZMNP* (1841), no. 11, p. xliii.

25. L. M. Bramson, *K istorii nachal'nago obrazovaniia evreev v Rossii* [To the history of primary education among Russian Jews] (St. Petersburg, 1896), p. 19; A. Beletskii, *Vopros ob obrazovanii russkikh evreev v tsarstvovanie Imperatora Nikolaia I* [The question of the education of Russian Jews in the reign of Emperor Nicholas I] (St. Petersburg, 1894), pp. 10–11.

26. Adolf Ehrlich, *Entwickelungsgeschichte der Israelitischen Gemeindeschule zu Riga* (St. Petersburg, 1894), pp. 2–10.

27. See, for example, Dubnov, vol. 2, pp. 46–58; Louis Greenberg, *The Jews in Russia* (New Haven, 1944), pp. 32–36, for the treatment in the two most popular histories of Russian Jewry.

28. See the most recent exposition of this point of view, Nicholas Riasanovsky, *Nicholas I and Official Nationality in Russia, 1825–1855* (Berkeley and Los Angeles, 1969), pp. 70–72, 126–27.

29. James Flynn, "S. S. Uvarov's 'Liberal' Years," *Jahrbücher für Geschichte Osteuropas* 20 (1972): pp. 48–91; idem, "Tuition and Social Class in the Russian Universities: S. S. Uvarov and 'Reaction' in the Russia of Nicholas I," *Slavic Review* 35 (1976): pp. 232–48; Cynthia H. Whittaker, "Count S. S. Uvarov: Conservatism and National Enlightenment in Pre-Reform Russia," Ph.D. diss., Indiana University, 1971.

30. M. Stepanov and F. Vermale, "Zhozef de Mestr v Rossii, no. 3: Pis'ma Zhozefa de Mestra k S. S. Uvarovu" [Joseph de Maistre in Russia, no. 3: Joseph de Maistre's letters to S. S. Uvarov], *Literaturnoe nasledstvo* 29/30 (1937): 677–712.

31. See his biography in the *Entsiklopedicheskii slovar'*, vol. 67, p. 419–20.

32. *Etudes de philologie et de critique* (Paris, 1845) and *Esquisses politiques et litteraires* (Paris, 1848).

33. Alexander Herzen, *My Past and Thoughts*, trans. Constance Garnett, abr. ed. (New York, 1974), vol. 1, p. 115.

34. S. S. Uvarov, *L'Empereur Alexandre et Buonaparte* (St. Petersburg, 1814), p. 13.

35. Cited in Riasanovsky, *Nicholas I*, pp. 70–71.

36. Stepanov and Vermale, "Joseph de Maistre," pp. 706–7.

37. Ibid., pp. 708–10: Whittaker, "Count S. S. Uvarov," pp. 99, 141.

38. From an 1818 speech cited by Whittaker, "Count S. S. Uvarov," p. 99.

39. S. S. Uvarov, *Extrait du compte-rendu du Ministère de l'instruction publique pour l'année 1837* (St. Petersburg, 1837), p. 27.

40. See, for example, Isaiah Berlin, *Vico and Herder* (New York, 1976), p. 159.

41. See his "Projet d'une academie orientale," republished in his *Etudes de philologie et de critique* (Paris, 1845), p. 35.

42. *ZMNP* 5 (1835): 178–80.

43. Cited by Beletskii, *The Question of Education*, pp. 22–23.

44. See pp. 64–65 for further discussion.

45. Shaul Ginzburg, *Amolike Peterburg* [St. Petersburg in the past] (New York, 1944), p. 77.

46. Ibid.

47. *Sbornik postanovlenii po Ministerstvu narodnago prosveshcheniia* [Collection of orders of the Ministry of National Enlightenment] (St. Petersburg, 1876), vol. 2, sec. 2, pp. 227–43.

48. See pp. 70–72 for further discussion.

49. Orders of the Ministry of National Enlightenment, p. 232.

50. Ibid.

51. Ibid., pp. 233–34. The last lines in Russian: ". . . tak chto stareishie evrei govoriat: 'Eti uchilishcha prekrasny, dukh v nikh chisto evreiksii, a uchen'e vedet v khristianstvu'; v smysle zakorenelykh priverzhentsev evreiskikh predrazsudkov i sueveriia, eta slova znachat: "uchen'e vo vnov' uchrezhdaemykh uchilishchakh dolzhno malo po malu unichtozhit' v evreiakh fanatizm raz'edineniia i priobshchit' ikh k obshchemu nachalu grazhdanstvennosti.' V etom otnoshenii, oni ne oshibaiutsia, ibo religiia kresta ne est' li chisteishii simvol grazhdanstvennosti vsemirnoi?" The penultimate word, critical to Uvarov, is very difficult to translate, as it can in various contexts mean civilization, civil society, civic spirit, et cetera. The problem stems from the very different conceptions of *civitas* in Russia and the West—or rather, the absence of that concept in Russia. This term has been rendered, with deliberate archaism, as "civility," in the sense both of "the state of being civilized" and "behavior befitting a citizen," as the Oxford English Language Dictionary defines the term.

52. See the frequently cited discussion of this passage in M. Morgulis, "K istorii obrazovaniia russkikh evreev" [On the history of the education of Russian Jews] in his *Voprosy evreiskoi zhizni* (St. Petersburg, 1903), p. 39. Interestingly, contemporary Russian Jews did not share the misreading of the report. Sh. Y. Fin cites it in his 1880 article, "Words to the Faithful," expressing some hesitation over Uvarov's views on the Talmud but stating "nonetheless, the main thrust of his words are true." For Fin, Uvarov's support of the Haskalah's approach to Hebrew and biblical studies was critical; this article was written as part of the *Kulturkampf* of the 1880s on whether enlightened Jews should use Hebrew or Russian, with Fin citing Uvarov in defense of Hebraism. After the pogroms of the 1880s, such a positive evaluation of Uvarov or any Russian minister was impossible for most members of the Russian-Jewish intelligentsia; only the "assimilationists" such as Bramson and Beletskii, in their works cited above, defended Uvarov and Nicholas's regime, and later Soviet-Jewish historians such as O. Margolis argued that the religious motive in the government's Jewish policy was merely a mask for economic oppression and was not unique to the Jews.

53. Orders of the Ministry of National Enlightenment, p. 521. In Russian, the line reads: "Tsel' obrazovaniia evreev sostoit v postepennom sblizhenii ikh s khristianskim narodonaseleniem, i v iskorenenii sueveriia i vrednykh predrazsudkov, vnushaemykh ucheniem Talmuda."

54. Thus, for example, Joachim Tarnopol used the term *sblizhenie* in his

1868 work calling for religious reform, *Opyt sovremennoi i osmotritel'noi reformy v oblasti iudaizma v Rossii*, in the following context:

> We must strive for the time when in response to our fulfillment of the obligations laid upon us by the state and society, we shall attain a greater and greater degree of participation in societal life, and the granting of civic rights. . . . In order to attain the first, i.e., internal emancipation, we must expunge everything that separates us from our brethren of different origins; only thus will a gradual *rapprochement* [*sblizhenie*] between us and the latter be possible [p. 251].

Clearly, Tarnopol, the fierce nationalist who resigned from *Rassvet* claiming that it was too critical of the Jews, did not advocate their conversion to Christianity. The term *sblizhenie* is neutral and nonspecific: it could mean anything to anyone.

55. Cited in Yakov Shatski, *Yidishe bildungs-politik in poyln fun 1806 biz 1866* [Jewish educational politics in Poland, 1806–1866] (New York, 1943), p. 82. In his introduction to *KEY*, Shaul Ginzburg unfairly ridiculed Uvarov's claim that the Russian Jews did not know Hebrew (p. lii). Clearly, Uvarov had learned this from the maskilim themselves, who continuously mocked the state of Hebrew in traditional Jewish society. Indeed, to at least some contemporary maskilim, Uvarov appeared as a positive reformer precisely because he supported Hebrew studies.

56. *ZMNP* (1835): sec. ix, pp. 715–16.

57. Orders of the Ministry of National Enlightenment, p. 243.

58. As he wrote in his *Essai sur la regeneration physique, morale, et politique des Juifs* (Metz, 1789), p. 132: "L'entiere liberté religieuse accordée aux Juifs, sera un grand pas en avant pour les réformer et j'ose le dire, pour les convertir; car la verité n'est persuasive qu'autant qu'elle est douce: la verité, dit-on, déchire quelquefois le sein qui l'enfante." On Grégoire's missionary hopes, see P. Grunebaum-Ballin, "Grégoire convertisseur? ou la croyance au 'Retour d'Israel'," *Revue des études juives* 121 (1962): 388, 397, and Ruth E. Necheles, "The Abbé Grégoire and the Jews," *Jewish Social Studies* 33 (1971): 122–24. A similar argument has recently been made regarding a later controversial figure on New York's Lower East Side: see Jeffrey S. Gurock, "Jacob A. Riis: Christian Friend or Missionary Foe—Two Jewish Views," *American Jewish History* 71 (1981): 37–56.

59. See Jacob Katz, *Out of the Ghetto*, pp. 218–19.

60. Lilienthal to Ludwig Philippson, *AZJ* 6 (1842): 603; O. M. Lerner, *Evrei v novorossiskom krae* [Jews in New Russia] (Odessa, 1901), pp. 25–28.

61. Lerner, *Jews in New Russia*, pp. 25–28.

62. Reproduced in B. Natanson, *Sefer ha-zikhronot, divre yemei havai Riba"l* [Book of memoirs. Biography of Isaac Ber Levinsohn] (Warsaw, 1878), pp. 53–54.

63. Lerner, *Jews in New Russia*, p. 29.

64. Lilienthal to Philippson, p. 603.

65. David Philipson, "Max Lilienthal in Russia," *Hebrew Union College Annual* 12–13 (1937–38): 828–29.

66. Ibid.

67. Letter to Dr. Loewi of Furth, Philipson, "Max Lilienthal in Russia," p. 838.

68. Max Lilienthal, "My Travels in Russia" in David Philipson, *Max Lilienthal, American Rabbi* (New York, 1915), pp. 247–48.

69. Philipson, "Max Lilienthal in Russia," pp. 833–37.

70. *Iggerot Shada"l* [Correspondence of S. D. Luzzatto] (Roka, 1894), Letter 299, p. 738, and 302, p. 753.

71. *Sbornik postanovlenii po Ministerstvu narodnago prosveshcheniia* [Collection of orders of the Ministry of National Enlightenment] (St. Petersburg, 1876), vol. 2, sec. 2, p. 229.

72. Ben-Zion Katz, *Rabanut, ḥasidut, haskalah* [Rabbinism, Hasidism, Haskalah] (Tel Aviv, 1958), p. 240.

73. Lilienthal to Philippson, p. 603.

74. *KEY*, pp. 86–88.

75. Shaul Ginzburg Materials, Rivkind Archive, The National and University Library, The Hebrew University of Jerusalem, Collection 4°, 1281A file 24/8, folios 6–8.

76. *KEY*, pp. 103.

77. Lilienthal, "My Travels," p. 261.

78. See, for example, Louis Greenberg, *The Jews in Russia* (New Haven, 1944), p. 35.

79. See pp. 86–96 for further discussion.

80. Lilienthal to Philippson, p. 603.

81. *HLM*, p. 25.

82. Lilienthal, "My Travels," pp. 309–11.

83. L. Levanda, "Shkoloboiazn' " [Fear of schools], *Evreiskaia biblioteka* 5 (1875): 85–88.

84. Lilienthal to Philippson, p. 605.

85. *HLM*, pp. 30–32.

86. Ginzburg Materials, Rivkind Archive, file 13/1, no. 25, p. 22

87. Ibid., no. 39, p. 52.

88. *PSZ* 17: 15,771/Lev 462.

89. His instructions from the ministry are reproduced in Lilienthal, "My Travels," pp. 331–33.

90. A. B. Gottlober, "Ha-gizrah ve-habiniah" [The cutting and the building], *Ha-boker 'or* 3 (1878): 912–13, on Fin translating the work. *Maggid yeshuʿah* was published in Vilna, 1842, and is available in a reprint in *Ha-pulemus ʿal "ha-haskalah mi-taʿam" be-rusiah, 1842–1843* (no editor listed) (Jerusalem, 1966).

91. *Maggid yeshuʿah*, pp. 7–12, in particular.

92. Joseph I. Schneersohn, *The "Tzemach Tzedek" and the Haskalah Movement* (Brooklyn, 1969), p. 50.

93. Ginsburg Materials, Rivkind Archive, file 13/1, no. 11, p. 21, contains Lilienthal's report to Uvarov on the trip; see also Lilienthal, "My Travels," pp. 343–63, and David Philipson, *Max Lilienthal*, pp. 30–35.

94. Lilienthal described his meeting with Rabbi Yiẓhak in a letter to Nisan Rosenthal, Rivkind Archive, file 17/4, no. 1, and Lilienthal, "My Travels," pp. 343–53. The Orthodox version is quite different: see *MB*, vol. 2, pp. 1076–78; *MB* vol. 4, pp. 1920–21; and Yaʿakov Halevi Lifshiẓ, *Zikhron Yaʿakov*, pp. 82–83.

95. M. Y. Berdichevsky, "Toledot yeshivat ʿeẓ-hayim" [History of the Volozhin yeshivah], *He-'asif* 3 (1886): 239–40; Lilienthal reported that Rabbi Yiẓhak told him, "After the service I explain to them some chapters of the *sidrah* of the week, and the *haphtarah* with the commentary of *Rashi*, adding some free explanations of my own, into which I interweave some remarks from the commentary of *Moshe Dessau* (Mendlessohn)." Lilienthal, "My Travels," p. 348.

96. *MB*, vol. 2, pp. 1076–78.

97. *HLM*, pp. 41–42.

98. *KEY*, pp. 66–68.

99. See Iulii Gessen's article (under spelling J. Hessen), "Die russische Regierung und die westeuropäischen Juden, Zur Schulreform in Russland 1840–1844," *Monatsschrift für Geschichte und Wissenschaft des Judentums* 57 (1913): 257–71, 482–500.

100. *KEY*, pp. 68–69.

101. *KEY*, pp. 71–72.

102. Ibid.

103. *KEY*, p. 68.

104. *KEY*, p. 70.

105. A. Sh. Heilman, *Sefer Bet rebi* [House of my master] (reprint ed. Tel-Aviv, 1965), pt. 3, p. 229.

106. See pp. 84–85 for further discussion.

107. Iu. Gessen, "Prosveshchenie" [Enlightenment], *Evreiskaia entsiklopediia*, vol. 13, p. 47. In his work on the education of Jews in Nicholas's time, A. Beletskii also added some unprovable details about the rabbis' ideas; see his *Vopros ob obrazovanii russkikh evreev v tsarstvovanie Imperatora Nikolaia I* [The question of the education of Russian Jews in the reign of Emperor Nicholas I] (St. Petersburg, 1894), pp. 70–72.

108. Schneersohn, *The "Tzemach Tzedet,"* p. 46.

109. Ibid., p. 47.

110. Ibid., pp. 53–54.

111. Rabbi Shelomo Zalman of Neustadt, *Sefer bet 'avot* [House of fathers] (Berlin, 1838–39), p. 244. I am indebted for this citation to Dr. Emanuel Etkes of the Hebrew University.

112. Lifshiẓ, *Zikhron Yaʿakov*, pp. 101–2.

113. See letter cited in *KEY*, p. 70.

114. *HLM*, pp. 43–44.

115. *PSZ* 19: 18,240/Lev 505.

116. Published in the Orders of the Ministry of National Enlightenment, pp. 521–67.

117. Ibid., art. 1.

118. Ibid., arts. 5, 6.

119. Ibid., art. 7.

120. Ibid., art. 10.

121. Ibid., arts. 4, 16.

122. Ibid., art. 17.

123. Ibid., art. 23.

124. Ibid., supplementary instructions on the elementary schools, arts. 14, 49.

125. Ibid., general regulations, arts. 13–25.

126. Ibid., temporary rules, arts. 3–11.

127. Ibid., arts. 18–20, 37–43.

128. Ibid., arts. 28–36.

129. Dubnov, vol. 2, p. 59; Baron, p. 37; David Philipson, "Max Lilienthal, 1815–1915," *Centenary Papers and Others* (Cincinnati, 1919), pp. 162–65, are the best-known examples.

130. Aharon Surski, *Toledot ha-ḥinukh ha-torati be-tekufah ha-ḥadashah* [History of Torah education in the modern era] (Bnei Brak, 1967), p. 39.

131. Gessen, "Die russische," p. 500.

132. M. Morgulis, "K istorii obrazovaniia russkikh evreev" [On the history of the education of Russian Jews] in his *Voprosy evreiskoi zhizni* (St. Petersburg, 1903), pp. 69–71.

133. Ibid.

134. Philipson, *Centenary Papers*, p. 45.

135. David Kahana, "Lilienthal ve-haskalat ha-yehudim be-rusiah" [Lilienthal and the Russian Haskalah], *Ha-shiloaḥ* 27 (1912): 555.

136. Morgulis, "On the History of Education," pp. 69–71.

137. Philipson, *Centenary Papers*, p. 45.

138. "Max Lilienthal," *Encyclopedia Judaica*, vol. 11 (1971), p. 244.

139. These memoranda are found in the Ginzburg Materials, Rivkind Archive, Jerusalem, file 13/1, no. 11.

140. Ibid.

141. See p. 104 for further discussion.

142. He even published a paean to Uvarov's hero, Herder, in *ZMNP* 65 (1844): pt. v, pp. 1–30.

143. *AZJ* 10 (1846): 56.

144. *AZJ* 10 (1846): 98.

145. "Russische-jüdische Skizzen," *AZJ* 11 (1847): 154–55, 213–15, 226–30, 547–49, 615–19, 683–86; 12 (1848): 232–33.

146. Ibid., p. 232.

147. Ibid., p. 231.

148. Lilienthal, "My Travels," p. 266.

149. "The Russian Government and the Russian Jews: My Personal Experience," *Jewish Times* 1 (1870): 3–4.

150. *PSZ* 19: 17,503/Lev 484.

151. Philipson, *Max Lilienthal*, p. 155.

152. Ibid., pp. 157–58; full text of letter in Sophie Lilienthal, *Lilienthal Family Record* (San Francisco, 1930), p. 51; see p. 91 for further discussion.

153. Lilienthal, *Family Record*, p. 52.

154. See, for example, Iu. Gessen, "Tsadik Mendel Liubavichskii" [The Tsadik Mendel of Liubavich], *Voskhod* 25 (1905): 119.

155. *KEY*, p. 118; *Family Record*, pp. 50, 53.

156. *KEY*, p. 118.

157. Ibid.

158. Philipson, *Max Lilienthal*, p. 48.

159. Ibid., p. 133, n. 1.

160. I am indebted to Prof. Jacob Rader Marcus for first bringing this work to my attention.

161. Philipson, *Max Lilienthal*, p. 145; full text in Lilienthal, *Family Record*, p. 26.

162. Ibid., pp. 23–24.

163. Ibid., p. 20.

164. See Lilienthal's salary record in *KEY*, p. 106, and recall Henry Adams's report that John Quincy Adams was unable to live up to the standards of St. Petersburg society.

165. *KEY*, pp. 105–6.

166. Ginzburg Materials, Rivkind Archive, file 13/1, no. 9, 15–16; Morgulis, "On the History of Education," p. 54–55.

167. Ibid., p. 55.

168. Schneersohn, The "Tzemach Tzedek," pp. 50–51: see also I. Binshtok, "Russko-evreiskaia narodnaia shkola v sviazi s istoricheskim khodom obrazovaniia evreev v Rossii" [Russian-Jewish folk school in connection with the historical development of the education of the Jews in Russia], Voskhod 17 (1893): 95.

169. Maggid 'emet (Leipzig, 1843), pp. 5–6. This pamphlet is reproduced in the Ha-pulemus ʿal "ha-haskalah." It was published under the pseudonym Yonah ben Amitai, but there is no doubt that it was written by Ginzburg. See Yosef Klausner, Historiah shel ha-sifrut ha-'ivrit ha-hadashah [History of modern literature] (Jerusalem, 1953), vol. 3, pp. 130–31.

170. Maggid 'emet, p. 7.

171. Ibid., pp. 10–11.

172. HLM, pp. 40–41.

Chapter 4

1. KEY, p. 104; AZJ 5 (1841): 293; AZJ 6 (1842): 89; described by Max Lilienthal, "My Travels in Russia," in David Philipson, Max Lilienthal, American Rabbi (New York, 1915), pp. 288–89.

2. Ibid., pp. 372–77; KEY, pp. 200–201.

3. See Adolph Ehrlich, Entwickelungsgeschichte der Israelitischen Gemeindeschule zu Riga (St. Petersburg, 1894), pp. 13–23.

4. KEY, p. 247; A. Beletskii, Vopros ob obrazovanii russkikh evreev v tsarstvovanie Imperatora Nikolaia I [The question of the education of Russian Jews in the reign of Emperor Nicholas I] (St. Petersburg, 1894), pp. 125–26, 147; L. M. Bramson, K istorii nachal'nago obrazovaniia evreev v Rossii [To the history of primary education among Russian Jews] (St. Petersburg, 1896), p. 34; Joachim Tarnopol, Notices historiques et caractéristiques sur les israélites d'Odessa (Odessa, 1855), p. 190; I. Cherikover, "Kazennye evreiskie uchilishcha" [State Jewish Schools], Evreiskaia entsiklopediia, vol. 9, pp. 110–15.

5. ZMNP 79 (1851): supp. 1, pp. 12–16.

6. KEY, p. 247; Beletskii, The Question of Education, pp. 125–26, 147; Bramson, History of Primary Education, p. 34; Tarnopol, Notices historiques, p. 190; Cherikover, "State Jewish Schools," pp. 110–15.

7. See, for example, Iu. Gessen, "Tsadik Mendel Liubavichskii" [The Tsadik Mendel of Liubevich], Voskhod 25 (1905): 119.

8. YIVO Archives, Vilna Collection on Jewish Education and Child Care, box VI, file 10, folio 5.

9. Mikra-kodesh ʿim bi'ur ve-targum germani be-'otiot 'ivriot be-tosefot "be-urim hadashim" shel Ada"m Ha-kohen u-"be'urim yeshanim"shel R' Yehudah Bohak [The Holy Scriptures with a commentary and translation into German in Hebrew letters. Supplemented with "New Exegeses" by Ada"m Ha-kohen and "Old Exegeses" by Yehudah Bohak], 17 vols. (Vilna, 1849–52).

10. See KEY, p. 525; M. Morgulis, "K istorii obrazovaniia russkikh evreev" [On the history of education of Russian Jews], Voprosy evreiskoi zhizni (St. Petersburg, 1903), pp. 95–147.

11. ʿEize halakhot mi-yad ha-hazakah la-'adoneny morenu ha-Ramba"m (German title page read: Auszuge aus dem Buche Jad-Haghasakkah, die starke

Hand, Handbuch der Religion, nach dem Talmud zusammengestellt von Rabbi Moscheh-be-Maimon, gen. Moses Maimonides, aus Spanien), 5 bks. (St. Petersburg, 1850). See my article "The Tsarist Mishneh Torah: A Study in the Cultural Politics of the Russian Haskalah" to be published in the forthcoming 1981 volume of the *Proceedings of the American Academy for Jewish Research.*

12. These were: (1) "Kevod ha-melekh" (anonymous); (2) V. Heidenheim, "Bikoret kelallit ʿal pi din Torah bi-khevod u-mishpat ha-ʿamim 'asher be-zemanenu"; (3) "Divrei ha-rabanim de-k"k Vilna"; and (4) "Mikhtav ha-rav . . . Yehiel Heller. . . . le-harav A. M. Strashun." All four of these essays were also issued separately in one volume entitled *Shenei perakim* [Two chapters] (St. Petersburg, 1850).

13. For a recent overview of these views, see Jacob J. Schacter, "Dina De-Malkhuta Dina—A Review," *Dine Israel* 8 (1978): 77–95.

14. Insert to "Heʿarah le-dinei mamonot" [Note on the laws of money], pt. 4, unpaginated.

15. Insert to "He-ʿarah le-hilkhot ʿaku"m" [Note on laws of idolators], pt. 1, between pp. 176–77.

16. See pp. 112–13 for further discussion.

17. See p. 183 for further discussion.

18. Vilna Collection, file 30, folio 1, 10; *Key*, pp. 216–19.

19. The YIVO Archives contain the Archive of the Rabbinical School and Jewish Teachers' Seminary in Vilna. The *formuliarnye spiski* (service records) of each teacher can be found in Record Group 24.

20. M. Morgulis, "Iz moikh vospominanii" [From my memoirs], *Voskhod* 15 (1895): 105–6.

21. On Shulman, see Vilna Collection, file 31, folios 8–9, and file 24, folio 7; on Mapu, see an anonymous unpublished study in the Vilno Collection "Lite," file 1399, folio 63,925; on Gottlober, see his "Zikhronot ʿal sofrei yidish ve-sifreihem," in the R. Goldberg edition of his memoirs, vol. 2, p. 15; on Gordon, see his correspondence in *'Iggerot Yala"g* (Warsaw, 1894), pp. 5–181.

22. See p. 113, and R. Kulisher's letter on the offer to Levinsohn, in the Ginzburg Materials, Rivkind Archive, file 22/11, no. 22. Following the myth of the powerfulness of the maskilim, Russian Jews—and later historians—truly believed that Levinsohn was close to the government and enjoyed great political clout, when in fact he was a destitute, psychologically ill (referred to generally as suffering from "sickness of the nerve") recluse who had to beg for every ruble of support he got. Yosef Klausner, for example, wrote that "Levinsohn almost always spoke in German with the Ministers of Russia" (*Historiah shel ha-sifrut ha-ʿivrit ha-ḥadashah* [History of modern literature] [Jerusalem, 1953], vol. 3, pp. 31)—as though this were a frequent occurrence rather than something that might have taken place two or three times during Levinsohn's life, when he applied for grants from the regime.

23. *Sbornik postanovlenii po Ministerstvu narodnago prosveshcheniia* [Collection of orders of the Ministry of National Enlightenment] (St. Petersburg, 1876), vol. 2, pt. 2, no. 428, 897. This ordinance was obviously not known even to the best-informed Russian-Jewish historian, Iulii Gessen; see his German article (under spelling J. Hessen), "Die russische Regierung und die westeuropäischen Juden, Zur Schulreform in Russland 1840–1844," *Monatsschrift für Geschichte und Wissenschaft des Judentums* 57 (1913): 499, n. 1.

24. *KEY*, pp. 243, 299, 157.

25. See *ZMNP* 39 (1843): 2–4; Sh. Y. Fin in "Safah le-ne'emanin" [Words to the faithful] *Ha-karmel* 4 (1880): 598; M. Morgulis, "Memoirs," p. 76.

26. Fin, "Words to the faithful," pp. 664–65; Tugendhold's service record found in Teachers' Seminary in Vilna, Record Group 24, file 51, 161–65.

27. See Y. Ben-Ya°akov's letter to Levinsohn in *Ha-kerem* (1887), p. 43.

28. P. Marek, *Ocherki po istorii prosveshcheniia evreev v Rossii* [Studies on the enlightenment of the Jews in Russia] (Moscow, 1909), p. 80.

29. YIVO Institute, Vilna Rabbinical School Archive, File: miscellaneous items, no. v.

30. *KEY*, pp. 220–21.

31. See his "Memoirs," p. 109.

32. Gessen, "Ravvinskie uchilishcha v Rossii" [Rabbinical seminaries in Russia], *Evreiskaia entsiklopediia*, vol. 13, p. 259; *KEY*, p. 209, lists 271 students in the Zhitomir seminary in February 1854.

33. M. Bann, *Geschichte des Jüdisch-Theologischen Seminar in Breslau* (Breslau, undated), p. 134.

34. See biography of each in the *Evreiskaia entsiklopediia*.

35. *Ḥaṭ'ot ne°urim* [Sins of my youth], ed. Sh. Breiman (reprinted, Jerusalem, 1970), pt. 1, pp. 103–4.

36. Ya°akov Gurland, *Kevod ha-bayit* [Honor of the house] (Vilna, 1858), p. 28–34.

37. On Jews in the elementary schools, see the letter from Uvarov to Kiselev in the Ginzburg Materials, Rivkind Archive, SG 13/6, no. 6 (which contradicts Ginzburg's assertion in 2:50, that only forty-eight Jews attended Russian elementary schools). On Jews in the gymnasiums, see Lilienthal's comments in SG 13/1, no. 11, II/iii, 53–58, and M. Kosven, "K voprosu o vysshem obrazovanii russkikh evreev" [To the question of the higher education of Russian Jews], *Evreiskaia zhizn'*, no. 7 (July 1904): 171. No reliable figures have been published on Jews in Russian universities in this period. The names of these students have been culled from the list of maskilim described in note 38. In order properly to evaluate these figures, it is important to note that in this period, the total enrollment in Russian gymnasiums and universities was minuscule: in 1847, the total gymnasium enrollment in the empire was 18,911, and there were all of 4,566 at the universities. After the upheavals of 1848, these numbers dropped by one-fourth. See Patrick Alston, *Education and the State in Tsarist Russia* (Stanford, 1969), p. 26.

38. It is impossible to know how many maskilim there were in Russia at this—or any—time. Statements are based on an admittedly rough method: a card was kept on every maskil mentioned in any source, thus identifying about three hundred maskilim, not including the students in the schools.

39. Morgulis, "Memoirs," p. 116.

40. Isaiah Berlin, "A Marvelous Decade," pt. 1, *Encounter* (1955), p. 29.

41. Jacob S. Raisin, *The Haskalah Movement in Russia* (Philadelphia, 1913), p. 11.

42. The most consequential such analysis is Y. Tsinberg, *History of Jewish Literature* (New York, 1966), bk. 9, chap. 5, pp. 166–99.

43. See Richard Pipes, *Struve: Liberal on the Left* (Cambridge, Mass., 1970), pp. 29–30.

44. *TB*, p. viii.

45. Ibid., p. ix.

46. Ibid., and Levinsohn's letter to Shishkov in Iulii Gessen, *Perezhitoe* 1 (1908): documentary section, pp. 23–27.

47. Published by Iu. Gessen, "Iz letopisi minuvshago" [From past chronicles], *Perezhitoe* 1 (1908): 11–13.

48. *TB*, pp. 57, 87, 121, 122, 138–42, and E. Etkes' introduction to this edition, p. 18.

49. S. M. Ginzburg, "Iz zapisok pervago evreia-studenta v Rossii (L. I. Mandelshtam, 1839–1840gg.)" [From the notes of the first Jewish student in Russia (L. I. Mandelshtam, 1839–1840)], *Perezhitoe* 1 (1908): 27–28.

50. Ibid., p. 37.

51. Ibid.

52. Ibid., p. 39.

53. See Klausner, *Historiah*, vol. 4, pp. 190–93, for a bibliography on Lilienblum.

54. Beletskii, *The Question of Education*, pp. 22–23.

55. Morgulis, "Iz vospominanii" [Memoirs], p. 76; Rabbi Mazeh cited in Azri'el Shochat, *Mosad "ha-rabanut mi-ta'am" be-rusyah* [The institution of the "Crown Rabbi" in Russia] (Haifa, 1975), p. 36.

56. Ben-Ya'akov's letter to Levinsohn, pp. 18–49.

57. Tarnopol, *Notices historiques*, pp. 14–15.

58. Ibid., p. 17.

59. *TB*, pp. 29–39.

60. *Die Semitiche Nachklänge* (?, 1848), which cannot be located. See Fin, "Words to the faithful," p. 665.

61. *TB*, pp. 36, 16–17.

62. Ibid., pp. 51–52.

63. Y. Tsinberg, *History of Jewish Literature* (New York, 1966), bk. 8, pt. 2, p. 145.

64. Introduction to *Shirei sefat kodesh* [Songs of the holy tongue] (Vilna, 1861), p. 9. The original edition of 1841 cannot be located, but this citation is from the introduction to that first edition.

65. *HLM*, pp. 4–5.

66. Ibid.

67. See Dan Miron, *A Traveler Disguised* (New York, 1973). Recently, Miron has argued that "the great shift in the development of Hebrew belles-lettres in the nineteenth century" occurred in this period, with the appearance in 1851 of Micah Joseph Lebensohn's *Shirei bat-Zion* and in 1853 of Abraham Mapu's *Ahavat Zion*. Particularly relevant is his statement that in Lebensohn's work "Haskalah poetry came as close as it could to the modern Hebrew poetry initiated forty years later by Bialik and Tchernichowsky." See his "Rediscovering Haskalah Poetry," *Prooftexts* 1 (1981): 297–98.

68. Cited in Ginzburg, vol. 1, p. 78.

69. Ibid., pp. 80–82.

70. See Miron, "A Traveler," pp. 34–36.

71. Tsinberg, *History of Jewish Literature*, bk. 9, chaps. 1–2, passim.

72. Tarnopol lists the following Jewish authors in Odessa until 1855: in Hebrew, Eichenbaum, Pinsker, Werbel; in Russian, O. Rabinovich, Finkel, Bertensohn; in German, Stern, Wolfsohn, J. Hurovitz; in French: E. Loevensohn, J. Tarnopol; in Italian, Derblich and Wahltuch (*Notices historiques*, p. 183).

73. Yosef Y. Yerushalmi, *The Lisbon Massacre of 1506 and the Royal Image in the Shebet Yehudah* (Cincinnati, 1976), p. xii.

74. *TB*, unpaginated preface.

75. Ibid., p. 183.

76. "Toledot ploni 'almoni ha-kazavi" [Story of the deceitful Mr. X], *Yalkut Riba"l* (Warsaw, 1878), p. 12.

77. "Di hefker-velt," *Yidishe folks-bibliotek* (Berdichev, 1888), p. 145.

78. Tarnopol, *Notices historiques*, p. 52.

79. *HLM*, p. 7.

80. Ginzburg, "From the Notes," p. 18.

81. Ibid., p. 20.

82. O. M. Lerner, *Evrei v novorossiskom krae* [Jews in New Russia] (Odessa, 1901), p. 40.

83. Published by S. M. Ginzburg in *Perezhitoe* 3 (1911): 367–77.

84. See Moshe Perlmann, "Razsvet, 1860–61: The Origins of the Russian-Jewish Press," *Jewish Social Studies* 24 (1962): 162–83.

Chapter 5

1. *PSZ* 19: 18,545/Lev 509.

2. Ibid., 18,559/Lev 510.

3. I shall use the word "kahal" without italics, and the artificial form 'kahals' for the plural; the Russian forms are *kagal* and *kagaly*, the Hebrew *kahal* and *kehalim*.

4. *PSZ* 19: 18,545/Lev 509, art. 1.

5. Ibid., art. 12.

6. Ibid., art. 16.

7. Ibid., arts. 16, 17.

8. Levitats, *The Jewish Community in Russia* (New York, 1943), p. 26, claims that the Senate's decision of May 7, 1786, "abolished the judicial autonomy granted the Jews by the Placard (of Catherine II)." This is not correct: that decision merely forbade the establishment of any *new* Jewish courts on the model of other "estate" courts and had no bearing on the existing Jewish judicial institutions. Indeed, as Levitats himself notes, the 1786 law specifically permitted the Jews to continue to adjudicate all matters regulated by Jewish religious law as they had always done, and the 1804 Statute officially recognized the *bet din* as a court of arbitration in cases between Jews. Thereafter, the judicial autonomy of Jewish life remained intact, buttressed by official support.

9. See p. 132. Theoretically, of course, it would have been possible for the Russian government to continue to hold the Jews responsible for their tax arrears after their communities were abolished, on the model of the postrevolutionary French governments. But the tsarist bureaucracy was in no way as efficient or rational as the French.

10. For example, I. G. Orshanskii, *Russkoe zakonodatel'stvo o evreiakh* [Russian legislation on the Jews] (St. Petersburg, 1877), p. 201, and Gessen, vol. 2, pp. 94–95.

11. See Azri'el Shochat, "Ha-hanhagah be-kehilot rusyah ʿim bitul ha-kahal" [The administration of the communities in Russia after the abolition of the kahal], *Zion* 44 (1979): 161–65.

12. Ibid., pp. 211–24.

13. Cited in ibid., p. 159.

14. See L. Loewe, ed., *Diaries of Sir Moses and Lady Montefiore* (London, 1890), vol. 1, p. 364.

15. Cited in D. Pines, "Bor'ba s khaperami" [Battle with the *khappers*]; *ES* 8 (1915): 398.

16. Ginzburg, vol. 1, pp. 267–68.

17. Yeḥezkel Kotik, *Mayne zikhroynes* [My memoirs] (Berlin, 1922), vol. 1, p. 182.

18. Archival material reproduced by O. Margolis, *Geshikhte fun yidn in rusland* [History of the Jews in Russia] (Moscow, 1930), pp. 401–2.

19. Ibid., pp. 402–4; Raphael Mahler, *Divrei yemei yisra'el* [History of the Jews], vol. 2, bk. 1, p. 130.

20. See p. 184 for further discussions.

21. *MB*, vol. 1, p. 965.

22. Ginzburg, vol. 1, pp. 242–43.

23. Police report published by S. Dubnov in *Perezhitoe* 1 (1908): document 1, pp. 1–7; Ginsburg, vol. 3, pp. 178–87 for additional, if unverifiable details.

24. David Fajnhaus, "Konflikty społeczne wśród ludności żydowskiej na Litwie i Białorusi w pierwszej polowie xix wieku" [Social conflicts among Jews in Lithuania and Belorussia in the first half of the 19th century], *Biuletyn żydowskiego instytutu historycznego*, no. 52 (1964): pp. 13–14.

25. Margolis, *History of the Jews in Russia*, document 92, pp. 341–46.

26. Ibid., document 93, pp. 347–52, document 94, pp. 353–58.

27. Ibid., document 91, pp. 337–41.

28. Sh. Rombakh, "Di yidishe balmelokhes in rusland in der ershter helft fun xix y.h." [Jewish artisans in Russia in the first half of the 19th century], *Tsaytshrift* 1 (1926): 29.

29. Ibid.

30. See pp. 183–84.

31. Petition reproduced in E. Tsherikover, "Fun di rusishe arkhivn: Kantonistn" [From the Russian archives: Cantonists], *Historishe shriftn* 1 (1929): 688; on this petition see p. 184.

32. *PSZ* 25: 24,718/Lev 638.

33. Margolis, *History of the Jews in Russia*, pp. 113–14.

34. Tsherikover, "From the Russian Archives."

35. A. Fridberg, "Zikhronot mi-yimei neᶜurai" [Memoirs of my youth], *Sefer ha-shanah* 3 (1901): p. 84.

36. For a summary of these laws see Azri'el Shochat, *Mosad "ha-rabanut mit-ta'am" be-rusyah* [The institution of the "Crown Rabbi" in Russia] (Haifa, 1975), pp. 9–12.

37. *PSZ* 10: 8054/Lev 304, art. 90.

38. See Shochat, *"Crown Rabbi,"* pp. 12–13 for several examples.

39. Ibid. Shochat does attempt to sort out the situation in this period, but he is not successful. See my review of the work in *Association for Jewish Studies Newsletter*, no. 19 (February 1977): 19–20.

40. Yiẓhak Aizik Bohorad, *She'eilot u-teshuvot Penei Yiẓhak* [Responsa 'The Face of Isaac'] (Vilna, 1909), responsum 4, p. 15. This work was pointed out to me by Professor Chimen Abramsky of University College, London.

41. Emanuel Etkes makes this point in a different fashion in his article "Parashat ha-'haskalah mi-taᶜam' ve-ha-temurah be-maᶜmad tenuᶜat ha-haskalah be-rusyah" [Compulsory enlightenment as a crossroads in the history of the Haskalah movement in Russia], *Ẓion* 43 (1978): 265–66.

42. Cited in Yosef Klausner, *Historiah shel ha-sifrut ha-ʿivrit ha-ḥadashah* [History of modern Hebrew literature] (Jerusalem, 1953), vol. 3, p. 29.

43. See p. 136. In addition, Rabbi Shik was renowned for a novel exegesis on Isaiah 42:24, "Who was it gave Jacob away for despoilment/ And Israel to plunderers?" The term "Jacob," claimed Shik, is used to designate the Jewish people as a whole, while Israel refers to its leaders. Moreover, the Hebrew for despoilment, *meshisah*, is a regular noun, while *bozezim*, plunderers, is an active participle. Thus the sentence correctly read, suggested Shik, is "Who caused the masses to be despoiled, and the leaders of the Jews to be the plunderers?" *MB*, p. 965.

44. Ibid.

45. Y. L. Levin, "Zikhronot ve-raʿayanot" [Memoirs and thoughts], *Sefer ha-yovel li-khvod Naḥum Sokolov* (Warsaw, 1904), p. 358.

46. Emanuel Etkes, "R' Yisra'el Salanter ve-reishitah shel tenuʿat ha-musar" [Rabbi Israel Salanter and the origins of the Musar movement] (Ph.D. diss., Hebrew University, 1975), p. 247.

47. Fridberg, "My Youth," p. 87.

48. See pp. 149–51 for further discussion.

49. Shochat, "The Administration of the Communities" pp. 216–17 citing others.

50. Kotik, *My Memoirs*, vol. 1, p. 153.

51. *AZJ* 4 (1840): 339.

52. Joachim Tarnopol, *Notices historiques and caractéristiques sur les israélites d'Odessa* (Odessa, 1855), p. 105. In the same year, the most important Reform temple in Eastern Europe was founded in Lwów. See M. Bałaban, *Historia Lwowskiej Synagogi Postępowej* [History of the progressive synagogue of Lwów] (Lwów, 1937), chap. 2.

53. *AZJ* 6 (1842): 265–66; B. Natanson, *Sefer ha-zikhronot, divre yemei ḥayai Riba"l* [Book of memoirs: Biography of Isaac Ber Levinsohn] (Warsaw, 1878), p. 67; Osip Rabinovich, "Novaia evreiskaia sinagoga v Odesse" [New Synagogue in Odessa], in his *Sochineniia* [Works] (Odessa, 1888), vol. 3, pp. 373–74.

54. Rabinovich, "New Synagogue," pp. 377–79.

55. *HLM*, p. 79, Etkes, "Rabbi Israel Salanter," p. 127.

56. Klausner, *Historiah*, vol. 3, p. 184.

57. *HLM*, pp. 84–88.

58. Etkes, "Compulsory Enlightenment."

59. *HLM*, p. 81.

60. Tarnopol, *Notices historiques*, p. 106.

61. Rabinovich, "New Synagogue," p. 378.

62. Ibid.

63. There is only one monograph on the subject which deals solely with its literary aspect in the later period: G. Katzenelson, *Ha-milḥamah ha-sifrutit bein ha-ḥaradim ve-ha-maskilim* (Tel Aviv, 1954).

64. Interestingly, in Poland there did arise a group of Jews who called themselves "Poles of the Mosaic persuasion" and articulated a German-style Reform ideology. A comparative study of the two Jewries on this point (like so many others) would be most important.

65. On the problem of rabbinical positions for the graduates of these seminaries see Yehudah Slutsky, "Bet ha-midrash la-rabanim be-vilnah" [The rabbinical seminary in Vilna], *Ha-ʿavar* 7 (1960): 72–79.

66. Klausner, *Historiah*, vol. 3, p. 184, and relevant articles on each of these cities in the *Encyclopedia Judaica*.

67. The most reliable statistics available are those collected by Shaul Ginzburg from Synod archives, found in his materials in the Rivkind Archive, Hebrew University, Jerusalem, file 6, no. 6. These correspond with the statistics published by J. F. A. de Le Roi, *Judentaufen im 19 Jahrhundert* (Leipzig, 1899), and roughly corroborate the estimates of N. Samter, *Judentaufen im 19ten Jahrhundert* (Berlin, 1906), p. 91, all listing approximately 30,000 Jewish converts to various denominations of Christianity in Russia. This figure is further corroborated by the one official published source located, the report of the Procurator of the Holy Synod for 1825–55: "Otchet Ober-Prokurator Sviateishago Sinoda, 1825–1855," *Sbornik Imp. russkago istoricheskago obshchestva* 98 (1890): 457–60, which lists 22,324 conversions to Russian Orthodoxy alone during Nicholas's reign. Unfortunately, no official information is available on baptisms in the Catholic and Protestant churches. The German works mentioned contain data on such conversions only for the second half of the century, and the synod would not have kept such information in its files. Sporadic figures are given in the yearly reports of the Ministry of the Interior in its journal, *Zhurnal Ministerstva vnutrennikh del*, but these are suspect, as the data on conversions to Russian Orthodoxy do not match those of the synod, which knew better. In this memoirs, Max Lilienthal wrote "I met several converted Jews, of whom there are about forty thousand in Petersburg and Moscow" ("My Travels in Russia," in David Philipson, *Max Lilienthal, American Rabbi* [New York, 1915], p. 162). Either the synod's figures were drastically low, or Lilienthal was engaging in his customary hyperbole; the latter seems more likely.

68. Based on the calculations cited on p. 25, such an assumption would yield 25,000 converts rather than the 22,324 claimed by the synod. Therefore, the number of voluntary apostates may have been as high as 7,676.

69. These are: (1) YIVO Institute, Archives of the Lithuanian Consistory in Vilna—Conversions Records, which contain the files of Jews who converted to Russian Orthodoxy in Lithuania from the 1830s to the Second World War; and (2) the Papers of the Church's Mission to the Jews, formerly the London Society for the Promotion of Christianity among Jews, at the Bodleian Library, Oxford, which contain fascinating materials on conversions in Russia in the last decades of the nineteenth and first decades of the twentieth century.

70. These are found in boxes 1–7 of the Archives of the Lithuanian Consistory.

71. These were Moshe Motus of Grodno, act 2, box 2, and Haim Borisevich of Vilna, act 10, box 3.

72. Act 130, box 4, on dissolution of marriage of Sloyme Karon and wife.

73. Act 122, box 3, case of Berek Leibovich, seven-year-old son of converted wife of Jewish noncommissioned officer.

74. Act 53, box 5; act 91, box 7; act 96, box 2; act 36, box 1.

75. It is assumed that those who did not list any profession did not have one.

76. Only those who signed their names with x's or who had someone else sign for them, usually their priest, were counted as illiterate.

77. Act 42, box 3. One other woman, A. Itskovich, may have converted purely out of religious motives: she appealed for baptism on her deathbed (act 114, box 5).

78. Act 187, box 3.

79. See correspondence on the readmission of the Society to Poland during the reign of Alexander II, in Papers of the Church's Mission to the Jews, file d. 51.

80. The most famous such renegade, Ya'akov Brafman, was born in 1824 in Minsk Province but converted in 1858.

81. These were collected into the following volumes: Sh. L. Tsitron, *Avek fun folk* [Away from the nation] (Vilna, undated), 4 vols.; Shaul Ginzburg, *Meshumodim in tsarishn rusland* [Apostates in tsarist Russia] (New York, 1946). Tsitron was an excellent storyteller, but it is impossible to know where he found his material. Ginzburg based most of his accounts on Tsitron but added his substantial historical abilities; unfortunately, he too gave no sources for his facts.

82. See Ginzburg, *Meshumodim*, pp. 251–54, the details of which can be corroborated in A. B. Gottlober's "Zikhronot mi-yemei ne'urai" [Memoirs of my youth] in his *Zikhronot u-masa'ot*, ed. R. Goldberg (Jerusalem, 1976), and in the letter from Grinboim.

83. Published in *ES* 3 (1911): 414–16.

84. Gottlober taught in the school in Kamenets-Podol'sk.

85. *KEY*, p. 404–5, p. 115; *Evreiskaia entsiklopediia*, vol. 15, pp. 584–87; Ginzburg, *Meshumodim*, pp. 120–21.

86. Ginzburg, *Meshumodim*.

87. Ibid.

88. I. Itskovich, "Vospominaniia arkhangel'skago Kantonista" [Memoirs of an Arkanagel'sk Cantonist], *ES* 5 (1912): 23.

89. Cited from the official history of the University of Kiev by Sh. Ginzburg in *Perezhitoe* 1 (1908): 2, n. 2. Tsimmerman's story as relayed by Ginzburg and Tsitron is one of the most fascinating and dramatic of the lot: yeshivah boy meets factory manager on father-in-law's estate who is a disguised maskil; seduced into heresy; wife dies, marries factory-manager's daughter, who induces him to convert; new father-in-law dies from heart attack when visits children on Easter and finds them returning from church. Unfortunately, none of these facts can be established from any authenticated sources.

90. *PSZ* 25: 23,905/Lev 615.

91. *ES* 2 (1909): 273.

92. Yehezkel Kaufmann, *Golah ve-nekhar* [Diaspora and alien lands] (Tel Aviv, 1961), vol. 2, p. 34.

93. Ibid.

94. Etkes, "Rabbi Israel Salanter," p. 60, makes a similar point but does not elaborate on conditions or results of this change.

95. S. Y. Fin, "Dor ve-doreshav" [A generation and its seekers], *Ha-karmel* 4 (1879): p. 195–96.

96. Joseph I. Schneersohn, *The "Tzemach Tzedek" and the Haskalah Movement* (Brooklyn, 1969), p. 57; evidence from this work has been accepted only when it refers directly to actions taken by Rabbi Menahem Mendel.

97. Ginzburg, vol. 1, pp. 35–47.

98. Schneersohn, *The "Tzemach Tzedek."*

99. Shemu'el Bialoblutski, *Yahadut Lita* [Lithuanian Jewry], vol. 1 (1959), pp. 190–91.

100. M. Y. Berdichevsky, "Toledot yeshivat ez-hayim" [History of the Volozhin yeshivah], *Ha-'asif* 3 (1886): 233–34.

101. See Aharon Surski, *History of Torah Education in the Modern Era* (Bnei Brak, 1967), pp. 287–88.

102. A. H. Glitsnshtein, *Rabenu ha-Ẓemah-Ẓedek* [Our rabbi the "Tsemakh-Tsedek] (Brooklyn, n.d.), p. 143; for some reason this quote is not included in Schneersohn, *The "Tzemach Tzedek,"* which reproduces most of the material in this book.

103. Glitsnshtein, *Our Rabbi,* pp. 143–45; Schneersohn, *The "Tzemach Tzedek,"* p. 59.

104. Ibid., pp. 60–61.

105. H. A[leksandrov], "Kazyone yidishe shuln un rekrutchine" [The government Jewish schools and the draft], *Tsaytshrift* 4 (1930): 125–32.

106. See Baron, p. 121.

107. Etkes, "Rabbi Israel Salanter," pp. 218–19, 230–31, 363–65. This dissertation is far more successful and useful than the previous works on the subject.

108. Yeḥiel Heller, *ʿAmudei 'or* [Pillars of light] (reprint ed., Jerusalem, 1968–69), unpaginated, second page of introduction.

Chapter 6

1. S. Ginsburg and P. Marek, *Evreiskie narodnye pesni v Rossii* [Jewish folk songs in Russia] (St. Petersburg, 1901), p. 53.

2. *PSZ* 19: 18,562/Lev 512.

3. Cited in O. M. Lerner, *Evrei v novorossiskom krae* [Jews in New Russia] (Odessa, 1901), pp. 48–49.

4. Ibid., pp. 49–50.

5. Ibid., p. 52.

6. Gessen, vol. 2, p. 101.

7. *AZJ* 10 (1846).

8. Ibid.

9. Ibid.

10. Ibid.

11. *PSZ* 26: 25,766/Lev 660.

12. *PSZ* 27: 26,315/Lev 672.

13. Yeḥezkel Kotik, *Mayne zikhroynes* [My memoirs] (Berlin, 1922), pp. 92–93.

14. Ibid.

15. Cited in J. Lestchinsky, "Di antviklung fun yidishn folk far di letste 100 yor" [The development of the Jewish people for the last hundred years], *Shriftn far ekonomik un statistik* 1 (1928): 5.

16. Ibid.

17. See his "Khoziaistvennoe ustroistvo i sostoianie evreiskikh obshchestv v Rossii" [The economic order of the Jewish community in Russia], *Zhurnal Ministerstva vnutrennikh del* 5 (1850): 417–19.

18. Lestchinsky, "Development of the Jewish People," p. 5.

19. See pp. 163–64 for further discussion.

20. The 1830 figures were published in *Zhurnal Ministerstva vnutrennikh del* (1830): 153; the 1838 figures in "Ueber die Zahl der Hebräer in Russland und deren Verhältniss zur übrigen Bevölkerung, in denjenigen Provinzen, wo

solche geduldet werden," *Bulletin scientifique publié par l'Académie Imperiale des Sciences de Saint-Peterbourg* 7 (1840): 92–96; the 1847 figures in Miliutin, "Economic Order," pp. 238–78; the 1851 figures in P. I. Koppen, *Deviataia reviziia. Issledovanie o chisle zhitelei v Rossii* [Ninth revision. Study of the number of inhabitants in Russia] (St. Petersburg, 1857), pp. 23–239.

21. Lestchinsky, "Development of the Jewish People," p. 4, Ben Zion Dinur, "Demutah ha-historit shel ha-yahadut ha-rusit u-va‘ayot ha-heker bah" [The historical character of Russian Jewry and problems in its study], *Zion* 22 (1937): 94.

22. Bernard Weinryb, in his *Neuste Wirtschaftsgeschichte der Juden in Russland und Polen,* 2nd ed. (New York, 1972), p. 52, prefers to accept the figures cited by A. Yuditsky, *Yidishe burzhuazie un yidisher proletariat in ershter helft xix y"h* [Jewish bourgeoisie and Jewish proletariat in the first half of the 19th century] (Kiev, n.d.), even though Yuditsky gives the source of his data only as an unidentified "manuscript copy of the Statistical Collection of 1852, found in the Kiev former University Library (Bibikov collection), no. 840" (p. 103). Baron, 86–87, accepts Weinryb's compilations of Yuditsky's figures, and these in turn are taken from Baron by William L. Blackwell, *The Beginnings of Russian Industrialization, 1800–1860* (Princeton, 1968), p. 251. Since there is no information on the author or provenance of Yuditsky's manuscript, there is no sound reason to accept it as preferable to the government's own official statistics.

23. See Patricia Herlihy, "Odessa: Staple Trade and Urbanization in New Russia," *Jahrbücher für Geschichte Osteuropas* 21 (1973): 184–95.

24. Compiled from the sources listed in n. 20.

25. No further detail is needed about the Jewish agriculturists in Nicholas's Russia, as this is the one subject studied in depth and with care by previous historians. The two best monographs on this subject are S. Y. Borovoi, *Evreiskaia zemledel'cheskaia kolonizatsiia v staroi Rossii* [Jewish agricultural colonization in Old Russia] (Moscow, 1923), and V. N. Nikitin, *Evrei zemledel'tsy* [Jewish farmers] (St. Petersburg, 1877).

26. J. Lestchinsky, *Dos yidishe folk in tsifern* [The Jewish people in numbers] (Berlin, 1922).

27. P. G. Ryndziunskii, *Gorodskoe grazhdanstvo doreformennoi Rossii* [City dwellers of pre-reform Russia] (Moscow, 1958), table 27, p. 295.

28. See archival material cited by Weinryb, *Neuste,* pp. 14–15.

29. See Baron, pp. 69–74.

30. See Max Lilienthal, "My Travels in Russia," in David Philipson, *Max Lilienthal, American Rabbi* (New York, 1915), p. 135 and *Zhurnal Ministerstva vnutrennykh del* 4 (1846): 14. Curiously, the Ministry of the Interior listed four-hundred odd Jews living in Moscow in 1839 and 1840 as "serving in the police." See its *Zhurnal* (1840) and (1841).

31. P. Marev, "K istorii evreev v Moskve" [To the history of the Jews in Moscow], *Voskhod* (1893): 85.

32. The worst Soviet offender is the study by Yuditsky "The Jewish Bourgeoisie" and various studies published in *Tsaytshrift* and other Soviet-Yiddish publications, listed in the bibliography. The best Soviet work, and the closest to an actual economic history of Russian Jewry is O. Margolis' *Geshikhte fun yidn in rusland* [History of the Jews in Russia] (Moscow, 1930), which at least provides the documentation to support its spurious conclusions. Weinryb's monograph is useful but accepts too much of the Soviet jargon and is uncritical in its use of published statistics. Raphael Mahler's chapters are the best on the subject but are marred by his attempt to salvage Marxist terminology and analysis from the

Soviets' orthodoxy. Baron's chapters on demography and economics are excellent summaries of highly flawed materials.

33. Figures calculated in Walter M. Pintner, *Russian Economic Policy under Nicholas I* (Ithaca, 1967), p. 77.

34. Unfortunately, there is no scholarly study of the liquor trade in the Russian Empire at this time. The best survey of governmental policy on this issue is in S. M. Seredonin, et al., *Istoricheskii obzor deiatel'nosti Komiteta ministrov* [Historical survey of the work of the Committee of Ministers], vol. 2, pt. ii, pp. 105–51.

35. First collection of *PSZ* 28: 21,547/Lev 59, art. 34.

36. *PSZ* 10: 8054/Lev 304, art. 64.

37. See, for example, *PSZ* 12: 10,012/Lev 340; *PSZ* 13: 11,315/Lev 373; and *PSZ* 17: 15,715/Lev 454.

38. *PSZ* 20: 19,289/Lev 527.

39. Ibid., secs. 2 and 3.

40. *PSZ* 24: 33,668/Lev 608.

41. *PSZ* 27: 27,322/Lev 694.

42. See Margolis, *History of the Jews in Russia*, p. 172.

43. The most effective expulsion of Jews from villages resulted, of course, from the infamous May Laws of 1882.

44. Blackwell, *Russian Industrialization*, p. 55.

45. Archival documents reproduced in Margolis, *History of the Jews in Russia*, p. 216.

46. *Zhurnal Ministerstva vnutrennykh del* (1844): 171–72.

47. See the fascinating article "Khlebnaia torgovlia v kievskoi gubernii, za 1847 god" [Grain trade in Kiev Province, 1847], *Zhurnal Ministerstva vnutrennykh del* (1849): 104–28.

48. Blackwell, *Russian Industrialization*, pp. 73–76.

49. Ibid.

50. On an 1820 ban, see Baron, p. 85; on a ḥerem in the 1840s, see the report in *Archives israélites* 5 (1844): 285.

51. *PSZ* 18: 16,767/Lev 475.

52. *PSZ* 19: 17,503/Lev 484.

53. Cited in Margolis, *History of the Jews in Russia*, p. 77.

54. See statistics cited by Kh. Korobkov, "Uchastie evreev vo vneshnei torgovle Pol'shi" [The participation of Jews in the foreign trade of Poland], *ES* 4 (1913): 197–220, and Baron, p. 85.

55. Cited in Blackwell, *Russian Industrialization*, p. 232.

56. Most of the studies of this question are based on Yuditsky's work in the Yiddish version, *The Jewish Bourgeoisie and Jewish Proletariat in the First Half of the 19th Century*, and, curiously, in a much less polemical article, "Evreiskaia burzhuaziia i evreiskie rabochie v tekstil'noi promyshlennosti pervoi poloviny xix v." [The Jewish bourgeoisie and Jewish workers in the textile industry of the first half of the 19th century], *Istoricheskii sbornik* 4 (1935): 107–33.

57. See Pintner, *Russian Economic Policy*, pp. 224, 106–08, and the standard Soviet economic history of Russia, P. I. Lyashchenko, *History of the National Economy of Russia* (New York, 1949), p. 336.

58. Compiled from archival sources by Yuditsky in his Russian article, "The Jewish Bourgeoisie and Jewish Workers," p. 133.

59. Ibid., pp. 123, 126.

60. For such useless computations, see ibid., p. 122.

61. On the later period see Ezra Mendelsohn, *Class Struggle in the Pale* (Cambridge, 1970). Even the orthodox Soviet historian P. V. Ryndziunskii is forced to concede that the industrial workers of pre-reform Russia cannot be considered a true proletariat. See his recent *Utverzhdenie kapitalizma v Rossii* [The consolidation of capitalism in Russia] (Moscow, 1978), pp. 26–33.

62. Weinryb, *Neuste Wirtschaftsgeschichte*, pp. 115–16.

63. 1804 statute, art. 23; 1835 statute, art. 62.

64. *PSZ* 2: 1115/Lev 152; *PSZ* 6: 4591/Lev 238.

65. Sh. Rombakh, "Di yidishe balmelokhes in rusland in der ershter helft fun 19tn y"h" [Jewish artisans in Russia in the first half of the 19th century], *Tsaytshrift* 1 (1926): 26–28.

66. *PSZ* 12: 10,255/Lev 346; *PSZ* 19: 18,234/Lev 499.

67. Rombakh, "Jewish Artisans."

68. *PSZ* 26: 25,766/Lev 660, art. 5.

69. Mahler, *History of the Jews*, supp. 2, p. 282.

70. *PSZ* 27: 26,171/Lev 669.

71. Simon Kuznets, "Economic Structure and Life of the Jews," *The Jews, Their History, Culture, and Religion*, ed. Louis Finkelstein, vol. 2, 3rd ed. (Philadelphia, 1960), pp. 1623–24.

Conclusions

1. Cited in W. Bruce Lincoln, *Nicholas I* (Bloomington and London, 1978), p. 294.

2. *PSZ* 25: 24,127/Lev 620.

3. *PSZ* 25: 24,678 and 24,769/Lev 639 and 640.

4. *PSZ* 26: 25,305/Lev 647. The only source that mentions this earlier increased quota and compares it to the Jewish case is A. M. Dik's 1871 story mentioned above, *Der erster (sic) nabor* [The first levy] (Vilna, 1871), pp. 19–20. Unfortunately, no historians picked up on Dik's comments and checked the legal sources that were at their disposal.

5. See the petitions reproduced by E. Tsherikover, "Fun di rusishe arkhivn: kantonistn" [From the Russian archives: Cantonists], *Historishe shriftn* 1 (1929): 789–99.

6. Both this decree and the next were never included in the *PSZ* and are extant only in the *Zhurnal Ministerstva vnutrennikh del* [Journal of the Ministry of the Interior] 1853: 31–32, chast' offitsial'naia.

7. Ibid., chast' offitsial'naia, no. 31, 20–21. Astonishingly, although every history of Russian Jewry mentions this extremely important law, no citation is given for it, its absence from the *PSZ* is never noted, and its text is never cited. Moreover, Iulii Gessen, usually the most reliable and authoritative student of governmental policy on the Jews, mistakenly gave the date of this decree as 1852, both in Gessen, vol. 2, p. 115, and in his article on the subject in the *Evreiskaia entsiklopediia*, vol. 12, p. 372. Other authors simply fudge the issue.

8. *PSZ* 29: 28,432/Lev 732.

9. Cited in Nicholas V. Riasanovsky, *Nicholas I and Official Nationality in Russia 1825–1855* (Berkeley and Los Angeles, 1969), p. 266.

Bibliography

Archival Documents

New York. YIVO Institute for Jewish Research
  Tcherikower Archives
  Materials from the Archive of Baron Günzburg and the Society for the Promotion
    of Enlightenment among the Jews of Russia
  Dubnov Archive
  Vilna Archive
    Archive of the Kehillah in Vilna
    Archive of the Rabbinical Schools and Jewish Teachers' Seminary in Vilna
    Collection Russia and Soviet Union
    Zamlung Vilna
    Lite
    Vilna Collection on Jewish Education and Child Care
    Archive of the Kehilla in Minsk
  Lithuanian Consistory in Vilna—Conversion Records
  Educational Alliance Archive
    Autobiography of the Cantonist T. Shkolnik
  Manuscript Collection
    Biography of Eli Goodman, a Cantonist in Nicholas I's army
Jerusalem. Jewish National and University Library
  Rivkind Archive
    Shaul Ginzburg Materials, Collection 4° 1281A
Oxford. Bodleian Library
  Papers of The Church's Ministry among the Jews, formerly the London Society
    for Promoting Christianity among the Jews, 1808–1970.

Unpublished Materials

Etkes, Emanuel. "R' Yisra'el Salanter ve-reishitah shel tenuᶜat ha-musar" [Rabbi
  Israel Salanter and the origins of the Musar movement]. Ph.D. dissertation,
  The Hebrew University of Jerusalem, 1975.
Haltzel, Michael Harris. "The Reaction of the Baltic Germans to Russification
  during the Nineteenth Century." Ph.D. dissertation, Harvard University,
  1971.

Levine, Hillel. "Menahem Mendel Lefin: A Case Study of Judaism and Modernization." Ph.D. dissertation, Harvard University, 1974.

Silber, Michael. "Absolutism, Hungary, and the Jews. A Comparative Study of Military Conscription of the Jews in the Hapsburg Lands, 1788–1815." Master's thesis, Columbia University, 1977.

Whittaker, Cynthia H. "Count S. S. Uvarov: Conservatism and National Enlightenment in Pre-Reform Russia." Ph.D. dissertation, Indiana University, 1971.

Primary Sources

Aleksandrov, H. "Fun arkhiv fun minsker kool" [From the archive of the Minsk kahal]. *Tsaytshrift* 1 (1926): 239–49; 2–3 (1928): 767–78.

Allgemeine Zeitung des Judentums. Leipzig, 1837–56.

Archives israélites de France: Revue mensuelle. Paris, 1811–55.

Assaf, Simha. *Mekorot le-toledot ha-hinukh be-yisra'el* [Sources on the history of Jewish education]. 4 vols. Tel Aviv, 1925–42.

Barats, G. "Dva dokumenta 1828 goda" [Two documents of 1828]. *Evreiskaia starina* 4 (1911): 89–95.

Beilin, S. "Razskazy byvshikh kantonistov" [Stories of former Cantonists]. *Evreiskaia starina* 8 (1915): 224–25.

Ben-Yaᶜakov, Yizḥak. "ᶜOlam ha-ᶜasiyah" [The world of action]. *Ha-kerem*, 1887, pp. 41–62.

Berman, Yekuti'el. "Shenot ra'inu raᶜah" [Years of evil]. *Ha-meliz*, 1861.

Bohorad, Yizḥak Aizik. *She'eilot u-teshuvot Penei Yizḥak* [Responsa]. Vilna, 1909.

Deynard, Ephraim. *Zikhronot bat ᶜami* [Memoirs of my people]. 2 vols. Arlington, N.J., 1920.

Dubnov, S. M. "Istoricheskie soobshcheniia: podgotovitel'nyia raboty po istorii russkikh evreev. No. 13: Biurokraticheskiia uprazheniia v reshenii evreiskago voprosa (1840–1841)" [Historical notices: preliminary works in the history of Russian Jews. no. 13: bureaucratic exercises in the solution of the Jewish question]. *Voskhod* 21 (1901): no. 4, 25–40; no. 3, 3–21.

———. "Iz moego arkhiva" [From my archive]. *Perezhitoe* 1 (1908): documentary section, pp. 1–9.

Dziennik Praw Królestwa Polskiego [Legal daily of the kingdom of Poland]. Warsaw, 1826–71.

Epstein, Barukh Halevi. *Sefer Mekor Barukh* [Spring of Barukh]. 3 vols., 4 pts. New York, 1954.

Fin, Sh. Y. " 'Iggerot Sh. Y. Fin" [Letters of Sh. Y. Fin]. *Pardes* 3 (1896): 149–56.

———. *Toledot leshon rusiyah* [History of the Russian language]. Vilna, 1847.

Fridberg, A. Sh. "Zikhronot mi-yimei neᶜurai, Ha-ḥatufim" [Memoirs of my youth. The Cantonists]. *Sefer ha-shanah*, 1892, pp. 82–101.

Galant, I. "Dokumenty iz epokhi Nikolaia I (iz Kievskikh arkhivov)" [Documents of the period of Nicholas I (from Kievan Archives)]. *Evreiskaia starina* 7 (1914): 104–6.

Gessen, Iu. I. "Iz sorokovykh godov. Graf P. Kiselev i Moisei Montefiore" [From the forties. Count P. Kiselev and Moses Montefiore]. *Perezhitoe* 4 (1913): 149–80.

———. "Zabytyi obshchestvennyi deiatel' " [A forgotten communal activist]. *Evreiskaia starina* 4 (1911): 391–402.

———. "Zapiska vilenskago kagala o nuzhdakh evreiskago naroda (1833)" [A memorandum of the Vilna kahal on the needs of the Jewish people (1833)]. *Evreiskaia starina* 4 (1911): 96–108.

Ginzburg, M. A. *'Avi^cezer.* Vilna, 1863.

———. *Devir* [Sanctuary]. Warsaw, 1883.

———. "Kikayon de-yonah" [Jonah's gourd]. *Ha-moriah,* 1878, pp. 38–48.

[Ginzburg, M. A.] Yonah ben Amitai. *Maggid 'emet* [Herald of truth]. Leipzig, 1843.

Ginzburg, S. M. "Iz sviazki pisem" [From correspondence]. *Perezhitoe* 1 (1908): 35–36; 2 (1910): 289–95; 4 (1913): 331.

———, ed. "Iz zapisok pervago evreia-studenta v Rossii (L. I. Mandel'shtam, 1830–1840 gg)" [From the notes of the first Jewish student in Russia (L. I. Mandelshtam, 1839–1840)]. *Perezhitoe* 1 (1908): 1–50.

———. "Ketavim u-te^cudot le-toledot ha-yehudim be-rusiyah" [Writings and documents on the history of the Jews in Russia]. *Ḥorev* 2 (1935): 108–11.

———. "Max Lilienthal's Activities in Russia: New Documents." *Publications of the American Jewish Historical Society,* no. 35 (1939): 39–51.

Ginzburg, S. M., and Marek, P. *Evreiskie narodnye pesni v Rossii* [Jewish folk songs in Russia]. St. Petersburg, 1901.

Gol'dberg, Sh. "Prisiazhnyi list evreiskago rekruta 1829 g." [The oath of a Jewish recruit in 1829]. *Perezhitoe* 2 (1910): 285–87.

Goldenshtayn, P. D. *Mayn lebns-geshikhte* [My life story]. Petaḥ-Tikvah, 1929.

Gol'dshtein, S. "Emmanuel Borisovich Levin—po avtobiograficheskikh zametkam (1820–1913)" [Emmanuel Borisovich Levin—according to autobiographical notes (1820–1913)]. *Evreiskaia starina* 9 (1916): 253–75.

Gottlober, A. B. "Iz perepiski A. B. Gotlobera" [From the correspondence of A. B. Gottlober]. *Evreiskaia starina* 3 (1910): 283–92, 411–18; 4 (1911): 299–303, 403–8.

———. "Zikhronot mi-yemei ne^curai" [Memoirs of my youth] *Zikhronot u-masa^cot,* edited by R. Goldberg. Jerusalem, 1976.

———. "Zikhroynes: erinerungen iber yidishe shrayber un sforim" [Memoirs of Yiddish writers and books]. *Di yidishe folks-bibliotek* 1 (1888): 250–59.

Heller, Yeḥiel. *Sefer ^camudei 'or. She'eilot u-teshuvot* [Pillars of light. Responsa]. Reprint ed. Jerusalem, 1967.

Herzen, Alexander. *My Past and Thoughts.* Translated by Constance Garnett. Abr. ed. New York, 1974.

Hurvits, E. L., and Fin, Sh. Y., eds. *Pirḥei ẓafon* [Flowers of the north]. Vilna, 1841 and 1844.

Itskovich, I. "Vospominaniia arkhangel'skago kantonista" [Memoirs of an Arkhangel'sk Cantonist]. *Evreiskaia starina* 5 (1912): 54–65.

Kagan, M. "Soobshcheniia—kvitantsiia 'poimannika' " [Communication—the receipt of a "captured one"]. *Evreiskaia starina* 3 (1910): 427.

Katsenelson, Y. L. (Buki ben Yagli). *Mah she-ra'u ^ceinai ve-shameu 'ozenai, zikhronot mi-yemei ḥayai* [What my eyes saw and my ears heard, memoirs of my life]. Jerusalem, 1947.

Katzenellenbogen, Hirsh Ẓvi. *Netivot ^colam* [Paths of the world]. Vilna, 1858.

Koppen, P. I. [Köppen, P. I.]. *Deviataia reviziia. Issledovanie o chisle zhitelei v*

Rossii. [Ninth revision. Study of the number of inhabitants in Russia]. St. Petersburg, 1857.

————. "Ueber die Zahl der Hebräer in Russland und deren Verhältniss zur übrigen Bevolkerung, in denjenigen Provinzen, wo solche geduldet werden." *Bulletin scientifique publié par l'Academie Impériale des Sciences de Saint-Peterbourg* 7 (1840): 92–96.

Kon, P. "Di gefunene teiln fun vilner koolishn arkhiv (1808–1845) mit tsvei reproduktsies" [The found parts of the Vilna kahal archive (1808–1845), with two reproductions]. *Historishe shriftn* 2 (1937): 538–42.

————. "Fun vilner arkhivn un bibliotekn: Yulian Kliatshko un zayn foter Hirsh" [From Vilna archives and libraries: Julian Kliaczko and his father Hirsh]. *Historishe shriftn* 1 (1929): 772–78.

————. "Materialn un notitsen: yidn in industrie un handl in vilne onheyb 19tn y"h" [Materials and notices: Jews in industry and trade in Vilna at the beginning of the 19th century]. *YIVO-Bleter* 8 (1935): 78–84.

Kotik, Yehezkel. *Mayne zikhroynes* [My memoirs]. Berlin, 1922.

Kukol'nik, Pavel. "Anti-Tsiprinus: vospominaniia o N. N. Novosil'tseve" [Anti-Tsiprinus: memoirs about N. N. Novosil'tsev]. *Russkii arkhiv* 1 (1873): 193–224.

Kulisher, R. "Itogi: nadezhdy i ozhidaniia peredovoi chasti russkikh evreev za poledniia 50 let" [Results: the hopes and expectations of the progressive part of Russian Jewry in the last fifty years]. *Voskhod* 11 (1891): 24–39; 12 (1892): 6–15; 13 (1893): 100–118; 14 (1894): 81–100, 40–53.

Lebenzon, A. et al. *Mikra kodesh ʿim beiʾur ve-targum germani beʾ-otiot ʿivriot, be-tosefot "beʾurim ḥadashim" shel Ada"m Ha-kohen u-"beʾurim ye-shanim" shel Rʾ Yehudah Bohak* [The Holy Scriptures with a commentary and translation into German in Hebrew letters. Supplemented with "New Exegeses" by Ada"m Ha-kohen and "Old Exegeses" by Yehudah Bohak]. 17 vols. Vilna, 1849–52.

Lebenzon, A. *Shirei sefat kodesh* [Songs of the holy tongue]. Vilna, 1861.

Levanda, L. "Shkoloboiazn' " [Fear of schools]. *Evreiskaia biblioteka* 5 (1875): 65–88.

————. "Tipy i siluety (vospominaniia shkol'nika kontsa sorokovykh godov)" [Types and silhouettes (memoirs of a schoolboy at the end of the forties)]. *Voskhod* 1 (1881): no. 1, 32–59; no. 2, 120–29; no. 3, 1–23; no. 4, 49–94.

Levanda, V. O. *Polnyi khronologicheskii sbornik zakonov i polozhenii, kasaiu-shchikhsia evreev* [Complete chronological collection of laws concerning Jews]. St. Petersburg, 1874.

Levin, Yehudah, Leib. "Zikhronot ve-raʿayanot" [Memoirs and thoughts]. *Sefer ha-yovel huval le-shai Naḥum Sokolov*. Warsaw, 1934, pp. 354–67.

Levin, E. B. "Zapiska o poimannikakh (1855)" [Memorandum on captives (1855)]. *Evreiskaia starina* 8 (1915): 216–24.

Levinsohn, I. B. *Bet ha-ʾozar (Shoreshei Levanon)* [Treasure house (rocks of Lebanon)]. Vilna, 1871.

————. *Bet yehudah* [The house of Judah]. Vilna, 1839.

————. "Di hefker-velt" [World of lawlessness]. *Di yidishe folks-bibliotek* 1 (1888): 133–47.

————. *ʾEfes damim*. Translated from the Hebrew by Dr. L. Loewe. London, 1841.

————. "Pis'mo I. B. Levinzona k admiralu A. S. Shishkovu" [Letter of I. B.

Levinsohn to Admiral A. S. Shishkov]. Edited by Iulii Gessen. *Perezhitoe* 1 (1908): documentary section, pp. 23–27.

———. *Te͗udah be-yisra'el* [Testimony in Israel]. Vilna, 1828.

———. "Toledot peloni 'almoni ha-kozavi" [History of the deceitful Mr. X]. *Yalkut Riba"l*. Warsaw, 1878.

Lifshiz, Ya͗akov Halevi. *Zikhron Ya͗akov* [Memoirs of Jacob]. Kovna, 1924.

Lilienblum, M. L. *Ḥat'ot ne͗urim* [Sins of my youth]. Reprint ed. Jerusalem, 1970.

Lilienthal, Max. *Freiheit, Frühling and Liebe. Gedichte.* Cincinnati, 1857.

———. "Gerder" [Herder]. *Zhurnal Ministerstva narodnago prosveshcheniia* 45 (1844): pt. 5: 1–30.

———. [Letter]. *Archives israélites* 3 (1842): 552–57.

———. [Letter]. *Allgemeine Zeitung des Judentums* 6 (1842): 602–11.

———. *Maggid yeshu͗ah* [Herald of salvation]. Vilna, 1842.

———. "My Travels in Russia." In David Philipson, *Max Lilienthal, American Rabbi, Life and Writings*, pp. 159–367. New York, 1915.

———. "Family Letters." In David Philipson, *Max Lilienthal, American Rabbi, Life and Writings*, pp. 133–58. New York, 1915.

———. "Pis'mo d-ra Lilientala o svoei missii (1842)" [Letter of Dr. Lilienthal about his mission]. *Evreiskaia starina* 5 (1912). 91–94.

———. *Predigten für Sabbathe und Festtage.* Munich, 1839.

———. "Russisch-jüdische Skizzen." *Allgemeine Zeitung des Judentums* 9 (1845): 525–26, 537–39, 552–54, 569–72, 586–88, 600–602; 11 (1847): 154–55, 213–15, 226–30, 547–49, 615–19, 683–86; 12 (1848): 232–33.

———. "The Jews in Russia under Nicolai I." *Asmonean* 10 (1854): 84–85, 93–94, 101.

———. "The Russian Government and the Russian Jews: My Personal Experience." *Jewish Times* 1, no. 48: (1870), 3–4.

Lilienthal, Sophie. *The Lilienthal Family Record.* San Francisco, 1930.

Lozinskii, S. G., ed. *Kazennye evreiskie uchilishcha.* (*Opisanie del byvshego arkhiva Ministerstva narodnogo prosveshcheniia*) [Government Jewish Schools (description of the files of the former Ministry of National Enlightenment)], vol. 1. Peterburg [sic], 1920.

Lurie, A. "Di tsvoe fun a pinsker balebos onheyb 19tn y"h" [The will of a Pinsk homeowner, beginning of the 19th century]. *YIVO-Bleter* 13 (1938): 390–428.

Lutski, Y. Sh. *'Iggeret teshu͗ah yisra'el* [Epistle of salvation to Israel]. Guzlav, 1841.

Luzzatto, S. D. *Iggerot Shada"l* [Letters of S. D. Luzzatto]. Cracow, 1894.

Maggid, D. G. "Iz semeinago arkhiva: K istorii kagala" [From a family archive: to the history of the kahal]. *Perezhitoe* 2 (1910): 126–30.

Maimonides, Moses. *'Eize halakhot mi-yad ha-ḥazakah la-'adonenu morenu ha-Ramba"m* [German title page: Auszüge aus dem Buche Jad-Haghasakkah, die Starke Hand, Handbuch der Religion, nach dem Talmud zusammengestellt von Rabbi Moscheh-ben-Maimon, gen. Moses Maimonides, aus Spanien]. Compiled by L. Mandelshtam. 5 vols. St. Petersburg, 1850.

Mandelshtam, Binyamin. *Ḥazon la-mo͗eid* [A prophecy for our time]. Vienna, 1867.

Mandelshtam, L., ed. *Shenei perakim* [Two chapters]. St. Petersburg, 1852.

Marek, P. "Iz arkhivnoi kollektsii: Pis'mo Lilientala" [From an archival collection: a letter of Lilienthal]. *Evreiskaia starina* 1 (1909): 110–12.

Merimzon, M. "Razskaz starago soldata" [The story of an old soldier]. *Evreiskaia starina* 5 (1912): 290–301, 406–22; 5 (1913): 86–95, 221–32.

[Miliutin, B.] "Khoziaistvennoe ustroistvo i sostoianie evreiskikh obshchestv v Rossii" [The economic order and state of the Jewish communities of Russia]. *Zhurnal Ministerstva vnutrennikh del* 28 (1849): 67–92, 197–254, 429–69; 29 (1850): 52–85, 238–78, 417–35; 31 (1850): 153–210.

Montefiore, Moses. *Diaries of Sir Moses and Lady Montefiore*. Edited by L. Loewe. 12 vols. London, 1890.

Morgulis, M. "Iz moikh vospominanii" [From my memoirs]. *Voskhod* 15 (1895), no. 2: 108–29; no. 4: 21–35; no. 7: 140–54; no. 9: 97–122; nos. 11–12: 81–103; 16 (1896), nos. 5–6: 169–90; 17 (1897), no. 4: 65–87; no. 6: 86–100.

Opis' del arkhiva Gosudarstvennago soveta [Description of the files of the archive of the State Council]. 16 vols. St. Petersburg, 1908–10.

"Otchet Ober-prokurora Sviateishago Sinoda, 1825–1850" [Report of the head of the Holy Synod, 1825–1850]. *Sbornik Imp. russkago-istoricheskago obshchestva* 98 (1890): 457–60.

Paperna, A. I. "Iz Nikolaevskoi epokhi" [From the Nicholaevan era]. *Perezhitoe* 2 (1910): 1–53.

———. "Vospominaniia" [Memoirs]. *Perezhitoe* 3 (1911): 264–364.

———. "Zikhronot" [Memoirs]. *Sefer ha-shanah* 1 (1900): 60–75.

———. "Zikhronot u-shemu^cot" [Memoirs]. *Reshumot* 1 (1918): 148–65.

Polnoe sobranie zakonov rossisskoi imperii [Complete collection of laws of the Russian Empire]. Second Collection: 1825–55. 30 vols. St. Petersburg, 1830–56.

Rabinovich, Osip. "Shtrafnoi" [The penal conscript]. In his *Sochineniia*. Odessa, 1880, 1: 1–74.

———. "Novaia evreiskaia sinagoga v Odesse" [New Synagogue in Odessa]. In his *Sochineniia*. Odessa, 1888, 1: 373–80.

Sbornik postanovlenii po Ministerstvu narodnago prosveshcheniia [Collection of orders of the Ministry of National Enlightenment], vol. 2 (1825–1855). St. Petersburg, 1875–76.

Shelomoh Zalman of Neustadt. *Sefer Bet 'avot* [House of fathers]. Berlin, 1838–39.

Shpigel', M. "Iz zapisok kantonista" [From the notes of a Cantonist]. *Evreiskaia starina* 4 (1911): 249–59.

Simonov, M. "Iz vospominanii russkago vracha. Pravoslavnoe dukhovenstvo i evrei" [From the memoirs of a Russian doctor. The Russian Orthodox clergy and the Jews]. *Evreiskaia starina* 2 (1909): 71–75.

Slonimski, H. S. *Mosedei ḥokhmah* [The foundations of wisdom]. Vilna, 1834.

———. *Kokhva de-shavit* [Comet]. Vilna, 1835.

Stepanov, M., and Vermale, F. "Zhozef de Mestr v Rossii." Pis'ma Zhozefa de Mestra k S. S. Uvarovu" [Joseph de Maistre in Russia. Joseph de Maistre's letters to S. S. Uvarov]. *Literaturnoe nasledstvo* 29/30 (1937): 677–712.

Svod voennykh postanovlenii [Code of military orders]. 12 vols. St. Petersburg, 1838.

Svod zakonov rossisskoi imperii [The code of laws of the Russian Empire]. 15 vols. St. Petersburg, 1842.

Takones-sho: vi men zol brengen di yidishe yeshives, lernanshtalten, khadorim, un melamdim unter der hashgokhe fun der ministerstva narodnaho prosvesh-cheniie [Orders of the day: how to bring the Jewish yeshivot, educational institutions, ḥeders, and melamdim under the supervision of the Ministry of National Enlightenment]. Vilna, undated.

Tarnopol, Joachim. *Notices historiques et caractéristiques sur les israélites d'Odessa, précédées d'un aperçu général sur l'état du peuple israélite en Russie*. Odessa, 1855.

Tsherikover, E. "Der arkhiv fun Shimen Dubnov" [The archive of Shimen Dubnov]. *Historishe shriftn* 2 (1937): 591–600.

————. "Fun di rusishe arkhivn" [From the Russian archives]. *Historishe shriftn* 1 (1929): 779–92.

Tsh[erikover], E. "Fun der YIVO-arkhiv" [From the YIVO archive]. *Historishe shriftn* 2 (1931): 668–73.

Tsinberg, S. L. "Pis'mo d-ra M. Lilientalia k G. Katsenelenbogenu" [Letter of Dr. Lilienthal to G. Katzenellenbogen]. *Perezhitoe* 3 (1911): 379–81.

Tsiprinus. "Kaleidoskop vospominanii 1811–1871: N. N. Novosil'tsev" [A kaleidoscope of memories 1811–1871: N. N. Novosil'tsev]. *Russkii arkhiv* 10 (1872): 1704–69.

Tsunzer, Eliakum. *Tsunzer's biografie, geshribn fun im aleyn. A Jewish Bard, Being the Biography of Eliakum Zunser, Written by Himself and Rendered into English by Simon Hisdansky*. New York, 1905.

"Tsvei proshenies fun mohilever un grodner kehiles tsu Nikolai dem ershtn" [Two petitions from Mogilev and Grodno kahals to Nicholas I]. *Tsaytshrift* 2/3 (1928): 759–64.

Tugendhold, V. *Ha-musar, 'o 'aḥarit ha-reshᶜa* [The moral, or the end of evil]. No publication information.

————. *Poᶜel ẓedek* [Labor of justice]. Vilna, 1842.

Uvarov, S. S. *Desiatiletie Ministerstva narodnago prosveshcheniia, 1833–1843* [Ten years of the Ministry of National Enlightenment, 1833–1843]. St. Petersburg, 1864.

————. *Etudes de philologie et de critique*. 2nd ed. Paris, 845.

————. *Esquisses politiques et littéraires*. Paris, 1848.

————. *Extrait du compte-rendu du Ministère de l'instruction publique pour l'année 1837*. St. Petersburg, 1838.

————. *Funeral Ovation on Moreau*. Translated from the French by G. H. Neuville. New York, 1814.

————. *L'Empereur Alexandre et Buonaparte*. St. Petersburg, 1814.

————. "Podvigaetsia li vpered istoricheskaia dostovernost'?" [Is historical truth advancing?] *Sovremennik* 25 (1851), no. 2: 121–28.

Wengeroff, Pauline. *Memoiren einer Grossmutter. Bilder aus der Kultur-Geschichte der Juden Russlands im 19. Jahrhundert*. 2 vols. Berlin, 1908–10.

Zhurnal Ministerstva narodnago prosveshcheniia [Journal of the Ministry of National Enlightenment]. 88 vols. 1834–1855.

Zhurnal Ministerstva vnutrennikh del [Journal of the Ministry of the Interior]. St. Petersburg, 1829–55.

Secondary Works

Alabin, P. V. "Iz dnevnika P. V. Alabina: I. B. Levinzon" [From the diary of P. V. Alabin: I. B. Levinzohn]. *Russkaia starina* 25 (1878): 223–30.

Aleksandrov, H. "Kazyone yidishe shuln un rekrutchine" [The government Jewish schools and the draft]. *Tsaytshrift* 4 (1930): 125–32.

———. *Tsu der geshikhte fun folks-bildung bay yidn in rusland in der tsayt fun Nikolai dem ershtn* [To the history of the folk-education of the Jews in Russia in the time of Nicholas I]. Minsk, 1929.

Alston, Patrick. *Education and the State in Tsarist Russia.* Stanford, 1969.

Aristov, N. Ia. "Istoricheskie anekdoty" [Historical anecdotes]. *Istoricheskii vestnik,* 1882, pp. 245–48.

Bałaban, Majer. *Historia Lwowskiej Synagogi Postępowej* [History of the progressive synagogue of Lwów]. Lwów, 1937.

———. *Herz Homberg i szkoły józefińskie dla żydów w Galicji* [Herz Homberg and the "Josephite" schools for Jews in Galicia]. Lwów, 1906.

Barnard, Frederick M. "Herder and Israel." *Jewish Social Studies* 28 (1966): 25–33.

Baron, Salo W. "Newer Approaches to Jewish Emancipation." *Diogenes* 29 (1960): 56–81.

———. *The Russian Jew under Tsars and Soviets.* New York, 1964.

Beilin, S. "Anekdoty o evreiskom bezpravii" [Anecdotes about Jewish rightlessness]. *Evreiskaia starina* 2 (1909): 269–81.

———. "Byl ili vymysel?" [Truth of fiction?]. *Evreiskaia starina* 7 (1914): 106–8.

———. "Iz istoricheskikh zhurnalov" [From historical journals]. *Evreiskaia starina* 4 (1911): 417–19, 588–90; 5 (1912): 340–41; 6 (1913): 408–12, 540–42; 7 (1914): 492–94.

———. "Iz razskazov o kantonistakh" [From stories about Cantonists]. *Evreiskaia starina* 2 (1909): 115–20.

Beletskii, A. *Vopros ob obrazovanii russkikh evreev v tsarstvovanie Imperatora Nikolaia I* [The question of the education of Russian Jews in the reign of Emperor Nicholas I]. St. Petersburg, 1894.

Berdichevsky, M. Y. "Toledot yeshivat ᶜeẓ-ḥayim" (History of the Volozhin yeshivah]. *Ha-'asif* 3 (1886): 231–42.

Berger, Mordehai. "Mas neirot ha-shabbat be-rusyah" [Sabbath-candle tax in Russia]. *He-ᶜavar* 19 (1972): 127–242.

Berlin, Isaiah. *Vico and Herder.* New York, 1976.

———. "A Marvelous Decade." *Encounter* 26 (1955).

Berlin, Me'ir. *Raban shel yisra'el: Rabenu Naphtali Ẓvi Yehudah Berlin—ha-Neẓiv, toledotav, korotav* [Israel's rabbi: rabbi Naphtali Ẓvi Yehudah Berlin, his biography]. New York, 1943.

Berlin, P. A. *Russkaia burzhuaziia v staroe i novoe vremia* [The Russian bourgeoisie in old and modern times]. Moscow, 1922.

Berz, L. "Aritmetishe lernbikher in yidish, 1699–1831" [Arithmetic textbooks in Yiddish, 1699–1831]. *YIVO-Bleter* 19 (1942): 59–79.

Bialoblutsky, Shemu'el. "Merkazei ha-torah be-lita" [Torah centers in Lithuania]. *Yahadut Lita* 1 (1959): 185–205.

Binshtok, I. "Russko-evreiskaia narodnaia shkola v sviazi s istoricheskim khodom obrazovaniia evreev v Rossii" [Russian-Jewish folk school in connection with the history of the education of the Jews in Russia]. *Voskhod* (1893), no. 8: 82–100; nos. 10–11: 262–77; no. 12: 26–40.

Blackwell, William L. *The Beginnings of Russian Industrialization, 1800–1860.* Princeton, 1968.

Borovoi, S. Ia. *Evreiskaia zemledel'cheskaia kolonizatsiia v staroi Rossii* [Jewish agricultural colonization in Old Russia]. Moscow, 1928.

Bramson, L. M. *K istorii nachal'nago obrazovaniia evreev v Rossii* [To the history of primary education among Russian Jews]. St. Petersburg, 1896.

Brezhgo, B. "Yidishe shules in vitebsker gubernie 1849–1863" [Jewish schools in Vitebsk Province, 1849–1863]. *Shriftn far ekonomik un statistik* 1 (1928): 183–85.

Brodskii, David. "Iak do Khresta privodili kantonistiv zhidiv" [How Jewish Cantonists were converted]. *Zapiski istorichno-filologiches'koho vidilly Ukrains'koi Akademii Nauk* 12 (1927): 297–304.

Curtiss, John S. *The Russian Army under Nicholas I*, Durham, 1965.

Custine, Marquis de. *La Russie en 1839*. 8 bks. in 4 vols. Brussels, 1843.

Czynski, Jean. "Juifs de la Russie et de la Pologne." *Archives israélites* 4 (1843): 40–44, 163–72, 238–42, 365–73, 497–505, 617–23; 5 (1844): 135–42, 333–37, 479–85, 721–24, 778–80; 6 (1845): 238–44.

Dereviansky, Y. D. "Di batsiung fun der gezelshaft un di regirungs-krayzn tsu der rabiner-shul" [The attitude of society and the authorities to the rabbinical school]. *YIVO-Bleter* 10 (1936): 14–19.

Dik, A. M. *Ha-'oreaḥ* [The visitor]. Königsberg, 1860.

———. *Der erster (sic) nabor vos var in dem yor 5588–1828 [The first levy in 1828]*. *Vilna, 1871.*

———. *Ha-behalah* [The panic]. *He-ʿavar* 2 (1954): 37–44.

Dinur, B. "Demutah ha-historit shel ha-yahadut ha-rusit u-veʿayot ha-ḥeker bah" [The historical character of Russian Jewry and problems in its study]. *Zion* 22 (1957): 93–118.

Doroshenko, D. *Narys istorii Ukrainy* [Outline of the history of the Ukraine]. Vol. 2. Warsaw, 1933.

Dubnov, S. M. "Iz khroniki mstislavskoi obshchiny" [From the chronicle of the Mstislavl' community]. *Voskhod* 19 (1899), no. 9: 33–59.

———. "Kak byla vvedena rekrutskaia povinnost' dlia evreev v 1827g" [How the recruit duty was introduced for Jews in 1827]. *Evreiskaia starina* 2 (1909): 256–65.

———. "K istorii goneniia na evreiskiia knigi (1848)" [To the history of persecutions against Jewish books (1848)]. *Evreiskaia starina* 2 (1909): 112–14.

———. *History of the Jews in Russia and Poland*. Translated by I. Friedlaender. 3 vols. Philadelphia, 1916–26.

Dubnov, Volf. "Tsu der ekonomisher geshikhte fun di yidn in rusland" [To the economic history of the Jews in Russia]. *Shriftn far ekonomik un statistik* 1 (1928): 92–97.

Ehrlich, A. *Entwickelungsgeschichte der Israelitischen Gemeindeschule zu Riga*. St. Petersburg, 1894.

Eisenbach, Artur. *Kwestia równouprawnienia Żydów w Królestwie Polskim* [The question of the equal rights of the Jews in the Kingdom of Poland]. Warsaw, 1972.

Eliav, Mordehai. *Ha-ḥinukh ha-yehudi be-germaniah bi-yemei ha-haskalah ve-ha-'emanẓipaẓiiah*. [Jewish education in Germany in the period of enlightenment and emancipation]. Jerusalem, 1961.

Epstein, M. B. "Religioznyi motiv v russkom zakonodatel'stve o evreiakh" [The religious motive in Russian legislation on the Jews]. *Evreiskaia letopis'* 3 (1924): 119–23.

Etkes, Emanuel. "Ha-Gr"a ve-ha-haskalah: tadmit u-mezi'ut" [The Gaon of Vilna and the Haskalah: image and reality], *Perakim be-toledot ha-ḥevrah ha-yehudit be-yimei ha-beinayim u-veᶜet ha-ḥadashah mukdashim le-prof'* Ya-ᶜakov Kaẓ, pp. 192–217 (Jerusalem, 1980).

——. "Parashat ha-'haskalah mi-taᶜam' veha-temurah be-maᶜamad tenuᶜat ha-haskalah be-rusyah" [Compulsory enlightenment as a crossroads in the history of the Haskalah movement in Russia]. *Ẓion* 43 (1978): 264–313.

Ettinger, Shemu'el. "Ha-yesodot ve-ha-megamot be-ᶜitsuv mediniut ha-shilton ha-rusi kelapei ha-yehudim ᶜim ḥalukat polin" [The bases and orientation in the shaping of policy toward the Jews with the partition of Poland]. *He-ᶜavar* 19 (1972): 20–34.

——. "Takanat 1804" [The statute of 1804]. *He-ᶜavar* 22 (1977): 87–110.

Fajnhaus, David. "Konflikty społeczne wśród ludności żydowskiej na Litwie i Białorusi w pierwszej połowie xix wieku" [Social conflicts among Jews in Lithuania and Belorussia in the first half of the 19th Century]. *Biuletyn Żydowskiego instytutu historycznego* (1964), no. 52:3–15.

Fin, Sh. Y. "Safah le-ne'emanim" [Words to the faithful]. *Ha-karmel* 4 (1879–1880): 51–64, 591–98, 657–79.

——. "Dor ve-doreshav" [A generation and its seekers]. *Ha-karmel* 4 (1879–1880): 9–15, 73–80, 193–201, 259–66, 331–38, 461–71.

——. *Kiriah ne'emanah* [A faithful city]. Vilna, 1915.

Flynn, James T. "S. S. Uvarov's 'Liberal' Years." *Jahrbücher für Geschichte Osteuropas* 22 (1972): 48–91.

——. "Tuition and Social Class in the Russian Universities: S. S. Uvarov and 'Reaction' in the Russia of Nicholas I." *Slavic Review* 35 (1976): 232–48.

Fridkin, A. *Avrohom-Ber Gottlober un zayn epokhe* [Abraham Ber Gottlober and his era]. Vilna, 1925.

Gelber, N. M. "Di hishtadles fun Baron Salomon Rotschild in Vien letoyves di russiche yidn in 1846" [The lobbying of Baron Solomon Rothschild in Vienna on behalf of the Russian Jews in 1846]. *Historishe shriftn* 1 (1929): 803–10.

Gershenzon, M. D., ed. *Epokha Nikolaia I* [The era of Nicholas I]. Moscow, 1911.

Gessen, Iulii I. [Hessen, J.] "Die russiche Regierung und die westeuropäische Juden, Zur Schulreform in Russland, 1840–1844," *Monatsschrift für Geschichte und Wissenschaft des Judentums* 57 (1913): 257–71, 482–500.

——. *Galleria evreiskikh deiatelei* [A gallery of Jewish activists]. St. Petersburg, 1898.

——. *Istoriia evreiskogo naroda v Rossii* [History of the Jewish people in Russia]. 2 vols. 2nd ed. Leningrad, 1925–27.

——. "Iz letopisi minuvshago" [From past chronicles]. *Perezhitoe* 1 (1908): documentary section, pp. 10–34.

——. "K istorii evreiskikh tipografii" [To the history of Jewish publishers]. *Evreiskaia starina* 2 (1909): 251–55.

——. "K istorii korobochnago sbora v Rossii" [To the history of the "korobka" tax in Russia]. *Evreiskaia starina* 3 (1911): 305–47, 484–512.

——. "K sud'be evreev-vrachei v Rossii" [On the fate of Jewish doctors in Russia]. *Evreiskaia starina* 3 (1910): 612–23.

——. "Moskovskoe getto (po neizdannym materialam)" [The Moscow ghetto, according to unpublished materials]. *Perezhitoe* 1 (1908): 51–65.

————. "Mstislavskoe buistvo (po arkhivnym materialam)" [The Mstislavl' riot, according to archival materials]. *Perezhitoe* 2 (1910): 54–77.

————. "Popytka emantsipatsii evreev v Rossii (po neizdannym materialam)" [An attempt at emancipating the Jews of Russia, according to unpublished materials]. *Perezhitoe* 1 (1908): 144–63.

————. "Ravvinskie uchilishcha v Rossii" [Rabbinical seminaries in Russia]. *Evreiskaia entsiklopediia*, vol. 13, p. 259.

————. "Smena obshchestvennykh techenii: I. B. Levinson i d-r M. Liliental" [The shift in societal trends: I. B. Levinsohn and Dr. M. Lilienthal]. *Perezhitoe* 3 (1911): 1–37.

————. "Sotsial'no-ekonomicheskaia bor'ba sredi evreev v Rossii v 30–50-kh godakh 19go veka" [The socioeconomic war among Jews in Russia in the 30s–50s of the 19th century]. *Evreiskaia letopis'* 4 (1926): 45–56.

————. "Stranitsy iz istorii obshchestvennago samoupravleniia evreev v Rossii (po arkhivnym materialam)" [Pages from the history of the communal autonomy of the Jews of Russia, according to archival materials]. *Voskhod* 24 (1904), no. 7: 50–78, no. 8: 56–93.

————. "Sud'by Volozhinskago eshibota" [The fortunes of the Volozhin yeshivah]. *Perezhitoe* 1 (1908): documentary section, pp. 19–22.

————. "Tsadik Mendel Liubavichskii (epizod iz prosvetitel'noi epokhi)" [The Tsadik Mendel of Liubavich (an episode from the period of enlightenment)]. *Voskhod* 25 (1905), no. 1: 106–20.

————. "V temnykh uglakh evreiskoi obshchestvennoi zhizni" [In the dark corners of Jewish communal life]. *Evreiskaia mysl'* 1 (1922): 102–14.

————. *Zakon i zhizn'* [Law and life]. St. Petersburg, 1911.

Ginzburg, Shaul [S. M.]. *Amolike Peterburg* [St. Petersburg in the past]. New York, 1944.

————. "Di antshteyung fun der yidisher rekrutchine" [The beginnings of Jewish recruitment]. *Tsaytshrift* 2/3 (1928): 89–106.

————. *Historishe verk* [Historical works]. 3 vols. New York, 1934.

————. "K semidesiatiletiiu 'Teudo beisroel' " [To the seventieth anniversary of Teᶜudah be-yisra'el]. *Voskhod* 18 (1898), no. 4: 132–51, no. 5: 50–64.

————. "Le-korot ha-behalah' be-shenat 5595" [To the history of the panic of 1835]. *He-ᶜavar* 2 (1918): 34–37.

————. *Meshumodim in tsarishn rusland* [Apostates in tsarist Russia]. New York, 1946.

————. "Mucheniki-deti (iz istorii kantonistov-evreev)" [Child-martyrs (from the history of the Jewish Cantonists)]. *Evreiskaia starina* 13 (1930): 50–79.

————. "Vilenskii samozvanets proshlago veka" [A Vilna imposter of the last century]. *Perezhitoe* 2 (1910): 236–47.

————. "Vilner materialn in mayn arkhiv" [Vilna materials in my archive]. *YIVO-Bleter* 8 (1935): 275–76.

Glitsnshtein, A. H. *Rabenu ha-"Tsemakh-Tsedek"* [Our rabbi the "Tsemakh-Tsedek]. Brooklyn, 1976.

Golitsyn, Nikolai N. *Istoriia russkago zakonodatel'stva o evreiakh* [The history of Russian legislation on the Jews]. St. Petersburg, 1886.

Gordon, Y. L. *Sikhes-khulin* [Small talk]. Warsaw, 1886.

————. "Ha-ᶜazamot ha-yeveishot" [Dry bones]. In *Kitvei Yehudah Leib Gordon: Prozah*. Tel Aviv, 1960.

Gordon, L. O. "Lebenzon i Levinzon" [Lebenzon and Levinsohn]. *Russkaia starina* 26 (1879): 159.

Gosudarstvennyi sovet, 1801–1901 [The state council, 1801–1901]. St. Petersburg, 1901.

Gottlober, A. B. "Ha-gizrah ve-habiniah" [The cutting and the building]. *Haboker 'or* 3 (1868): 353–59, 405–12, 467–73, 527–32, 582–89, 640–48; 4 (1869): 691–98, 735–43, 779–83, 841–48, 909–24, 973–76.

Greenberg, L. S. *A Critical Investigation of the Works of Rabbi Isaac Ber Levinsohn.* New York, 1930.

Greenberg, Louis. *The Jews in Russia. The Struggle for Emancipation.* 2 vols. New Haven, 1944 and 1951.

Grunebaum-Ballin, P. "Grégoire convertisseur? ou la croyance au 'Retour d'Israel'." *Revue des études juives* 121 (1962): 383–98.

Grunwald, C. de. *Tsar Nicholas I.* New York, 1954.

Gurland, Ya'akov. *Kevod ha-bayit* [Honor of the house]. Vilna, 1858.

Halant, Illia [Galant, I.]. "Izgnanie evreev iz Kieva po offitsial'noi perepiske (1828–1831 goda)" [The expulsion of the Jews from Kiev according to official correspondence (1828–1831)]. *Evreiskaia starina* 7 (1914): 465–85.

———. "K istorii kievskago getto i tsenzury evreiskikh knig 1854–1855 gg.) [To the history of the Kiev ghetto and the censorship of Jewish books (1854–1855)]. *Evreiskaia starina* 6 (1913): 264–78.

———. "Vyselennia zhydiv iz 50-verstovoho uzhranychchia na Volyni i Podilli v pershii polovyni XIX v." [The expulsion of the Jews from the 50-versts border-region of Volhynia and Podolia in the first half of the 19th century]. *Zbirnyk prats' zhydivs'koi istorychno-arkheohrafichnoi komisii* 1 (1928): 123–48.

———. "Vyselennia zhydiv iz Kyiva roku 1835-go" [The expulsion of the Jews from Kiev in 1835]. *Zbirnyk prats' zhydivs'koi istorychno-arkheohrafichnoi komisii* 1 (1928): 149–97.

Hadashevich. K. "Der 'razbor' fun der yidisher bafelkerung in vitebsker gubernie" [The 'sorting' of the Jewish population of Vitebsk Province]. *Tsaytshrift* 4 (1930): 139–45.

Halperin, Yisra'el. "Nisu'ei behalah be-mizrah 'eiropah" [Panic marriages in Eastern Europe]. *Zion* 27 (1962): 36–58.

Hans, Nicholas. *History of Russian Educational Policy.* London, 1931.

Haxthausen, Auguste de. *Les forces militaires de la Russie.* Berlin, 1853.

Haxthausen, August von. *Studies on the Interior of Russia.* Edited and with an introduction by Frederick Starr. Translated by E. L. M. Schmidt. Chicago and London, 1972.

Haywood, Richard M. *The Beginnings of Railway Development in Russia in the Reign of Nicholas I, 1835–1842.* Durham, 1969.

Heilman, Avraham Shemu'el. *Sefer Bet Rebi* [House of my master]. 3 vols. Tel Aviv, 1965.

Herlihy, Patricia. "Odessa: Staple Trade and Urbanization in New Russia." *Jahrbücher für Geschichte Osteuropas* 21 (1973): 184–95.

———. "The Ethnic Composition of the City of Odessa in the Nineteenth Century." *Harvard Ukrainian Studies* 1 (1977): 53–78.

Istoricheskie svedeniia o vilensom ravvinskom uchilishche [(Historical information on the Vilna Rabbinical School)]. Vilna, 1873.

Johnson, W. H. E. *Russia's Educational Heritage.* Pittsburgh, 1950.

Kabuzan, V. M. *Narodonaselenie Rossii v XVIII-pervoi polovine XIX v (po materialam revizii)* [The population of Russia in the 18th and first half of 19th century (according to the materials of the revisions)]. Moscow, 1963.

Kahana, David. "Lilienthal ve-haskalat ha-yehudim be-rusiah" [Lilienthal and the Russian Haskalah]. *Ha-shiloaḥ* 27 (1912): 314–22, 446–57, 546–56.

Kantor, L. O. "Abram Mapu (1808–1867gg)." *Perezhitoe* 1 (1908): 315–24.

Katz, Ben-Zion, *Rabanut, ḥasidut, haskalah* [Rabbinism, Hasidism, Haskalah]. 2 vols. Tel Aviv, 1958.

Katz, Jacob. *Out of the Ghetto*. Cambridge, Mass., 1973.

———. *Tradition and Crisis*. New York, 1961.

Kaufmann, Yeḥezkel. *Golah ve-nekhar* [Diaspora and alien lands]. 2 vols. Tel Aviv, 1961.

Klausner, Yosef. *Historiah shel ha-sifrut ha-ʿivrit ha-ḥadashah* [History of modern Hebrew literature]. 6 vols. Jerusalem, 1953–58.

Kon, P. "Vilner roshei-hakool in di yorn 1802–1831" [Heads of the kahal of Vilna, 1802–1831]. *YIVO-Bleter* 7 (1934): 152–56.

———. "A. M. Dik vi a lerer in a kroinisher shul in Vilne" [A. M. Dik as a teacher in a crown school in Vilna]. *YIVO-Bleter* 3 (1931): 84–86.

———. "Di tsarishe makht un der rambam" [The tsarist government and Maimonides]. *YIVO-Bleter* 13 (1938): 577–82.

Korobkov, Kh. "Evreiskaia rekrutchina v tsarstvovanie Nikolaia I" [The recruitment of Jews during the reign of Nicholas I]. *Evreiskaia starina* 6 (1913): 70–85, 233–44.

Kosven, M. "K voprosu o vysshem obrazovanii russkikh evreev" [To the question of the higher education of Russian Jews]. *Evreiskaia starina* 7 (1904): 161–74.

Koyré, A. *La philosophie et le problème national en Russie au début du XIXe siècle*. Paris, 1929.

Kucherov, Samuel. "Administration of Justice under Nicholas I of Russia." *American Slavic and East European Review* 7 (1948): 125–38.

Kulisher, M. I. "Istoriia russkogo zakonodatel'stva o evreiakh v sviazi s sistemoi vzimaniia nalogov i otbyvaniia povinnostei" [History of Russian legislation on the Jews in connection with the system of collection of taxes and duties]. *Evreiskaia starina* 3 (1910): 467–503.

Kuznets, Simon. "Ecomonic Structure and Life of the Jews." In *The Jews, Their History, Culture, and Religion*, edited by Louis Finkelstein, vol. 2, 3rd ed. pp. 1397–666. Philadelphia, 1966.

Landau, Heinrich. "Der onteyl fun yidn in der rusish-ukrainisher tsuker industrie" [The participation of Jews in the Russian-Ukrainian sugar industry]. *Shriftn far ekonomik un statistik* 1 (1928): 98–104.

———. "Yidn un di antviklung fun kredit un transport in rusland" [Jews and the development of credit and transport in Russia]. *Ekonomishe shriftn* 2 (1932): 93–105.

Leontovich, F. "Istoricheskii obzor postanovlenii o evreiakh" [Historical review of laws on the Jews]. *Sion* (1861–62): 293–97, 309–14, 325–29, 341–45, 358–61, 373–79, 389–94, 405–10, 421–27, 641–47, 653–57, 669–73.

Lerner, O. M. *Evrei v Novorossiskom krae* [Jews in New Russia]. Odessa, 1901.

Lestchinsky, Yakov. "Bardichever yidishe kehile fun 1789 biz 1917" [The Berdichev Jewish community from 1789 to 1917]. *Bleter far yidishe demografie, statistik, un ekonomik* 2 (1923): 37–48.

———. "Di antviklung fun yidishn folk far di letste 100 yor" [The development of the Jewish people for the last 100 years]. *Shriftn far ekonomik un statistik* 1 (1928): 1–64.

————. *Dos yidishe folk in tsifern*. [The Jewish people in numbers]. Berlin, 1922.

Levanda, L. "Po povodu stat'i M. G. Morgulisa (pis'mo k izdatel'stve 'Evreiskaia biblioteka') [On the article of M. G. Morgulis (a letter to the publishers of 'Evreiskaia Biblioteka')]. *Evreiskaia biblioteka* 3 (1873): 365–77.

Levin, Avrohom. *Kantonistn* [Cantonists]. Warsaw, 1934.

Levin, Mordehai. *'Erkhei ḥevrah ve-kalkalah be-'ideologiah shel tekufat ha-has-kalah*. [Social and economic values in the ideology of the age of the Haskalah]. Jerusalem, 1975.

Levitats, Isaac. *The Jewish Community in Russia 1772–1844*. New York, 1943.

Libman, Yehudah Yidl. *Zevi be-'erez ha-ḥayim* [A deer in the land of life]. Vilna, 1839.

Lifshiz, Yaʿakov Halevi. *Sefer toledot Yizḥak* [The biography of Isaac]. Warsaw, 1897.

Lifshits, Y. "Englishe un amerikaner rayznder fun 18tn un ershter helft 19tn y"h vegn yidn in poyln un rusland" [English and American travelers of the 18th and early 19th centuries on the Jews in Poland and Russia]. *YIVO-Bleter* 3 (1932): 313–29.

————. "Englishe rayznders fun onheyb 19tn y"h vegn mizrekh-eyropeisher yidn" [English travelers of the early 19th century on East European Jews]. *YIVO-Bleter* 16 (1940): 59–66.

Lincoln, W. Bruce. "The Daily Life of St. Petersburg Officials in the Mid-19th Century." *Oxford Slavonic Papers*, n. s. 8 (1975): 82–100.

————. "Count P. D. Kiselev: A Reformer in Imperial Russia." *Australian Journal of Politics and History* 16 (1970): 177–88.

————. "The Ministers of Nicholas I: A Brief Inquiry into Their Backgrounds and Service Careers." *Russian Review* 34 (1975): 308–23.

————. *Nicholas I, Emperor and Autocrat of All the Russias*. Bloomington and London, 1978.

————. "Russia's 'Enlightened' Bureaucrats and the Problem of State Reform, 1848–1856." *Cahiers du monde russe et sovietique* 12 (1971): 410–21.

————. "The Composition of the Imperial Russian State Council under Nicholas I." *Canadian-American Slavic Studies* 10 (1976): 369–81.

————. "The Genesis of an 'Enlightened' Bureaucracy in Russia, 1825–1856." *Jahrbücher für Geschichte Osteuropas* 20 (1972): 321–30.

Litovskii, G. "Uchastie russkikh evreev v otpravlenii pravosudiia" [The participation of Russian Jews in the administration of justice]. *Perezhitoe* 3 (1911): 158–98.

L[oeb], I[sidore]. "Chronique: M. Lilienthal et la Russie." *Revue des études juives* 4 (1882): 308–19.

Lyashchenko, Peter I. *History of the National Economy of Russia to the 1917 Revolution*. New York, 1949.

Maggid, David (Schteinschneider). *Sefer toledot mishpaḥat Ginzburg* [History of the Günzburg family]. St. Petersburg, 1899.

Mahler, Raphael. *Der kamf tsvishn haskole un khsides in Galitsie in der ershter helft fun 19tn yorhundert* [The battle between Haskalah and Hasidism in Galicia in the first half of the 19th century]. New York, 1942.

————. *Divrei yimei yisra'el: dorot 'aḥaronim* [History of the Jews: modern times]. 4 vols. Merhaviah, 1962.

Maor, Yitshak. " 'Eliyahu Orshanski u-mekomo be-historiografiyah shel yehudei rusyah" [Eliyahu Orshanskii and his place in the historiography of Russian Jewry]. *He-ʿavar* 20 (1975): 49–61.

Marek, P. "Iz istorii evreiskago pechatnago dela v Rossii" [From the history of Jewish printing in Russia]. *Voskhod* 8 (1888), no. 4: 76–91.

———. "K istorii evreev v Moskve" [To the history of the Jews of Moscow]. *Voskhod* 13 (1893), no. 6: 73–91.

———. *Ocherki po istorii prosveshcheniia evreev v Rossii* [Studies on the enlightenment of the Jews in Russia]. Moscow, 1909.

———. "Vnutrennaia zhizn' shkol v tsartsvovanii Imperatora Nikolaia I" [The internal life of the schools in the reign of Nicholas I]. *Evreiskii ezhegodnik za 1902/1903g,* pp. 156–83.

Margolis, O. *Geshikhte fun yidn in rusland (1772–1861)* [History of the Jews in Russia (1772–1861)]. Moscow-Kharkov-Minsk, 1930.

McGrew, Roderick E. *Russia and the Cholera, 1823–1832.* Madison, 1965.

Meyer, Michael A. "Where Does the Modern Period of Jewish History Begin?" *Judaism* 26 (1975): 329–38.

Miron, Dan. *A Traveler Disguised.* New York, 1973.

Mirsky, Shemu'el. "Yeshivat Volozhin" [The Volozhin yeshivah]. In his *Mosedot torah be-'eiropah.* New York, 1957.

Monas, Sidney. "Bureaucracy in Russia under Nicholas I." *The Structure of Russian History,* edited by Michael Cherniavsky, pp. 269–81. New York, 1970.

———. *The Third Section: Police and Society in Russia under Nicholas I.* Cambridge, Mass., 1961.

Morgulis, M. G. "K istorii obrazovaniia russkikh evreev" [On the history of the education of Russian Jews]. In his *Voprosy evreiskoi zhizni,* pp. 1–195. St. Petersburg, 1903. Published in a "corrected" Hebrew edition as *Dor ha-haskalah be-rusyah.* Vilna, 1910.

Mysh, M. I. "Bor'ba pravitel'stva s piteinym promyslom evreev v selakh i derevniakh" [The battle of the government against the Jewish liquor trade in the villages]. *Voskhod* 1 (1881), no. 9, 1–21.

Nadav, Mordehai. "Toledot kehilat Pinsk 1506–1880" [History of the community of Pinsk, 1560–1880]. In his *Pinsk, sefer ʿeidot ve-zikaron,* pp. 195–295. Tel Aviv, 1973.

Natanson, B. *Sefer ha-zikhronot, divrei yimei ḥayei Riba"l* [Book of memoirs. Biography of Isaac Ber Levinsohn]. Warsaw, 1875.

Necheles, Ruth E. "The Abbé Grégoire and the Jews." *Jewish Social Studies* 33 (1971): 126–40.

Nikitin, V. N. *Evrei zemledel'tsy* [Jewish farmers]. St. Petersburg, 1887.

———. *Mnogostradal'nye* [The long-suffering]. St. Petersburg, 1895.

Orlovsky, Daniel T. "Recent Studies on the Russian Bureaucracy." *Russian Review* 35 (1976): 445–67.

Orshanskii, I. G. *Russkoe zakonodatel'stvo o evreiakh* [Russian legislation on the Jews]. St. Petersburg, 1877.

———. *Evrei v Rossii. Ocherki ekonomicheskago i obshchestvennago byta russkikh evreev* [The Jews in Russia. Studies of the economic and communal life of Russian Jews]. St. Petersburg, 1877.

Peikazh, M. *Ḥasidut Braẓlav* [Bratslav Hasidism]. Jerusalem, 1972.

Perlmann, Moshe. "Razsvet 1860–61: The Origins of the Russian-Jewish Press." *Jewish Social Studies* 24 (1962): 162–83.

Philipson, David. *Max Lilienthal, American Rabbi, Life and Writings.* New York, 1915.

———. "Max Lilienthal, 1815–1915." *Centenary Papers and Others,* pp. 149–90. Cincinnati, 1919.

Pines, A. "Bor'ba s khaperami" [Battle with the *khappers*]. *Evreiskaia starina* 8 (1915): 396–98.

Pintner, Walter M. *Russian Economic Policy under Nicholas I*. Ithaca, 1967.

———. "The Social Characteristics of the Early Nineteenth Century Russian Bureaucracy." *Slavic Review* 29 (1970): 429–43.

Pipes, Richard. "Catherine II and the Jews: The Origins of the Pale of Settlement." *Soviet Jewish Affairs* 5 (1975): 3–20.

———. *Russia under the Old Regime*. New York, 1974.

———. *Russian Conservatism in the Second Half of the Nineteenth Century*. 13th International Congress of Historical Sciences, Moscow, August 16–23, 1970. Moscow, 1970.

Pogodin, M. "Dlia biografii grafa S. S. Uvarova" [For the biography of Count S. S. Uvarov]. *Russkii arkhiv* 10 (1871): 2078–112.

Polievktov, M. *Nikolai I, biografiia i obzor tsartsvovaniia* [Nicholas I, biography and survey of his reign]. Moscow, 1918.

Pozner, S. V. *Evrei v obshchei shkole* [Jews in the general schools]. St. Petersburg, 1914.

Presniakov, A. E. *Emperor Nicholas I of Russia. The Apogee of Autocracy, 1825–1855*. Edited and translated by J. C. Zacek, Gulf Breeze, Florida, 1974.

Pugachev, V. V. "K voprosu o politicheskikh vzgliadakh S. S. Uvarova v 1810e gody" [To the question of the political views of S. S. Uvarov in the 1810s]. *Uchenye zapiski Gor'kovskogo gosudarstvennogo universiteta* 72 (1964): 125–32.

Rabinovich, Osip. *Sochineniia* [Works]. 3 vols. Odessa, 1888.

Rafalovich, A. "Meditsinskaia statistika Odessy za 1842 god" [Medical statistics of Odessa for 1842]. *Zhurnal Ministerstva vnutrennikh del* (1843): 344–85.

Raisin, Jacob S. *The Haskalah Movement in Russia*. Philadelphia, 1913.

Riasanovsky, Nicholas V. *Nicholas I and Official Nationality in Russia 1825–1835*. Berkeley and Los Angeles, 1969.

Roi, J. F. A. de le. *Judentaufen im 19 Jahrhundert*. Leipzig, 1899.

Rogger, Hans. "Government, Jews, Peasants, and Land in Post-Emancipation Russia." *Cahiers du monde russe et sovietique* 27 (1976): 5–25, 171–211.

———. "Russian Ministers and the Jewish Question." *California Slavic Studies* 8 (1975): 15–76.

———. "Tsarist Policy on Jewish Emigration." *Soviet Jewish Affairs* 3 (1973): 26–36.

Romanovich-Slavatinskii, A. *Dvorianstvo v Rossii* (The nobility in Russia]. St. Petersburg, 1870.

Rombakh, Sh. "Di yidishe balmelokhes in rusland in der ershter helft fun 19tn y"h" [Jewish artisans in Russia in the first half of the 19th century]. *Tsaytshrift* 1 (1926): 25–30.

Rosenfel'd, S. Ia. "R. Isroel' Salanter (Lipkin), ego deiatel'nost' i posledovateli" [Rabbi Israel Salanter (Lipkin), his work and followers]. *Perezhitoe* 1 (1908): 66–104.

Rozhdestvenskii, S. V. *Istoricheskii obzor deiatel'nosti Ministerstva narodnago prosveshcheniia 1802–1902* [Historical survey of the works of the Ministry of National Enlightenment, 1802–1902]. St. Petersburg, 1902.

Ryndziunskii, P. G. *Gorodskoe grazhdanstvo doreformennoi Rossii* [City dwellers of pre-reform Russia]. Moscow, 1958.

Samter, N. *Judentaufen in 19ten Jahrhundert*. Berlin, 1906.

Schacter, Jacob J. "Dina De-Malhuta Dina—A Review," *Diné Israel* 8 (1978): 77–95.

Scheinhaus, Leon. "Ein Deutscher Pionier [Dr. Lilienthal's Kulturversuch in Russland]." *Allgemeine Zeitung des Judentums* 75 (1911): 404–5, 415–17, 426–28, 437–39, 452–54.

Schiemann, Theodor. *Geschichte Russlands unter Kaiser Nikolaus I*. 4 vols. Berlin, 1904–19.

Schmid, Georg, ed. *Goethe und Uwarow und ihr Briefwechsel*. St. Petersburg, 1888.

Schneersohn, Joseph I. *The "Tzemach Tzedek" and the Haskalah Movement*. Translated by Z. I. Posner. Brooklyn, 1969.

Seredonin, S. M. et al. *Istoricheskii obzor deiatel'nosti Komiteta ministrov* [Historical survey of the work of the Committee of Ministers]. 7 vols. St. Petersburg, 1902.

Shatski, Yakov. *Yidishe bildungs-politik in poyln fun 1806 biz 1866* [Jewish educational politics in Poland from 1806 to 1866]. New York, 1943.

———. *Geshikhte fun yidn in varshe* [History of the Jews in Warsaw]. 3 vols. New York, 1947–53.

———. *Kultur-geshikhte fun der haskole in lite* [Cultural history of the Haskalah in Lithuania]. Buenos Aires, 1950.

Shchepetil'nikov, B. B. *Stoletie Voennago ministerstva 1802–1902. Glavnyi shtab. Istoricheskii ocherk* [One hundred years of the Ministry of War. Head staff. Historical study]. St. Petersburg, 1907.

Shil'der, N. K. *Imperator Nikolai I, ego zhizn' i tsarstvovanie* [Emperor Nicholas I, his life and reign]. 2 vols. St. Petersburg, 1903.

Shiuts, P. "Nechto o evreiakh severo-zapadnykh gubernii" [On the Jews of the northwestern provinces]. *Zhurnal Ministerstva vnutrennikh del* 7 (1844): 167–85.

Shochat, Azri'el. "Ha-hanhagah be-kehilot rusyah ᶜim bitul ha-'kahal' " [The administration of the communities in Russia after the abolition of the kahal]. *Zion* (1979): 143–223.

———. *Mosad "ha-rabanut mi-taᶜam" be-rusyah* [The institution of the "Crown Rabbi" in Russia]. Haifa, 1975.

Shohetman, B. "Odessa." ᶜArim ve-'imahot be-yisra'el 2 (1948): 58–108.

Shteynberg, Yehudah. *Ba-yamim hahem. Sipuro shel zaken* [In those days. The story of an old man]. Jerusalem-Berlin, 1923.

Shteinshnaider, Hillel Noah Maggid. *ᶜIr vilna* [The city of Vilna]. Vilna, 1900.

Sistematicheskii ukazatel' literatury o evreiakh na russkom iazyke so vremeni vvedeniia grazhdanskago shrifta (1708g) do dekabria 1889 [A systematic index of literature on the Jews in the Russian language from the introduction of civil print (1708) to 1889]. St. Petersburg, 1892.

Sliozberg, G. B. *Baron G. O. Gintsburg: ego zhizn' i deiatel'nost'* [Baron H. O. Günzburg: his life and work]. Paris, 1933.

Slonimsky, Nicolas. "My Grandfather Invented the Telegraph." *Commentary* 63 (1977): 56–60.

Slutsky, Yehudah. *Ha-ᶜitonut ha-yehudit rusit be-meᵓah ha-19* [Russian-Jewish press in the 19th century]. Jerusalem, 1970.

———. "Bet ha-midrash la-rabanim be-vilnah" [The rabbinical seminary in Vilna]. *He-ᶜavar* 7 (1960): 29–48.

———. "Yuli Gessen." *He-ᶜavar* 20 (1973): 72–79.

Sosis, Y. *Di geshikhte fun di yidishe gezelshaftlekhe shtremungen in rusland in*

19tn y"h [The history of social trends in Russia in the 19th century]. Minsk, 1929.

Stanislavskii, S. "Iz istorii i zhizni odnoi evreiskoi shkoly (1826–1853gg.)" [From the history of one Jewish school (1826–1853)]. *Voskhod* 4 (1884): 126–49.

———. "K istorii kantonistov" [To the history of the Cantonists]. *Evreiskaia starina* 2 (1909): 266–68.

Starr, S. F. *Decentralization and Self-Government in Russia*. Princeton, 1972.

Strakhovsky, L. *L'Empereur Nicolas et l'esprit national russe*. Louvain, 1928.

Surski, Aharon. *Toledot ha-ḥinukh ha-torati be-tekufah ha-ḥadashah*. [History of Torah education in the modern era]. Benei-Brak, 1967.

Torke, Hans J. "Das russische Beamtentum in der ersten Hälfte des 19. Jahrhunderts." *Forschungen zur osteuropäischen Geschichte* 13 (1967): 7–345.

Trivus, M. "Ritual'nye protsessy doreformennago russkago suda" [Ritual trials in the pre-reform Russian court]. *Evreiskaia starina* 5 (1912): 246–62.

Tsherikover, Eliyahu. "He-hamon ha-yehudi, ha-maskilim ve-ha-memshalah be-yimei nikolai ha-rishon" [The Jewish masses, the maskilim, and the government in the time of Nicholas I]. In his *Yehudim be-ʿitot mahapekhah*, pp. 107–26. Tel Aviv, 1957.

"Tsenzura v tsarstvovanii Nikolaia I" [Censorship in the reign of Nicholas I]. *Russkaia starina* 114 (1903): 658–69.

Tsinberg, Yisroel [Zinberg, Israel]. *Di geshikhte fun der literatur bay yidn* [History of Jewish literature]. 9 vols. New York, 1943. Issued in a Hebrew translation by Sh. Z. Ari'eli et al. with new notes as *Toledot sifrut yisra'el*. Tel Aviv, 1960.

Tsinberg, S. L. "Isaak Ber Levinzon i ego vremia" [Isaac Ber Levinsohn and his time]. *Evreiskaia starina* 3 (1910): 504–41.

———. "Predtechi evreiskoi zhurnalistiki v Rossii" [Precursors of Jewish journalism in Russia]. *Perezhitoe* 4 (1913): 119–48.

Tsitron, Sh. L. *Avek fun folk* [Away from the nation]. 4 vols. Vilna, undated.

———. [Z̧itron, Sh. L.]. *Mei-'aḥarei ha-pargod* [Behind the curtains]. 2 vols. Vilna, 1923–25.

Varadinov, N. *Istoriia Ministerstva vnutrennikh del* [History of the Ministry of the Interior]. 8 vols. St. Petersburg, 1862.

Weinryb, Bernard Dov. *Neuste wirtschaftsgeschichte der Juden in Russland und Polen von der 1. polnischen Teilung bis zum Tode Alexanders II* (1772–1881). 2nd ed. Hildesheim, N.Y., 1972.

Weiss, I. H. "Reishit ẓemiḥat ha-haskalah be-rusyah" [The beginnings of the flowering of the Haskalah in Russia]. *Mi-mizraḥ u-mi-maʿarav* 1 (1894): 9–16.

Wilkinson, Samuel. *In the Land of the North—The Evangelization of the Jews in Russia*. London, 1905.

Wortman, R. S. *The Development of a Russian Legal Consciousness*. Chicago and London, 1976.

Yakhnison, Y. *Sotsial-ekonomisher shteyger ba yidn in rusland in xix y"h* [The socioeconomic condition of the Jews in Russia in the 19th century]. Kharkov, 1929.

Yaney, George. *The Systematization of Russian Government: Social Evolution in the Domestic Administration of Imperial Russia 1711–1905*, Urbana, 1975.

Yerushalmi, Yosef Haim. *The Lisbon Massacre of 1506 and the Royal Image in the Shebet Yehudah*. Cincinnati, 1976.

Yuditsky, A. "Evreiskaia burzhuaziia i evreiskie rabochie v tekstil'noi promyshlennosti pervoi poloviny XIX v." [The Jewish bourgeoisie and Jewish
workers in the textile industry of the first half of the nineteenth century].
Istoricheskii sbornik 4 (1935): 107–33.

————. *Yidishe burzhuazie un yidisher proletariat in ershter helft xix y"h*
[Jewish bourgeoisie and Jewish proletariat in the first half of the 19th
century]. Kiev, undated.

Zaionchkovskii, P. A. "Vysshaia biurokratiia nakanune Krymskoi Voiny" [The
high bureaucracy on the eve of the Crimean War]. *Istoriia SSSR* (1974):
154–64.

Index

intelligentsia, Jewish (*continued*)
  see also education, Haskalah-based;
    Haskalah; maskilim
"ironclad" code, 11

Jewish Committee, 8–11, 79
Jewish legislation codified by, 11, 35
Jewish communities:
  autonomy and self-government of, 9,
    125, 185–86
  child-recruits drafted by, 25, 28–31
  communal organization of, 8–9
  conscription's effect on, 17, 22, 32–
    34, 166, 184–88
  discriminatory conscription prac-
    tices in, 28–29, 106, 130–31
  economic stratification in, 180–82,
    186
  ideological split in, 42–43, 187–88
  internal taxes of, 40–41, 123–26,
    129–33
  poor members conscripted in, 28,
    106, 130–31
  recruitment procedures required of,
    20
  role of kahal in, 9, 124
  separatist movements in, 131–33
  social discipline essential in, 113
  unrestricted court system of, 126–
    27
  see also economy, Jewish; Pale of
    Settlement; population, Jewish
Jewish Enlightenment movement, *see*
  Haskalah
Jews, Russian:
  dual community membership of, 8,
    125
  forced resettlement of, 35–37
  gentile authority distrusted by, 32
  legal restrictions on residence of, 6–
    8, 11, 35–36, 158
  marriages of, 37
  in municipal elections, 37–39, 158
  objections to conscription of, 14–15
  outlawed traditional garb of, 44, 47,
    123, 158, 183
  Siberian land grants to, 39–40

"useful" vs. "nonuseful" categories
  of, 45, 47, 156–59, 184
  see also Jewish communities
Joseph II, Holy Roman Emperor, 13
Jost, Isaac, 71
*Journal of the Ministry of National En-
  lightenment* (ed. Uvarov), 67–68,
    100
Judaism:
  orthodox society consolidated in, 55,
    148–54, 187
  religious reforms of, 137–41
  see also education, private; kahal;
    rabbis
Jüdisch-Theologisches Seminar (Bres-
    lau), 107

kahal:
  abolition of, 43–44, 47, 123–27, 186
  defined, 9
  dissatisfaction with, 127–33
  lost status of, 132–33
  mass riots against, 128–29
  poor Jews' denunciations of, 28, 106,
    130–31
  protest in synagogues of, 127–28
  see also Jewish communities
Kankrin, E. F.:
  colonization encouraged by, 39–40
  as pragmatic traditionalist, 10
Katzenellenbogen, Ḥaim Leib, 97
Katzenellenbogen, Hirsh Zvi, 63, 103,
    138
Kaufmann, Yeḥezkel, 149
khappers (child-recruit abductors), 29–
    33, 128, 136
Khvolson, Daniel, 146–47
Kiev, 36, 39
Kiselev, P. D., 10, 59, 78
  as objective pragmatist, 10
  reforms of, 43–48, 123–26, 183
Kishinev, school of maskilim in, 64–
    66
Kliaczko, Hirsh, 93, 103
korobka (tax), 40–41, 44, 47
  abolition of, 43–44, 47, 123–27, 186
  revision of, 123–26

peasants, conscription of, 14
Philippson, Ludwig, 59, 70–71, 74, 87
Poland, Kingdom of, 14, 169, 174
  foreign missionaries in, 143
  Jews in, 14
  military service of inhabitants in, 17
Polish Uprising of 1830, 47–48
population, Jewish:
  calculations of females in, 164
  calculations of males in, 163–64
  concealment of statistics on, 160–64
  increases in, 164
  migrations of, 165–70
  urbanization of, 167–69
  see also Jewish communities; Pale of Settlement
Prussia, 45, 56, 156, 169, 175

rabbiners, 134
rabbis:
  censorship duties of, 42, 58
  conscription exemption of, 19
  governmental role of, 133–37
  oath of allegiance required of, 37
  provincial chief, 44, 47
  rabbiners vs., 134
  see also education, private; Hasidism; Judaism; kahal
Rabinovich, Osip, 140
razbor (reclassification) project, 155–60, 166, 176, 179–80, 182, 184
  abandonment of, 159–60
  announcement of, 157–59
  Jewish reaction to, 159
  opposition to, 156–57
Recruitment Statute of the Jews (August 1827), 11, 16–34
  amendment to (1828), 28
  opposition to, 15–16
  summary of, 18–21
  violations of, 22–30
  see also conscription, Jewish; military service, Jewish
Riga, 64–66, 72, 91–92, 98
  new congregation formed in, 138–41
Rosenthal, Nisan, 63, 93, 94, 97

Russian Legislation on the Jews (Orshanskii), 6–7
Russian Orthodoxy, conversions to, 141–48
  foreign missionaries and, 143
  Jewish origins and, 147–48
  Lithuanian Consistory on, 141
  of maskilim, 146–48
  military service as means of, 15, 16
  psychological incentives for, 23–24
  rates of, 22–23, 24, 141–42
  social status gained by, 143, 147–48
  torture as incentive for, 24
  tsar's missionary motives and, 15, 19, 22–25, 35
  unauthorized baptisms in, 22
  youths' susceptibility to, 25
Russian Revolution, 141
  role of Jews changed in, 4
"Russifier," 110, 115
Ryndziunskii, P. G., 168–69

Salanter (Lipkin), Israel, 136, 146, 156
Schneersohn, Menahem Mendel, 78–81, 135, 150–52
secret police, Russian, 15, 19, 40, 42
Sefer Hasidim (Aksenfeld), 117
Sforno, Obadiah, 101
Shik, Eliyahu, 129, 136
Shirinskii-Shikhmatov, Prince P. A., 183
Shishkov, A. S., 53–54
Society for the Promotion of Enlightenment among Russian Jews, 147
Society of Seekers after Enlightenment, 55, 58
Statute of 1804, 8, 36–38
  Jewish liquor trade forbidden by, 171
Statute of 1827, see Recruitment Statute of the Jews
Statute on the Jews (April 1835), 9, 35–42
  Jewish liquor trade allowed by, 171–72
  recommendations for, 35–36